Work in Progress

thinking|media

Series Editors:
Bernd Herzogenrath
Patricia Pisters

Work in Progress

Curatorial Labor in Twenty-First-Century American Fiction

Rieke Jordan

BLOOMSBURY ACADEMIC
NEW YORK • LONDON • OXFORD • NEW DELHI • SYDNEY

BLOOMSBURY ACADEMIC
Bloomsbury Publishing Inc
1385 Broadway, New York, NY 10018, USA
50 Bedford Square, London, WC1B 3DP, UK

BLOOMSBURY, BLOOMSBURY ACADEMIC and the Diana logo
are trademarks of Bloomsbury Publishing Plc

First published in the United States of America 2019
Paperback edition first published 2021

Copyright © Rieke Jordan, 2019

For legal purposes the Acknowledgments on p. vii constitute
an extension of this copyright page.

Cover design: Daniel Benneworth-Gray
Cover image © Paolo Sanfi lippo

All rights reserved. No part of this publication may be reproduced or
transmitted in any form or by any means, electronic or mechanical,
including photocopying, recording, or any information storage or retrieval
system, without prior permission in writing from the publishers.

Bloomsbury Publishing Inc does not have any control over, or responsibility for,
any third-party websites referred to or in this book. All internet addresses given
in this book were correct at the time of going to press. The author and publisher
regret any inconvenience caused if addresses have changed or sites have
ceased to exist, but can accept no responsibility for any such changes.

Library of Congress Cataloging-in-Publication Data
Notes109
Names: Jordan, Rieke, author.
Title: Work in progress: curatorial labor in twenty-first century American fiction / Rieke Jordan.
Description: New York, NY: Bloomsbury Academic, 2019. |
Series: Thinking media | Revision of author's thesis (doctoral)–Freie Universitèat Berlin,
2016, titled Work in progress: curation and creativity in 21st century
American fiction. | Includes bibliographical references and index.
Identifiers: LCCN 2019007195 (print) | LCCN 2019016981 (ebook) |
ISBN 9781501347733 (ePub) | ISBN 9781501347740 (ePDF) |
ISBN 9781501347726 (hardback: alk.paper)
Subjects: LCSH: American fiction–21st century–History and criticism. |
Reader-response criticism.
Classification: LCC PS380 (ebook) | LCC PS380.J67 2019 (print) |
DDC 813/.609–dc23
LC record available at https://lccn.loc.gov/201900719

ISBN: HB: 978-1-5013-4772-6
PB: 978-1-5013-7545-3
ePDF: 978-1-5013-4774-0
eBook: 978-1-5013-4773-3

Series: Thinking Media

Typeset by Deanta Global Publishing Services, Chennai, India

To find out more about our authors and books visit
www.bloomsbury.com and sign up for our newsletters.

Contents

List of Figures	vi
Acknowledgments	vii
Preface: When the Internet Dropped Its Capital "I"	viii
1 Work in Progress: Curatorial Labor	1
2 A Tale of Two Buildings: Chris Ware's *Building Stories*	39
3 The Broken Record: Beck Hansen's *Song Reader*	81
4 *Kentucky Route Zero*'s Netherworld of Slowness	125
Coda: What's the Matter, Media?	163
Bibliography	175
Index	188

Figures

2.1	*Building Stories'* box	40
2.2	*Building Stories*, spread out	40
2.3	Overlapping panels or inset panels	61
2.4	The zoetrope in *Jimmy Corrigan*	64
2.5	*The Multi-Story Building Model*	73
3.1	*Song Reader*	84
3.2	Beck Hansen and his puppet doppelgänger	88
3.3	"Title of this Song" cover of sheet music song	110
3.4	Hambeck's "Paper Beck and with Cameron" (2009)	122
3.5	Paper Beck assembly manual	123
4.1	*Kentucky Route Zero* screenshot	134
4.2	*Limits & Demonstrations* screenshot	142
4.3–4.5	The glitch in *Kentucky Route Zero*	147–148

Acknowledgments

This book used to be a clutter of Word and Open Office documents or maybe even TextEdit files that used to be Notes on my phones or notes scribbled on legal pads and the back of envelopes. Once the process is a product, well, I guess that's the moment of letting go.

My own work in progress could have not ever be turned into a book without the generosity and support of Laura Bieger and Frank Kelleter, to whom I am deeply thankful for their encouragement and trust throughout the years. Gabi Bodmeier, David Bosold, and my colleagues and fellow cohort members of the Graduate School of North American Studies have been supportive since I started working on this project in 2012. Thanks to my students and colleagues in Frankfurt for their fresh perspectives on old ideas. Johannes Voelz and Bernd Herzogenrath have given me new thoughts and inspiration for this project—and for projects to come. Thank you to Patricia Pisters. At Bloomsbury, thanks to Katie Gallof and Erin Duffy. For my family and my friends: thank you for taking care of me. Thanks to the wonderful Joshua Rahtz. Thank you to Maria Sulimma for rocket coffee and units. Unending modern thanks to Sarah Wasserman; your help and support means more than you can imagine.

I am grateful for having been able to present my ideas during workshops and conferences at FU Berlin, Johns Hopkins University, Ohio State University, University of Freiburg, University of Delaware, University of Erfurt, and Goethe-University Frankfurt.

Copyright acknowledgments

Chapter 2: Images of the *Multi-Story Building Model* used with permission by Drawn and Quarterly (thanks to Peggy Burns)

Chapter 3: The cover of "Title of This Song" from *Song Reader* used with permission by McSweeney's (thanks to Kristina Kearns); Beck cut outs used with permission by the artist (thanks to Ham); Creative Commons licensing for the Beck concert photograph (image by Scott Beale/Laughing Squid—laughingsquid.com)

Chapter 4: Screengraps from *Kentucky Route Zero* used with permission by Cardboard Computer (thanks to the Cardboard Computer team)

Preface: When the Internet Dropped Its Capital "I"

On June 1, 2016, a *New York Times* headline proclaimed, "It's Official: The 'Internet' Is Over." "Oh no," I thought, looking up from the news app on my beaten up iPhone 4—screen cracked, loading time slow like honey, storage full. But the internet did not fall out of style in the summer of 2016, instead, *The New York Times* joined *The Associated Press* in a changing of their style rule: to lowercase the term "the internet." This small change, so the announcement went, facilitates a smoother reading flow for the peruser of the newspaper. But the choice to lowercase the term signals a broader shift in the understanding of the internet in everyday life. It suggests that the internet is not a "new" medium anymore: it is "a common tendency to capitalize newly coined or unfamiliar terms. Once a term becomes familiar and quotidian, there is a tendency to drop the capital letter," as the announcement says (Corbett 2016, n.p.). The dropping of its capital letter by the year 2016 marks the moment the internet turned into a familiar and commonplace medium that orchestrates life, love, and labor—it is not *new* anymore but has created routines, habits, and addictions for many users. In this book I turn toward cultural objects that emerge around this very moment when the capital letter "I" slowly made way for the lowercase "i," when the internet started to be culturally coded as commonplace and ordinary.[1] I am interested in this shift toward a restructuring of an ever-present present, or, rather, a present that keeps on refreshing itself. *Work in Progress: Curatorial Labor in Twenty-First-Century American Fiction* aligns a conceptual rock album, a glitchy computer game, and an incomplete graphic narrative that toy with the dichotomy of staging themselves as digital media that remain decidedly offline and retro, working with the implications of commonplace media and retro newness.

The three case studies I turn to in this book incorporate *and* reject digital forms and practices—they borrow what they need not to replicate online experience, but to make it both legible and unfamiliar. In each chapter, I attempt to tease out the traces of earlier forms that reside in the newer ones: nineteenth-century sheet music in a twenty-first-century DIY musical release;

---

[1] It should be noted that not all English print outlets adhere to this new standard that was suggested by *The Associated Press*. *The Guardian* adopted the style change too, but as of August 2018, *The New Yorker* and *The Washington Post* still use the capital "I."

the antiquated paper cut out inside a digitally reproduced graphic-novel-in-a-box; DOS code from the 1980s appearing on the screen of a MacBook—these are medial oddities that become visible when we pay close attention by excavating the old from within the new. This helps to fully understand the layers of meaning that these objects encode and the experiences they make available: It is my assertion in this project that we must think of the object and the reader as flirting, knowingly or unknowingly, with the ghosts of the past. This relay between old and new is not limited to the texts' mediality. As decidedly contemporary texts, they combine recent innovations in printing, computing, and distribution with familiar modes of storytelling and reader engagement. Whether or not the reader of Beck Hansen's *Song Reader* knows much about nineteenth-century sheet music, the practices of reading, rehearsing, or performing nonetheless recall earlier modes of musical production encapsulated within practices enabled by YouTube or MP3s on our mobile devices. Whether or not the reader of *Kentucky Route Zero* is able to write code or is savvy in earlier computer technologies, she still surreptitiously, maybe unbeknownst to her, reproduces online activity by selecting pre-given options on the screen. She may easily be overwhelmed by the meandering plotline and the design of the computer game; she will, however, rely on familiar reading strategies of character identification, suture and closure, and following the plot.

But how does one begin even theorizing and interpreting works that emerge in this very moment of lowercasing the internet? What is the appropriate method for a "first responder"? It has been tempting in examining these texts from 2012 and 2013 to rely on Fredric Jameson's famous mandate to "always historize." In *Work in Progress* I do indeed often trace the historical developments—technological or aesthetic—that have led up to these current objects. But in the process of excavating the meaning from these texts, I have come to see that thinking in timelines and historical arcs may in fact be inadequate. These texts, when they are invested in the past, are invested in modes that cannot be neatly called "nostalgic," "historical," and "retro." Instead, they are often all of these things at once, while also staging themselves as hip and new. I am therefore less concerned with how a given work might have developed from a previous one and more interested in how a contemporary work might be said to *contain* an earlier one. This cadence of meaning is indicative, and I take my methodological cues from recent work in media studies by scholars such as Wolfgang Ernst, Lisa Gitelman, and John Durham Peters. In her book *Always Already New* (published in 2008), Lisa Gitelman claims that media are always historical subjects. By historical Gitelman means that "even the newest new media today come from somewhere" (Gitelman 2008, 5). But she also insists that media are historical "because they are functionally integral to a sense of pastness. Not only do people regularly learn about the past by means of media representations—books, films, and so on—using media also involves implicit encounters with the past that produced the representations in question" (Gitelman 2008, 5). I am convinced by her second point—the objects that I look at can rightly be called new, however, they also offer encounters with past, older incarnations. A text such as *Building Stories*, for example, could be read as the twenty-first century's result of a long history of comic books, dime novels, and graphic novels. But an analysis of *Building Stories* as an incomplete text that asks its readers to become collectors relies rather on the way that Ware's graphic narrative recalls the board game, the archive, and the collection—this approach can therefore unveil strategies of the texts that would otherwise remain invisible or opaque.

I argue that what may in fact be truly contemporary about these texts is precisely in the way that they combine the new and the old—the unfamiliar and the familiar, the timely with the untimely—and explore questions of media usage in the twenty-first century by way of toying with a "sense of pastness." *Work in Progress* approaches the (messy, muddy) media genealogy of American pop-culture in this fold of cultural studies and media studies, between old and new, between "I" and "i." *Work in Progress* outlines the switch from matter to materiality, from the emergence of newness to the ever-changing contemporary and the ever-present new, whose newness might be embedded in earlier media. Here, media is not only the *biological* matter in line with media-philosophical inquiries[2] but also the *social* matter of the twenty-first century, determining who we talk to, what we read, who we date. For media studies has long grappled with the question of what exactly *is* new about "new media," my investment is to help untangle the past from the present—or, rather, to illuminate how past and present (and future) will repeatedly be entangled and braided in and through media, literature, and reader interaction.

Critical inquiries into twenty-first-century aesthetic categories of the ever new and the ever changing, the slow, the banal are concurrent during

---

[2] It is noteworthy here that the term "medium" is used to also refer to "biological, physical, technological, institutional, and aesthetic media—a theoretical positioning that oscillates between physical properties, qualities, technologies, materialities, and artistic means of expression" (Herzogenrath 2015, 1). Work in line with Herzogenrath's suggestion relates to a more inclusive version of media studies that would "also have to focus on what cultural studies bracket off or only see as a retro-effect of the cultural constituted construction of the world: matter, materiality, or to call it by its name usually safeguarded by quotation marks—nature" (Herzogenrath 2015, 2). He elaborates that the "materiality of biological and social systems seen as self-organizing aggregates . . . allow for the emergence of newness" (Herzogenrath 2015, 2).

a moment that the academy struggles to find definitions for. In 2009, Giorgio Agamben asked, "What is the contemporary?" and concurs that it ultimately must be the disconnected and anachronistic who can truly grasp their own time.³ The critical reception of a world in flux and in flow and of the repercussions of globalization, political polarization, and digitization into the Western subjects' life have been categorized in terms of post-postmodernism, post-millennialism, digimodernism, pseudomodernism, and metamodernism. In 2018, while writing this preface, the public and private spheres have been faced with the conundrum in what way to grapple with the effects of alternative facts, fake news, and filters. The moment of the lowercase "internet" has thus also brought about critical shifts in the perception of the self and the realities the internet creates for its users—and how low the thresholds can be to say what one thinks.

But what do we talk about when we talk about contemporary literature within these parameters? In their survey that analyzes recent monographs by literary scholars, Emily Hyde and Sarah Wasserman denote the porous contours around (global) literature⁴ in and of the twenty-first century. They underline that discussions around the literary contemporary directly confront "the difficulty of historicizing the contemporary and distinguishing it as a period" (Hyde and Wasserman 2017, 1) and see it rather as a "moving target with a growing list of aliases" (Hyde and Wasserman 2017, 2). Similarly, Lutz Koepnick draws out a cultural moment that is too fast to keep up with. The contemporary, according to Koepnick, follows the "exhaustion of postmodernism in the course of the 1990s. It has come to describe pluralistic forms of artistic practice that are weary about any effort

---

³ In his essay "What Is the Contemporary?" published within *What Is an Apparatus?* (2009) Giorgio Agamben writes, "Those who are truly contemporary, who truly belong to their time, are those who neither perfectly coincide with it nor adjust themselves to its demands. They are thus in this sense irrelevant [*inattuale*]. But precisely because of this condition, precisely through this disconnection and this anachronism, they are more capable than others of perceiving and grasping their own time" (Agamben 2009, 40). He continues that contemporariness is

> a singular relationship with one's own time, which adheres to it and. at the same time, keeps a distance from it. More precisely, it is *that relationship with time that adheres to it through a disjunction and an anachronism*. Those who coincide too well with the epoch, those who are perfectly tied to it in every respect are not contemporaries, precisely because they do not manage to see it; they are not able to firmly hold their gaze on it. (Agamben 2009, 41)

⁴ In addition to this, Hyde and Wasserman not only ask what the literary contemporary is, but also *who* has the privilege to be considered as (a) contemporary. "The disparities of gender, race, and ethnicity in the emerging corpus of scholarship on the contemporary are especially glaring. The infrequent appearance of short fiction, poetry, and drama in the works we examined is also striking. To put it bluntly, most book-length works of criticism on contemporary literature are about novels by white men" (Hyde and Wasserman 2017, 3).

to label distinct movements, narratives, styles, and formal repertoires, yet are also—highly attuned to the fleetingness of the now—quite hesitant to denounce the pleasures of newness and the fundamental productivity of time" (Koepnick 2014, 5). In line with these inquiries of the untimely timeliness (or is it a timely untimeliness?) and the exhaustion (or is it the inhalation?) of the contemporary as such a porous category for literary and cultural analysis (and classification), it may seem at hand that new texts do not always perform wholly new work, but rather negotiate their contemporariness through (older) *forms*. This is a tension that Hyde and Wasserman point toward: "Form in the contemporary novel is never outside the messy histories that bring texts into the present. It is not the universal or transtemporal solvent that elevates the novel above the reader and her environment. Rather, form points reader to a present that is contingent upon specific pasts by disclosing how the contemporary novel itself is contingent upon specific literary precursors" (Hyde and Wasserman 2017, 13–14). Forms seem to not merely unearth the novel (pun intended), but likewise intensify the familiar.

I take "form" at face value, for the case studies of this book *do* something with the forms and formats of the contemporary book, the song, the computer. The form turns into a moving target, and my work attends to thinking contemporary forms of fiction as *works in progress*. What makes my case studies, *Building Stories*, *Song Reader*, and *Kentucky Route Zero*, such paradigmatic texts is their play with form and content; they rely on a provisional, if incomplete aesthetic experience that brings forward creative practices that are staged as new, digital, and contemporary, yet rely on earlier forms of interaction and participation which feel simultaneously open *and* predetermined. In this sense, these objects stage themselves as unfinished, "unformatted." When brought into proximity, these objects give us a picture of the *unfinished* as a dominant mode of cultural production and participation in the twenty-first century. Yet forms want to be formed, and I am invested in the ways that the texts at hand demand and shape *labor* of various kinds. It seems as if the figure of the modernist poet who assembles the fragments of a shifting world and the figure of the postmodernist author who understands these fragments as mirages that can conceal no truth have been displaced by—or rather subsumed in—the contemporary reader who adds her labor and dexterity in order to shuffle fragments into any order.

This exemplifies how these texts privilege an *experience* of building, interacting, rehearsing over one single coherent vision or product. My second mission in *Work in Progress* is thus to excavate a new reading position that, too, recalls earlier practices enfolded within the allegedly new. These objects,

I argue, demand and reward *curatorial labor* that postulates and positions the reader as curator toward the object. I borrow the idea of the curator from the museum context—this shift away from the museum toward hip niches signals in what way a reader of contemporary literature needs to see herself as an accomplice—perhaps even an accomplished one—who make the preset options contained within legible and comprehensible. She is an archivist, an archaeologist, who is to unearth earlier incarnations of contemporary pop-cultural entertainment. *Work in Progress* acknowledges the literal dismantling and "strange-making" of the media at stake that challenge tried and tested notions of media interaction and consumption. Likewise, the curator acknowledges that fiction (and her social reality) are planes to be curated to a degree of aesthetic sophistication. The curator, I wager, is an aestheticized subject position of the twenty-first century that unfolds in the literary imaginary.

Curation here unfolds on the plane of mending (curating as *cure*) and on the plane of tinkering with a tessellated, almost post-Fordist fragmentation of material,[5] matters, and bodies of work. A curator's job includes "exhibiting," "showing," "caring for"—like organizing an art exhibition. This draws a line from art to literature, from the rarified object to the mass-produced commodity. Curatorial labor vis-à-vis contemporary American fiction does not take a ready-made (hence an everyday, ordinary manufactured object) to reintegrate it into an artistic context. Rather, it performs an obverse operation. It decontextualizes the rarified object from an artist and makes it available for a wider audience for purchase. The reader position is not necessarily singular; curation enfolds practices of a musician/song reader and marionette (*Song Reader*), data-analyst (*Kentucky Route Zero*), or recollector (*Building Stories*). Nevertheless, the texts stage themselves as distant to the

---

[5] David Banash in his introduction to *Collage Culture* (published in 2013) excavates the significance of the collage aesthetics in relation to the individual and her social reality:

> What was once grasped as a totality was now seen as an assemblage of manipulable parts. This was not only applied to the parts and products fabricated on the assembly line, but through timestudies, the workers themselves were shattered, their own movements broken into the smallest possible parts. Cutting manufacturing processes into a series of irreducible operations, Fordism separated workers from any concrete grasp of a total process. (Banash 2013, 15)

> And, as I would argue, also from any concrete grasp of a total "body"—not only the body of work, but the work of the body. This dichotomy between the work of the body and the body of work will come back throughout my book: what is at stake here is the means by which the work of the body is performed and how the single pieces work phenomenologically. This idea can be traced in Siegfried Krakauer's writings on the mechanized body looks at representations of legs in modernity, for instance, or the fragmentation of the body on the Fordist assembly line. Mark Hansen's work on new media asks similar questions, if from a different vantage point.

reader, for she is not the collector of a text like *Building Stories*—but she purchases a ready-made collection and arranges its storylines. She is not the songwriter of *Song Reader*, but rehearses the song according to her skill set—nor is she the programmer of *Kentucky Route Zero*, but she selects text options and sifts through databases on the screen. She *implements* and reassembles the options made available—a role that is staged as an integral part in making these stories work out but, likewise, from a inferior position toward the authors'. The reader interacts and assembles and is rather an implementing entity.

My questions are, Why can contemporary graphic narratives, albums, and computer games afford to be unfinished, elusive, and fragmentary? And why are we so tempted to engage creatively with a text that appears unfinished? Why do we want to "get to work" and "figure them out"? Works in progress seek a reader who does not shy away from unfinished works but instead sees them as vehicles for new hobbies, new forms of labor, new forms of creative outlets, thus new ways of aestheticizing the self. They presuppose highly individualized reading strategies that cater to narrow niche audiences. She becomes an archivist, an excavating curator, well versed in the oddities and niches of the respective media in her hand. To a large extent, curation in the way I understand it hence includes acknowledging the implementing of the generic, mass-produced, commodified into the specific, artistic, idiosyncratic, creative. In a related question, I ask how creativity has become a requirement and asset for reading complex narratives. Within the discourse of creativity and the aestheticization of cultural techniques and practices in the twenty-first century, the reader is reconfigured as an accomplice in order to make the stories legible and comprehensible. She becomes a manager of the chaotic texts that arrive at her doorstep unsorted (*Building Stories*, Chapter 2), unsung (*Song Reader*, Chapter 3), and unplayed (*Kentucky Route Zero*, Chapter 4).

For this study emphasizes the interplay of technological attributes and traces in what way the book of the twenty-first century repeatedly and relentlessly refers back to its earlier incarnations, we must also wonder in what way do the texts claim that digital reading processes are necessary for a productive curation of the fragmented text. I am thus invested in the tension between the highly specialized, curating readers of contemporary American fiction and artistic visions of highly esteemed authors that are now mass-produced and purchasable in bookstores and on amazon. *Work in Progress* tackles them as works in *and* of progress. The work is in and for itself. These cadences of meaning are indicative. The improvisational, unfinished qualities of the texts allow us to consider what the role of reading is today—are the tasks elicited by these curious contemporary texts ostensibly different than those tasks that have come before? My analysis suggests that there are indeed material differences. Beck Hansen's *Song Reader*, for instance, is built upon oxymorons, juxtapositions, and paradoxes, starting with the title of the album. A song reader is, in the traditional sense, a book of song lyrics and music. Beck Hansen's album is precisely this, and yet there is more to the project. The irony here is that one cannot read a song by a pop artist, but must *hear* it. *Song Reader* plays with this irony: slippages and misreading are its predominant modes of production and consumption, and the moments of breakage may be the most productive ones.

The same rings true for Chris Ware's graphic narrative *Building Stories*: the reader is asked to build and shuffle pieces of a graphic narrative that comes in an oversized box, but not a single read-through will resemble the next. Instead the reader is invited to recollect and remember how the plotlines have previously come together. Yet, the little booklets are subject to tearing and breakage, making the haptic and aesthetic experience of *Building Stories* precarious at best. The meaning of the plot in Ware's story is not given or found, but must be constantly *produced* by the material activities of the reader. The computer game *Kentucky Route Zero* presents readers with a highly procedural, point-and-click narrative. When the screen suddenly turns black in mid-play, the computer seems to break down and reveal streams of code and data. The game contains a simulation of its own: XANADU serves as a meta-commentary that subverts the reader's expectations that *Kentucky Route Zero* can never be finished or completed. It defers its conclusion endlessly. Characters and readers alike meander through the computer game levels.

What henceforth emerges when thinking about curation is a way of thinking about the way these texts mediate the analog and the digital. As *Work in Progress* shows, one reason why these texts feel so contemporary is that they both draw upon and work against expectations of interactive art in the digital age. I maintain that the curator performs a set of interactive and aesthetic tasks especially suited to the present moment, borrowing from the past. This pertains to questions of interaction and participatory culture that not only are current in the contemporary moment but also relate back to the medium and its pastness. Particularly because terms like "interaction"/"interactivity" and "participation" connote tactile, quite literally "digital" tasks in relation to the media at stake (i.e., gluing together, sorting through, or reshuffling given components), *Work in Progress* explores the assumption interaction is always already based on and mediated through a "material desire." The objects expose how reading has turned into a complex cultural technique that surpasses the mere turning of the page.

The primary mode of this book is the case study. Media are changing all the time and their histories are hard to keep track of—the little nooks and crannies in their histories hold artifacts long lost and forgotten. *Work in Progress* caters to these nooks and crannies. The mode of the case study avoids mixing and mingling the different missions and comments the texts make on contemporary reading and curating practices. Yet aligning them also produces surprising parallels, tensions, foils. I treat these three examples as paradigms, for I believe *Building Stories*, *Song Reader*, and *Kentucky Route Zero* must be seen as objects to tell us something about changing consumer habits, questions pertaining to creativity and creative reading practices and processes, the current state of materiality vis-à-vis the internet, fan involvement, fragments and serials/serialization, authorship, niches, and the "project-ness" of fiction and life today—in short: buzz words in the advent of the lowercase "internet." These texts reflect on how the unfinished and the provisional is equally a productive *and* all-consuming dogma for the reader in the twenty-first century. Approached from this angle, ideas of provisionality and contingency become productive concepts for thinking about the role of the reader, narrative as well as material. Yet, with works in progress, who really is the producer? Who consumes? Ultimately, I insist that *Building Stories*, *Song Reader*, and *Kentucky Route Zero* must be seen as more than mere artifacts that cater to niche audiences who "get" these geeky texts and are in the know.

Chapter 1, "Works in Progress: Curatorial Labor," offers a calibrated overview of my theoretical inquiries pertaining to curatorial labor that I just outlined. By uniting critical inquiries from cultural studies, media studies, and sociology, this chapter lays the foundation for a new way of approaching open-ended, provisional fiction in and of the twenty-first century. I move from the idea of "narrative desire" to that of "material desire," acknowledging the medial and narrative interlacing of form and format. In this chapter, I develop the idea of the reader turning into an integral entity within those texts. By way of the reading position of the curator, who performs labor that is not restricted to the turning of the page, but to the managing, building, rehearsing of the objects at hand, I examine a highly aesthetized subject position that unfolds in the tension between product and process, author and amateur, narrative and material.

In Chapter 2, entitled "A Tale of Two Buildings: Chris Ware's *Building Stories*," I explore how Chris Ware's *Building Stories* functions as a collection that affords a readerly and material practice that likens curatorial labor to a set of interactive tasks that stand in stark contrast with today's notions of interactivity and participatory culture. The narrative *and* haptic interaction with the object indeed interrogates readerly practices in the digital age, and it does so by examining how we build stories and lives through figments, fragments, and fallacies. Yet *Building Stories* speaks to individualization of preset modules and components through tactility and memory. In the course of my reading, I will pay close attention to Ware's material strategies and meta-material efforts to interrogate how memory, material, and narrative unfold an interdependent reading experience. Here, I find the concept of *experimental memory* instructive and I will connect these ideas with the idea of *Building Stories* as a collection. This in turn will help us answer questions regarding how *Building Stories* negotiates the collection as a narrative and material concept. In order to do so, I will turn to Ware's other materials, like *Jimmy Corrigan* and the *Multi-Story Building Model*, to illustrate the strand of curatorial labor that his oeuvre predisposes. To build stories are multilayered, interactive, and participatory practices, deeply engrained within the comics medium.

Song Reader does something counterintuitive in our digitized moment: in Chapter 3, "The Broken Record: Beck Hansen's *Song Reader*," I discuss Beck Hansen's *Song Reader* as a case study that initiates questions about the contemporary reader as a documenter, fan, producer, and consumer and her relation to Beck Hansen as a rock star. *Song Reader* provokes a precarious positioning of the subject toward the object in her hand and the author who composed the songs. With Andreas Reckwitz's notion of the creativity dispositif in mind, *Song Reader* both outlines and undermines the concept of creativity and the demands and pleasures creativity indexes today. Ironically, the song reader must create something that is not hers to begin with. Beck Hansen's project seeks, no less, a song reader who appropriates and creates something not of her own making, who cannot claim authorship, but merely creative interpretation. As Andreas Reckwitz suggests, the creativity dispositif conjures up both creative *practices* and *competencies*; this draws a picture of a song reader who is to understand culture, leisure, and work as thoroughly creative—but who is also competent enough to appreciate the cultural merit (or, to speak more in Bourdieuian terms, cultural capital) of engaging with *Song Reader*. This chapter extends the questions of competences of and demands toward the curator; one of the more challenging questions will be about the interplay of materiality and immateriality that go hand in hand in *Song Reader*. The album is steeped in these strange convergences and tensions that I understand as (ir?)reconcilable antipodes of online and offline, material and ephemeral qualities of an object. I see these convergences and contingencies as fundamental expressions of the tensions between creative labor and leisure the subject has to navigate in contemporary culture.

The final case study is *Kentucky Route Zero*. In Chapter 4, entitled "*Kentucky Route Zero*'s Netherworld of Slowness," I interrogate aspects of slowness as both a narrative *and* medium-specific aesthetic principle to understand the implications toward contemporary media and our interaction with digital technology. The interaction with a computer channeled *through* a computer exemplifies how technological, cultural, and personal temporalities collide. Henceforth, the aspect of curation as a mode for reader interaction with the medium takes up redefined nuances within *Kentucky Route Zero*. These arise, as my discussion will show, within the fold between narrative and material strategies vis-à-vis the concept of slowness and slippages. (Please note that I will focus my discussion on the first three acts.) In this way, the concept of curation can be shifted toward thinking together restoration and conservation—of computers, of narrative, of material, of the practices digital devices encapsulate in the twenty-first century. And if and when the computer breaks entirely, what kind of commentary is this on our interaction with the medium? If *Building Stories* examines the collection and Beck Hansen's *Song Reader* the history of participatory/mass culture through sheet music, *Kentucky Route Zero* might be able to comment on daily routinized interaction with art and devices—through the lens of slow pre-internet life.[6]

From Labor to *Labo*: In the coda, I ask, "What's the Matter, Media?" and interrogate cardboard as a twenty-first-century material for digital media. Replicating, again, pastimes of the nineteenth century, objects made out of cardboard reveal interaction with digital media in a new guise. Cardboard is both sturdy and fickle, static and flexible, mass-produced and singular—it entices children's imagination to build fortresses and keeps cats busy for hours. We see a gamification of cardboard by turning to objects such as Google *Cardboard* and Nintendo *Labo*; I investigate the matter and the medium of (digitized) pastimes by way of cardboard being the material/medium for the amateur, not so much that of the author.

Works in progress challenge and entice us to question the nostalgic gestures of the texts. They reveal past media in the present, longings toward the highly contingent, and modernist art forms in the twenty-first century. They interrogate how the process of remembering might change in digital times and what is lost on the way. The objects, too, resist translation into digital spheres. Yet, by reproducing practices of online habits through their

---

[6] Wendy Chun's point of departure in *Updating to Remain the Same* is that new media and their temporalities are wonderfully creepy: "They are endlessly fascinating yet boring, addictive yet revolting, banal yet revolutionary" (Chun 2016, ix). She is interested in the habits of media interaction in what way these routines illuminate on "creepier, slower, more unnerving time" (Chun 2016, x).

convoluted, seemingly infinite structures, they ask us, the readers familiar with digital texts, how our current reading practices might reproduce earlier versions of reading, working, playing: the many things we like to do in our spare time. The three case studies ultimately play with the constellation of digitality and nostalgia—one that has become a hallmark of our contemporary moment. I understand them as objects of inquiry that reflect a certain digital zeitgeist of the twenty-first century, bringing the reader, the author, and the text into new haptic proximity. Terms central to my approach toward my case studies include not only curation, failure, taste, and distinction but also technology, glitches, the analog and digital, and archives and databases.

These concepts play toward challenges of overhaul, obsolescence, data rot, and glitches, revealing questions toward the readability of files and formats throughout the years. This ties these cultural objects back to not only the larger concepts of the novel and digitization processes but also how the contemporary moment keeps on overwriting itself. Works in progress comment on their own obsolescence, and as Brian Feldman remarks the "grooves in a record are eventually worn down by the needle, while an MP3 file retains its data structure. If you open a JPEG today and then again twenty years down the line, the photo will not have changed at all; it won't have yellowed or faded or have developed frayed edges" (Feldman 2014, n.p.). In line with Feldman's quote, works in progress may well, twenty years down the line, expose similar fault lines about market fads, durability of media and materiality, and glance critically at the rather quick overhauls in the twenty-first century. Feldman's example—the rise of the shitpic (another hallmark of the lowercase internet), that is, a deliberately bad image uploaded and circulated on platforms such as Instagram or Facebook—flirts with what "matters" on the internet.

The shitpic shows how digital files do indeed decay—as Feldman explains, "as files are put through a myriad of compression algorithms and Instagram filters, a new aesthetic of digital decay has started to emerge" (Feldman 2014, n.p.). The shitpic and its cultural momentum highlight artistic means of expression and compression of and for the digital age. This might give indication how the internet acknowledges its own aging, trying to find means and matters and ways to store its own (art) history. The curator, ultimately, is now allotted with the practices of *conservation*, too. The page of a "conventional" novel will have aged and yellowed over time, or its spine might be torn and broken. A CD or vinyl record might have gathered scratches over the years, and the floppy disks of an old point-and-click computer game might be illegible (my computer does not even have a CD drive anymore, and Apple has discontinued USB ports for some of its models). Works in progress, though, perform something different here, seemingly archiving, aestheticizing, acknowledging media's many histories and forms—not through faux decay, like the shitpic, but by resurrecting the past and repackaging it into contemporary texts that mark the decade the internet came of age.

1

Work in Progress: Curatorial Labor

Unfinished, fragmentary, elusive, provisional. These are adjectives we know from modernism but that we can use in a new way to describe forms of fictions in the twenty-first century. Some recent contemporary popcultural objects are often described as open-ended and nonlinear in the sense that they do not rely on a prescribed course, but that they defy any fully predefined narrative progression established by the author. Instead the composite forms and contents prevalent in graphic narratives, television series, novels, computer games, music albums, and movies are infused and influenced by unusual materialities and narrative. They do something new with the old: what I call *works in progress* are genre-bending, flexible objects of American fiction that lack a clearly defined or prescribed beginning or end. They are retro and nostalgic, while simultaneously staging themselves as contemporary, new, and hip. Narrative and material give form to life in and of the digitized moment through gestures toward their past. But they also give life to form: reading these texts connotes to practices such as building, curating, collecting, rehearsing—pastimes that are now transferred onto the act(ivity) of reading. Reading as a cultural technique in and of the twenty-first century turns into a means of interacting—with material and story and form(at). Interaction with the text extends from narrative toward *material* openness.

The ever-changing forms that the digital moment produces are negotiated and remediated through a kaleidoscope of obsolescence and retro-chic. These retro incarnations simultaneously reject *and* incorporate digital forms and practices. This is why they feel analog and digital at the same time, for they borrow what they need from online interaction to be both legible and unfamiliar. At hand, we have a comics book that is a collection of tear outs, a mute music album, and a retro point-and-click video game. They ask, In what way has reading become a technologically sophisticated, individualized pastime that entails a variety of processes exceeding the turning of the page? By connecting reading as a cultural technique to inquiries toward obsolete, forgotten and obscure side notes of technological innovation, works in progress mobilize older media forms and practices, in order, we might say, to historize the present. They combine the ever new and ever changing with overhauls in taste, trends, and technology. Interacting with these texts seems both foreign and familiar, both old and new, both adequate for the digital moment and peculiarly analog and retro.

In this chapter I think of these works in progress facilitating *curatorial labor*. I identify four components here—a slight shift of emphasis away from reader-response theory toward the material interaction with given components, rendering the reader as curator. This identifies a peculiar joy in and openness toward being overwhelmed, eschewing narrative closure but privileging narrative and material flexibility. Inherent within these questions of material and narrative interaction are aspects in and around creativity as a dispositif in the twenty-first century. Likewise, these inquiries shed light on the hierarchies between reader and author. The authors of the respective works recede into a rhetorics of failure and self-deprecation, whereas the curator's interaction with the objects at hand seems to legitimatize the scattered, fragmentary works left deliberately unfinished. My broader contextualization of curatorial labor will also shed light on material flexibility, from *product to process*. The intertwining of these different strands of inquiry—reader-response, creativity, the fragmentation of the body of work—outlines methods to read a digitized cultural landscape and a reader embedded within this matrix as consumer and curator.

This outlines new, highly aesthetized reading practices and the marketability of creativity and failure. It is to acknowledge the interactions of different strands of critical inquiry that all, in some way or another, relate contemporary subject positions toward *creativity* as a hallmark in the twenty-first century. Even more to the point, if fiction now is coined provisional and flexible, the means of how to understand and relate to the world are reconfigured and reassessed through the interaction with these open media and matters. This makes things of course not only so much more fun but also, at the same time, so much more precarious. What happens when this cultural practice of relating to the world is made porous and fickle and turns from one practice to several practices?

Curating "planned confusion"

The kind of provisional and fragmentary texts that I am interested in emphasize their material flexibilities alongside their narrative affordances. Acknowledging this allows for an extension of concepts regarding reception aesthetics; to initiate my inquiries toward curatorial labor, it is my intention to slightly tilt the theoretical framework from narrative to *material* reader interaction. Undoubtedly, fiction has always been one mode of sense-making for the reader, and particularly theories on reception aesthetics[1] postulate fiction as the glue for identities. It is tempting to see how reception aesthetics and reader-response theories go together with works in progress. Here, though, the text rather emerges through readerly interaction pertaining to *narrative* and *material*. The idea of "reception" here is rearticulated into the quite literal production *and* consumption of the text—in flexible, haptic terms. Notice how a shift within the terminology, from "reading" to "engaging," "performing," "interacting," is helpful to see the text as a(n overwhelming) *material, haptic,* yet *fragmentary* object. Hence, the works I discuss privilege the haptic engagement with the reshuffling of the preset components at hand.

Works in progress are playful subversions of the format of the book and offer colorful commentary on digitization processes. They explore what fiction should "do" in the twenty-first century, for the medium of the book has been

---

[1] Fiction has been understood as the sheltered realm where the subject can test out her identities, attach herself to different forms of narrative identity, abandon one, and create another. Doing so is always in reference to her own social being and agency. Fiction plays back to the reader the social reality she is embedded in, and reading can help articulate what has yet not been articulated. Thus, reading has been understood as something like a testing ground for who the reader is and who she *could* become—she can be herself *and* somebody else at the same time. Reading is an extremely productive and active way of sense making of the world and of the self. It articulates underlying assumptions of the world, it can alter reality, and it addresses how we represent ourselves, how the world is represented, and how to knit our identities together. To contextualize, Wolfgang Iser points out that the "literary text is a mixture of reality and the imagined. This interaction produces far more than just a contrast between the two . . . we discard the opposition of fiction and reality altogether and replace this duality by a triad: the real, the fictional and . . . the imaginary" (Iser 1986, 5–6). Out of this triad Iser sees the text emerging: it "cannot be confined to its real elements; nor can it be pinned down to its fictional features, for these in turn do not constitute an end in themselves but are the medium for the appearance of the imaginary" (Iser 1986, 5–6). The text articulates and extends the woolly and intangible imaginary, which is, consequently, made more tangible and accessible through fiction. The real, or rather the social reality as the reader perceives it, is extended and altered as well. Through fiction, Iser argues, "extratextual reality merges into the imaginary, and the imaginary merges into reality" (Iser 1986, 7). This reciprocal ability of a fictional text to alter the reader's social reality and articulate her imaginary brings forth "a transgressing of boundaries both of that which it organizes (external reality) and of that which is converts into a gestalt (the diffuseness of the imaginary)" (Iser 1986, 7). The triad of the fictive, the real, and the imaginary showcases how the aesthetic experience of fiction informs and extends the reader. More importantly, it gives her imaginary—thus her underlying assumptions of herself and the world and her identity—a gestalt.

well under pressure to compete with different forms of (digital) entertainment (and distractions, of course). What might be a first approach to this issue is to understand that "digital" means, literally, "performed with a finger." Works in progress set forth reading strategies that are decisively performed with hands and fingers (reception here pertains to manipulating the material), both in the way that they demand reader interaction and in the way in which they reflect upon the nature of the digital technologies that shape our contemporary moment (i.e., the practice of scrolling, zooming in, or swiping on the cellphone screen). Besides the extending of the meaning of reading and its reflection upon current poetics of readerly interaction and communication, works in progress intertwine leisure/spare time with workout.[2]

This allows for an emphasis on the unfinished, fragmentary nature of the objects that aim at reconceptualizing the *textual* transfer into a *cognitive* and *material* "working out." In this sense, the texts replicate hobbies and pastimes that are now reconfigured as reader-response and reader involvement, or, rather, as labor.[3] This evokes a cycle of *production* and *consumption*, of labor and leisure. The texts show the reader who she can *be* (i.e., the idea of transfer), and they also predetermine certain skill sets to tease out what she

---

[2] Steven Johnson in his book *Everything Bad Is Good For You*, published in 2005, calls attention to this: "Certain kinds of environments encourage cognitive complexity; others discourage complexity" (Johnson 2005, 11). He continues to explain that

> the forces at work in these systems operate on multiple levels; underlying changes in technology that enable new kinds of entertainment; new forms of online communications that cultivate audience commentary about works of pop culture; changes in the economics of the culture industry that encourage repeat viewing; and deep-seated appetites in the human brain that seek out reward and intellectual challenge. (Johnson 2005, 11).

Frank Rose in *The Art of Immersion* performs similar work. It is interesting that these are both "popular science" books, with Johnson's book carrying a blurb by Malcolm Gladwell on its dust jacket, for example, hence catering to a certain clientele of readers. This gives indication on the self-observing, self-referential qualities of pop-culture: for the books—popular science no less—watch the field they are embedded in.

[3] In *The Human Condition* Hannah Arendt famously distinguishes between labor and work. "The word 'labor,' understood as a noun, never designates the finished product, the result of laboring, but remains a verbal noun to be classed with the gerund, whereas the product itself is invariably derived from the word of work, even when current usage has followed the actual modern development so closely that the verb form of the word 'work' has become rather obsolete" (Arendt 1998, 80–81). What I offer is a variation of labor's estimation here—Arendt underlines that to labor "meant to be enslaved by necessity, and this enslavement was inherent in the conditions of human life" (Arendt 1998, 83–84). What I suggest, though, is a focus on the idea of how labor never designates a finished product, but refers back to its own productivity. (Arendt continues to distinguish between productive and unproductive labor—which carries, for her, the fundamental distinction between work and labor.) Arendt continues, "The productivity of labor power produces objects only incidentally and primarily concerned with the means of its own

can *do* to achieve a satisfactory performing of the text (i.e., playing a guitar or gluing together parts). Several media theorists have coined this phenomenon "prosumption"[4] (a portmanteau of production and consumption), or "playbor" (Diedrichsen 2010, 135). The reader is (re)cast as a prosumer or playborer (a rather cumbersome portmanteau of play and labor) who engages with texts actively—producing and consuming texts at the same time. I personally am not too sold on this term of the prosumer, but it helps fathom the multifarious roles the audience is now assigned to in their free time. It taps into this cycle of consumption and production that I diagnose as integral part of textual and material work.

Work in progress rely on and make available disorienting and overwhelming reading or viewing experiences. These experiences might even tie together readers and fans in their leisure time to solve puzzles and riddles surrounding the objects they engage in together. These objects allow for an active and what we might call, in reference to Umberto Eco, an "open" engagement. These interactive, medial forms of involving audiences[5] change and shape fan communities: fans labor together to create Wikis (i.e., the *Lostpedia* for the popular, puzzle-ridden television series *Lost*) to trace character developments or transcribe episodes, write fan fiction, or recap episodes online.[6] Social media and Web 2.0 offer a myriad of innovative means to tell stories[7] in a digital environment.

---

reproduction" (Arendt 1998, 88). Clearly Arendt is critiquing Karl Marx's idea of labor power here. What I find useful is the reproduction for its own sake—labor, after all, never produces anything but life.

[4] Processes of digitization with its facilitating of the interaction and manipulation of texts have bolstered the term "prosumption" and its inherent reader position of a producing consumer. For more on prosumption and the prosumer, see Bolin (2012), Ritzer and Jurgenson (2010), Scholz (2013), and Terranova (2008).

[5] I appreciate the prologue of Frank Rose's *The Art of Immersion*, in which he relates the marketing strategy for the blockbuster movie *The Dark Knight* (2008); the movie was preceded by an alternate reality game over a period of fourteen months, involving about ten million people worldwide. It was a scavenger hunt to help the Joker with his nefarious plans of world domination (or chaos). Participants had to pick up cakes from random bakeries, with cellphones baked into the cake the participants would receive calls to. This game, called "Why So Serious?", was, most importantly, nonlinear and presupposed that participants were connected with one via the internet to exchange information and compare clues (see Rose 2011, 10).

[6] Participatory culture has become part and parcel in discussions on digital media. For more on participatory culture, see Jenkins (2006, 2008), Rose (2011), and Wolf (2012).

[7] Here, *afternoon, a story* (1987) by Michael Joyce and *Patchwork Girl* (1995) by Shelley Jackson are among the most famous iterations of early electronic fictions. Digital fiction, interactive media, participatory culture, and the art of immersion have become buzzwords in media studies and cultural studies alike; digital fiction "encompasses any length of work, any form, any thematic subgroup, any software, and any degree of interaction with the work. . . . The material origin and intention of how the works are

Frank Rose calls this deep media—"stories that are not just entertaining, but immersive, taking you deeper than an hour-long TV drama or a two-hour movie or a 30-second spot will permit" (Rose 2011, 3). This is a reading experience of keeping the loose ends and cliffhangers neatly organized and comprehensible. Think here also of hashtags that appear on screen during TV shows and how they entice audience members to engage with each other. Even historical events, such as the Civil War, have been "live-tweeted" on the *New York Times* website. Jennifer Egan's short story "Black Box" (2012) was published on twitter, and Chris Ware's graphic novella *The Last Saturday* (2014), which will be discussed in the chapter on *Building Stories*, can be accessed for free on *The Guardian* website.

These media practices look current and new and decidedly *digital*, but what I suggest is that they indeed replicate reader interaction borrowed from other domains in life. These interactive practices of hunting for clues, solving the riddles in TV shows, or following disparate plotlines are traceable in earliest childhood experiences—think of scavenger hunts, building fortresses, collecting baseball cards, and, of course, Choose Your Own Adventure novels. These YA novels expose something equivalent to fusing literature with games. These "gamebooks" are written in second person point of view, and the reader (addressed as "you") has to choose her own path through an adventure (i.e., a cave exploration mission). At the end of a chapter, the reader is asked to choose how she would like to proceed in the narrative. She has to make a deliberate choice how the adventure is to unfold by following her own chosen path. The Choose Your Own Adventure books premise narrative progression on anticipation and retrospection: the reader must take into account what she already knows (say: the cave is dangerous) and, when faced with how to proceed, must make the wisest choice for progression (should I go deeper into the cave? Should I run away from the mysterious monster living in the depths of the caves or should I fight it?) as well as for closure.

created and received are foregrounded" (Engberg 2014, 139). It includes, as Engberg emphasizes, "a series of writing practices, including hypertext fiction, interactive fiction, multimedia fiction, distributed narratives, blog fiction, alternate reality games (ARGs), fan fiction, and cell phone fiction" (Engberg 2014, 140). Notice how Sarah Sloane and Janet Murray, among others, wrote about the narrative complexities of the personal computer at the end of the twentieth century, during the time of the dot-com bubble and the rise of the popularity of the personal computer in end-consumers' homes. Sarah Sloane, for example, underscored how "we need to focus on digital fiction as an unfamiliar version of a familiar social exchange between writers and readers, between invented self and real self, between world imagined and world around us" (Sloane 2000, 38).

Upon rereading the Choose Your Own Adventure novel, she is aware of the dangers that might await her in the dark cave. The next time around, she is able to plot out an entirely new story. In *Reading for the Plot*, Peter Brooks picks up on the question of the anticipation of retrospection. He asserts that a

> sense of a beginning, then, must in some important way be determined by the sense of an ending. We might say that we are able to read present moments—in literature and, by extension, in life—as endowed with narrative meaning only because we read them in anticipation of the structuring power of those endings that will retrospectively give them the order and significance of plot. (Brooks 1992, 94)

He calls this "narrative desire": at the "end of a narrative we can suspend time in a moment when past and present hold together in a metaphor . . . that moment does not abolish the movement, the slidings, the mistakes, and partial recognitions of the middle" (Brooks 1992, 92). Narrative desire,[8] according to Brooks, is a desire *for* the end, yet the reader comes to appreciate the twists and turns the story can take between beginning and end (see Brooks 1992, 52).

Narrative desire, closure, yet recognizing its twists and deferred endings—Is the contemporary reader in for something else than "for the end"? We might say that she reads for the *experience*. One gesture toward this idea is the appreciation of the slidings, glitches, mistakes, gaps, and riddles that Peter Brooks fleshes out. This recognizes Jason Mittell's "narrative complexity," a concept[9] he develops to discuss complex television

---

[8] I am tempted here to infuse Peter Brooks's idea of narrative desire with Paul Ricoeur's idea of appropriation—this appreciation of the twists and turns in between beginning and end might have hermeneutical potential to actualize the
> meaning as addressed to someone. It takes the place of the answer in the dialogical situation, in the same way "revelation" or "disclosure" takes the place of ostensive reference to the dialogical situation. The interpretation is complete when the reading releases something like an event, an event of disclosure, an event in the present time. As appropriation, the interpretation becomes an event. (Ricoeur 1991, 89)

The reader appropriates, in dialogue, by engagement, play, and interpretation; after all, in play, nothing is serious, but something is
> presented, produced, given in representation. There is thus an interesting relation between play and the presentation of a world. The relation is, moreover, absolutely reciprocal: on the one hand, the presentation of the world in a poem is a heuristic fiction and in this sense "playful"; but, on the other hand, all play reveals something true, precisely because it is play. To play, Gadamer says, is to play at something. (Ricoeur 1991, 91)

[9] Jason Mittell explores in his seminal essay "Narrative Complexity and Contemporary American Television" how and why narrative strategies have changed in and around the 1990s. He looks at the cultural (and medial) implications and repercussions of this shift.

serials that reject "the need for plot closure within every episode that typifies conventional episodic form, narrative complexity foregrounds ongoing stories across a range of genres" (Mittell 2006, 32). Instead, he allocates technological changes as well as a changing perception on the legitimacy of the medium as key factors for such narrative complexity to emerge. Mittell writes decidedly of television and its serialized structures, but here we can trace a shift toward narrative complexity within media that employ smaller units to unite to a larger fictitious universe. This could include an episode or a new installment of a comic strip or even a new action figure that needs to be insinuated into the logics of a story's universe. In my understanding, Mittell's ideas serve to identify a more systemic change visible in fiction and the "desire for the end" today. Planned confusion implies larger repercussions on the legitimacy of off-kilter genres and their legitimacy in academia or mainstream media, for instance. In terms of reader interaction and narrative complexity, Jason Mittell writes that

> one of the central shifts stemming from the rise of narrative complexity is television's growing tolerance for viewers to be confused, encouraging them to pay attention and put the pieces together themselves to comprehend the narrative. While television rarely features an avant-garde level of abstraction or ambiguity, contemporary programming has embraced a degree of planned confusion. (Mittell 2012, n.p.)

I appreciate this definition about episodic forms under the influence of grander serial narration techniques. In a sense, the text can change any time, reroute its plotline suddenly, or fall apart, and the reader is enticed to plot out, manage the story, and be confused for the sheer sake of it. This paints a picture of a reader/viewer who has (growing) tolerance for these confusing units embedded within a larger narrative. She is willing to "get to work" and "figure the text out." This draws an image of a reader who relishes in the ambiguity and precariousness of a text's narrative complexities, for this "workout"[10] is simultaneously (time-)consuming *and* (text-)productive.

Mittell allocates technological changes as well as a changing perception of the legitimacy of the medium as key factors for narrative complexity to emerge.

[10] Frank Kelleter calls attention to this overlapping of work and play specifically in television dramas such as *The Sopranos*, *Mad Men*, *Lost*, and *The Wire* in his newspaper article "Serien als Stresstest" (no English translation available):
> Wer mitbekommen möchte, muss aufpassen; bloßes Berieselnlassen wird zur Frustration führen.... Fernsehunterhaltung als prozedurales Problemlosetraining,... was [Steven Johnson in *Everything Bad Is Good For You*] kenntnisreich als "kognitives Workout" der jüngeren Populärkultur beschreibt, ruft offensichtlich

This layering of complexity gives a first idea of curatorial labor and the curator's tasks inherent within the text. Curation is to bring order to the unruliness of composite forms and formats. Confusion is part and parcel of media's respective *modus operandi*. The "sorting out" of a story becomes an ambiguous effort: it refers to untangling of the plotlines *and* the sifting through the material of the objects. So if we read for an ending, what happens if there is no end, but multiple possibilities of reassembly and combination? Or, rather, can we read for confusion, for sheer confusion's sake? If we can ascribe *narrative* desire, can we ascribe something similar to *material* desire as well? I wager that the idea of the reader as curator springs out of these questions. The texts remain unfinished, unsung, and unplayed lest the reader "gets to work" and sets the texts into provisional order.

This allows us to take another glance at Mittell's quote about planned confusion, and we might also emphasize the episodic, the fragment, the unit which stands alone but is embedded within a (if messy) whole. The curator pays attention to the processes and the respective dynamics of the texts, that they can be tinkered with and shuffled through, that they can be organized in one way, but then reassembled in another one.[11] To *curate*, then, connotes something else than to "merely" *read*: curation in this context entails repetition and interaction with given components. Curatorial labor thus indexes a reading position that describes the engagement with and the caring for the material and narrative at hand. Refigured as pastimes, these forms of fiction present a set of tasks toward its readership that entails more than the turning of a page. But I must stress that curating, too, connotes something different than contingency management: curatorial labor describes the implementation of an artistic vision and redefines the role of the reader in terms of the interactive and participatory notions within contemporary culture. Further, it caters to debates in and around creativity in the twenty-first century.

---

genau jene Fähigkeiten ab, die den neoliberalen Arbeitsalltag im Zeitalter der Digitalisierung kennzeichnen: Netzwerkdenken, situative Rückkopplung, verteilte Informationsabwicklung, Multitasking und nicht zuletzt die Bereitschaft, zwischen Arbeit und Freizeit nicht zu unterscheiden. (Kelleter 2012, n.p.)

[11] In *Bring on the Books for Everybody* Jim Collins emphasizes how also *in* the contemporary novel, collecting and cataloging have become predominant modes of sense-making for characters. He writes how the reader encounters characters engaged in the "relentless catalouging [sic] of books read, movies watched, music listened to, and clothes purchased" (Collins 2010, 201).

Creativity and the curating reader

It is my assumption that creativity must be seen as a quintessential structuring principle within and of these texts and of the reading practices that curatorial labor entails. The overlapping critical and theoretical investment of literary studies, cultural studies, media studies, and sociology in creativity is indicative. As Jim Collins, for example, points out in his study on recent changes within American media publics in *Bring on the Books for Everybody*, "we're all curators now, of words *and* images" (Collins 2010, 266). Stephan Porompka explores the dispositif of "making" in one of his lecture series (and accompanying podcast) *Making Of—Dispositiv des Machens*. Likewise media critic Alexander Galloway in *The Interface Effect* underlines that interfaces must be seen as zones of aesthetic gravity that the critic must resort to "new methodologies of scanning, playing, sampling, parsing, and recombining. The critic might then be better off as a sort of remix artist, a disc jockey of the mind" (Galloway 2012, 29). And, writing from a sociological perspective, Andreas Reckwitz's study of the creative ethos in late-capitalist societies unravels the societal processes behind the aesthetization of the subject position toward that of a curator.[12] The reader is more than just a page turner—she is somebody who is rewarded with an idiosyncratic, unique experience by way of curation.

How do we spend our free time, anyway? We meet friends, waste time on the internet, travel, do volunteer work, read and go to the movies, go shopping, work out at the gym or go running, do jigsaw puzzles, listen to podcasts, or partake in hobbies ranging from knitting to blogging (and blogging about knitting) to crocheting to partying to bouldering to going to the fleamarket to horseback-riding and geo-caching. The possibilities to fill these precious hours of free time are endless and maybe even a little overwhelming—for time off should certainly not be wasted or idled away. Theodor W. Adorno traces the significance of free time in his piece "Free Time" (1969)—free time *cannot* exist, as Adorno observes, without *unfree* time. He posits how leisure (the German word he uses here is *Muße*) "refers to a specific difference, that of unfree time, time occupied by labor, and one

---

[12] These books have all been published around the same time, at the beginning of the 2010s. The disc jockey of the mind meets its contemporary, the curator of words and images. This may give us an image of how different strands of inquiry make comparable assumptions about a late-capitalist subject position, and in what way this language has become, in slight variation, pervasive in critical inquiry. Whether she is a reader, a media-user of the interface, a disc jockey, or, more broadly speaking, somebody seeking the creative, aesthetic "ethos" in her life, the circumstance of this creative work seem to be of similar interest in media studies, sociology, and literary studies.

should add, time that is determined heteronomously. Free time is shackled to its contrary. This opposition, the relationship within which free time appears, even shapes some of its essential characteristics" (Adorno 1998, 167). He diagnoses that free time becomes a parody of itself: "people are at least subjectively convinced that they are acting of their own will, this will itself is fashioned by precisely what they want to shake off during their time outside of work" (Adorno 1998, 168). In his essay, Adorno imagines that we would have even more spare time in the future—his clairvoyance proved shaky, yet not entirely so.

At the beginning of the twenty-first century, free time has been incorporated into the work place. Particularly in creative industries we see free and unfree time mingle and merge (i.e., the Google campus in Silicon Valley offers all kinds of benefits to Google employees; freelance work is, as the cliché goes, done in hip cafés and turns communal spaces into offices; team-building exercises are allocated into the after hours; happy hours in bars to shake off the work day are spent with colleagues; team messaging apps such as Slack recreate group chats on the cellphone). And so-called leisure industries (building an industry *on* free time), and Adorno's argument still rings true here, are "specific phenomena of free time, like tourism and camping, [and] are established and organized for the same of profit. At the same time the difference between work and free time has been branded as a norm into people's consciousness and unconscious" (Adorno 1998, 169). Moreover, the flipside of Adorno's prophecy describes people who come home from a day at the office to watch *The Office* on television or shuffle their *Sims* avatar on the computer from work to home and back again.

What we can distill from Adorno's piece is how the boundaries between free time and unfree time have become almost unrecognizable. Unfree time has increasingly bled into free time in which we reproduce capitalist labor (i.e., like sending *Sims* avatar to work) and, of course, vice versa. Just think how bean bags, foosball tables, or ping pong tables have become clichés in offices—both infantilizing creative workers and allowing them to "hang loose." CEOs and employees alike wear Nike sneakers: Controlled rebellion in style, the countercultural self with a stock market portfolio.[13] Alongside

---

[13] I have always appreciated the assessment of the trend forecasting agency K-Hole about style choices in the creative industries. In issue #3, "Brand Anxiety Matrix," they develop a matrix with one factor of "Illegible Order" which
> works the hardest to maintain credibility. . . . At its peak, Illegible Order is the best version of normal. But nothing looks more desperate than someone else's old reasoning. 'What would you wear to a meeting with Comme des Garcons [sic]?' a colleague asked over burgers at the Time Warner center. 'Uniqlo and Nike,' we replied

this, I would like to develop an argument that outlines how this reciprocity of free time and unfree time becomes prevalent in contemporary fiction. I posit that the rise of planned confusion as a narrative and material strategy and the reading position of the curator who keeps the story lines in check is deeply indebted to and affected by the rise of creativity as a dispositif. Here, the concepts such as planned confusion or "material desire" map out how a book gestures toward specific skills the audience has honed and attained from hobbies and/or at work (i.e., playing the piano, using Excel). This tilts Adorno's reflections on free and unfree time slightly and helps think how activities allocated within free time cater to neoliberal processes of individualization and a means-ends-calculus.

"Unfree" time here also takes on another dimension, for seeming busy has turned into a peculiar symbol of status of its own right in the Western neoliberalized social realities. The marketing professor Silvia Bellezza explains in an interview with Joe Pinsker for the *Atlantic* how "bragging and complaining with others about how much we work . . . operates as a symbol of status in the eyes of others" (Bellezza 2017, n.p.). Being busy means having cultural capital, and having no time, or, rather, no *free* time, is considered to be an asset. Silvia Bellezza continues that "compared to farming and manufacturing, there's now a more competitive market for talent and human capital, such that the more you work, it must mean that you're very sought after in the market" (Bellezza 2017, n.p.). So neither failure nor reclusiveness (i.e., having *too much* free time) are to be understood as "status symbols" today—but being in demand, moving around, and being busy are the norm and a desirable mode of being.

Studies such as Richard Florida's *The Rise of the Creative Class* explore these implications of the overlapping of work and leisure, and of work and the creation of the self.[14] He draws out how life lived in flux and uncertainty is part and parcel of the everyday. Florida sees the shift toward the

---

simultaneously. Illegible Order is completely unhackable. It houses the black box brands that externalize your experiences to the point that you're just watching yourself wear Rag & Bone. Nonetheless, it feels nice to be taken care of. (K-Hole 2013, 26ff)

[14] Further discussions about creativity and the creative subject can be found, besides Andreas Reckwitz's work in *The Invention of Creativity* and Richard Florida's work on the creative class in *The Rise of the Creative Class—And How It's Transforming Work, Leisure, Community and Everyday Life* (New York: Basic Books, 2004). Richard Florida pays detailed attention to flexibility and (social) mobility, examining cities that attract "creative" work. Other points of reference offer Lenk (2000) and Joas (1996). Noteworthy is also the pop-cultural/self-help discourse vis-à-vis creativity (i.e., how to unleash it). Austin Kleon's book *Steal Like an Artist—10 Things Nobody Told You About Being Creative* is guide to unlock your creative potential and, interestingly, filed in the "Psychology and Counseling" section on amazon.com; Keri Smith's widely popular

importance of the individual's creativity in economic and societal spheres as key factors for this development (see Florida 2004, 4). Further, creativity *creates* new industries (i.e., start-ups). Florida's study helps acknowledge the *geographical* influences of creativity onto city landscapes and their infrastructure (he focuses on "creative cities" and in what way creative sectors reshape the city, that is, Austin as a tech hub; Berlin's "Silicon Allee"), but, even more importantly, he gives us an image how creativity entered both the work and leisure sector as an asset—not in the sense of the Romantic genius and its creative "musings" (think Adorno)—but rather as an imperative for capital flow and keeping companies afloat—and its workers happy and creative.

The intermingling of work (and never being truly *not* at work) and lifestyle (emphasis on individuality and individualization) becomes visible and prevalent (and this also pertains to the "styling" of an individual's life): Andreas Reckwitz continues this conversation in *The Invention of Creativity*. He notes how "the self" arises in an "experimental, quasi-artistic way, all facets of the self in personal relations, in leisure activities, in consumer styles and in self-technologies of the body and the soul. This preoccupation with creativity is often construed as a striving for originality, for uniqueness" (Reckwitz 2017b, 3). I appreciate Reckwitz's observation greatly for he pays attention to self-technologies enfolded within creative maxims. Self-culture[15] and "self-creativity" conjure up a subject position that is well aware of a risky, contingent life and the necessity to unfold it within creative parameters—in which busyness turns into business and where fickleness is an inherent vice.

In what way can the pastime of *reading* unfold in this overlap between free and unfree time, being busy *and* being creative? Referring back to the ideas of reader-response theory, reading has undoubtedly always been a "creative" and creating endeavor (i.e., character identification, reading for closure,

---

Wreck This Journal is a ready-made sketch book to let the reader's bottled-up creative juices flow; *The Gift—Creativity and the Artist in the Modern World* by Lewis Hyde is labeled as a modern classic.

[15] I borrow this term from Ulrich Beck and Elisabeth Beck-Gernsheim whose work has been instrumental in defining second modernity. The individual within second modernity is informed by a multitude of factors that restructure, limit, as well as liberate her in the quest to curate and create the self successfully: she has the freedom to autonomously designate and design her life in terms of self-responsibility, self-regulation, as well as the freedom to make choices and engage in risks: "The choosing, deciding, shaping human being who aspires to be the author of his or her own life, the creator of an individual identity, is the central character of our time" (Beck and Beck-Gernsheim 2002, 23). A creative ethos of life is based on contingency, flexibility, as well as fickle work commitments and market demands.

suturing, and keeping plotlines together) for giving the self a gestalt—but this has predominantly been a private effort. What curatorial labor indexes and layers on top of these considerations is a pronounced creative engagement with material—objects like *Building Stories*, *Song Reader*, and *Kentucky Route Zero* feed into these ideas of reading as a creative, yet laborious pastime and self-technique. Toolkits for creativity come in the shape of an oversized keepsake box, or in a blue folder, or as download—*Gesamtkunstwerke* in and for themselves, mirroring the system of relations that they are encapsulated within. *Building Stories*, for example, reflects upon individual life patterns that are reliant on multi-tasking and self-organized management. Ware's book tells the story of one woman who often rushes from one appointment to the next. She yearns for a creative outlet to make sense of her world (i.e., she writes short stories, arranges flowers, goes to art school). Notice the doubling: engaging in this story is staged as a creative pastime while the reader stitches together a life lived within a creative ethos—similar to watching *The Office* or *30 Rock* after work.

This adds a new facet to the curator: not only is she creative and busy but she also finds creative outlet *and* creative practice in the stories she builds. This ties into a double bind, though—without her creativity, there is no text, but without text, she cannot let her creative juices flow. What is evoked through such fragmented material is that this is a culturization and aesthetization of the intertwining of fiction, art, work, and labor on narrative *and* material levels. What I have done so far is to lay bare the sedimentations of critical inquiry toward creativity (i.e., sociology, literary and cultural studies, media studies) in the twenty-first century as both compulsion and pleasure for the individual. Ironically, none of these notions of creativity or the curation of life, love, labor, and fiction ever evoke images of urban bohemians or countercultural activists who "live for art" and lead unconventional, artistic lives in squatter's apartments. Much on the contrary, creativity is reconfigured into a process of societal and cultural aesthetization that attains to every body and every thing: it is a dispositif, a system of relations.[16]

---

[16] Michel Foucault's notion of the *dispositif* comes to the fore here. As he points out in the interview "The Confessions of Flesh":

> What I'm trying to pick out with this term is, firstly, a thoroughly heterogeneous ensemble consisting of discourses, institutions, architectural forms, regulatory decisions, laws, administrative measures, scientific statements, philosophical, moral and philanthropic propositions—in short, the said as much as the unsaid. Such are the elements of the apparatus. The apparatus itself is the system of relations that can be established between these elements. (Foucault 1980, 194)

> Seen from this vantage point, creativity is now part and parcel in organizing and orchestrating this very system of relations.

Andreas Reckwitz would coin the compulsion and pleasure[17] to be creative as "creativity complex": this "complex does not merely *register* the fact that novelty comes about; it systematically propels forward the dynamic production and reception of novelty as an aesthetic event in diverse domains. It elicits creative practices and skills and suggests to the observer the importance of keeping an eye out for aesthetic novelty and creative achievements" (Reckwitz 2017b, 6). The curator, I posit, is a highly aesthetized, stylized subject position which equally reflects, informs, and conforms to these societal *and* medial processes. What we must subsume is that these practices—curators of words and images, or shufflers and remixers—are inherent within the dispositif of creativity that have equally influenced culture and the academy.

And a quick glance around the American cultural landscape elucidates a shift away from artsy bohemia to the institutionalization of creativity as a structuring ethos of all spheres of life.[18] This institutionalization of creativity becomes prevalent particularly in Mark McGurl's work on (graduate) creative writing programs, for he underlines how such programs turn "writers into salaried writing professors and students into tuition-paying apprentices. . . . [The] graduate programs represented a dramatic escalation of the relationship between the profession of authorship and the school, a systematic coupling, without (as of yet) a final merging, of art and institution" (McGurl 2009, 4). The bolt of inspiration is bolstered by a paycheck. This gestures toward larger implications of whether creativity can be "taught" or obtained through adequate schooling. In the same vein, though, a creative writing program

---

[17] This also accounts for the creative and creating accounting for one's own (tightrope) biography, as Ulrich Beck would postulate, which has become the dictum of the reflexive conduct of life (see Beck 1992, 98). Biography, as Ulrich Beck defines it, ultimately connotes the "becoming [of] a reflexive project" (Beck 1992, 125). Even more to the point, the act and managing of "becoming" is a creative endeavor. The self can now be placed strategically among options, solely dependent on the successful and active configuration to constitute herself as such, as a free and flexible and creative individual. This echoes in Ulrich Beck's argument that we live in a multi-activity society which is "characterized by individualized life patterns[,] . . . a form of 'voluntary, self-organized labour, where what should be done, and how it should be done are in the hands of those who actually do it'" (Beck qtd. in McFall 2014, 13).

[18] There are self-help bestsellers to crafty online stores to YouTube channels dedicated to home improvement or yoga or knitting to "Design Thinking" schools in Stanford and Potsdam over to Creative Writing MFA programs at American universities. This debate of whether creative writing can be taught was partly initiated by the literary magazine *n + 1*. In *MFA v. NYC*, the author Chad Harbach traces the social and literary consequences

> to consider the fiction writer less as an utterly free artistic being, with responsibilities only to posterity and eternal truth (or whatever), and more as a person constrained by circumstance—a person who needs money, and whose milieu influences the way she lives, reads, thinks, and writes. A person whose work is shaped by education and economy and a host of other pressures, large and small. (Harbach 2014, 4)

at a university also comes with the "right social climate (liberal, diverse) for creativity" (McGurl 2009, 20). This double bind of the institutionalizing creativity and providing the right climate (notice here: liberal, diverse) unpacks several chicken-or-egg situations: Can creativity flourish in rigid structures, or can the right structures facilitate creative outbursts and bolts of inspiration?[19] Is creativity pushed into a mold of societal structures or does creativity change these structures and make them more pliable? And who, really, has the privilege to be among the creative?

As a dispositif, creativity infuses the very last nook and cranny in the matrix of marketability. Can we rephrase the previous statement and say: once creativity becomes the demand for the (successful) implementation of such texts (and life in general), is there a shift detectable toward creativity as market asset? On the flipside, does this not signal a depletion of creativity as a structuring principle? To be creative out of sheer creativity's sake touches on Max Horkheimer and Theodor W. Adorno's notion of *purposelessness*. In *Dialectic of Enlightenment* they draw out tensions that arise once the marketability of art becomes the demand, or, rather, once there is a shift toward art as *commodity*. (Put differently: once the unique, creative, idiosyncratic *objet d'art* turns into a commodity or market asset.) Horkheimer and Adorno write, and it is worth quoting at length here:

> The work of art, by completely assimilating itself to need, deceitfully deprives men of precisely that liberation from the principle of utility which it should inaugurate. What might be called use value in the reception of cultural commodities is replaced by exchange value; in place of enjoyment there are gallery-visiting and factual knowledge: the prestige seeker replaces the connoisseur. The consumer becomes the ideology of the pleasure industry, whose institutions he cannot escape. One simply "has to" have seen *Mrs. Miniver*, just as one "has to" subscribe to *Life and Time*. Everything is looked at from only one aspect: that it can be used for something else, however vague the notion of this use may be. No object has an inherent value; it is valuable only to the extent that it can be exchanged. The use value of art, its mode of being, is treated as a fetish;

[19] Remember how Jason Mittell ascertains the rise of planned confusion to both the *technological* advancements as well as the legitimacy of television as a medium. We can reroute his attention to craftsmanship and reader interaction by way of acknowledging how it has been mirrored (and legitimized!) by the rise and popularity of DIY crafts, like knitting, crocheting, and sewing (which have been commercialized, with websites like etsy.com capitalizing on handiness and craftsmanship of their users cum entrepreneurs) or the popularity of fermentation and pickling. These skills have enjoyed resurgence *because of* technological innovations, like e-commerce or easy digital payment methods, like PayPal.

and the fetish, the work's social rating (misinterpreted as its artistic status) becomes its use value—the only quality which is enjoyed. The commodity function of art disappears only to be wholly realized when art becomes a species of commodity instead, marketable and interchangeable like an industrial product. (Horkheimer and Adorno 1989, 158)

Horkheimer and Adorno's critique on mass culture from 1944 echoes loudly in the year of 2018: What else but social rating, uniqueness and singularity might legitimize the entire process of building, gluing together, or practicing the songs, or, speaking more broadly, inviting the creative ethos in one's life?

The bleakness that Horkheimer and Adorno describe as the "assembly-line character of the culture industry, the synthetic, planned method of turning out its products (factory-like not only in the studio but, more or less, in the complication of cheap biographies, pseudodocumentary novels, and hit songs)" becomes part and parcel of the curator's experience (Horkheimer and Adorno 1989, 163). In the German original, Horkheimer and Adorno use the term "Montagecharakter der Kulturindustrie," which I see as a blurring between the lines of the Fordist fragmentation of assembly-line work steps (i.e., the disassembly of the body in capitalism) and the aesthetics of modernist art and literature of the early twentieth century created out of fragments and objects from disparate sources (see later in the chapter my ideas about processes and products). Horkheimer and Adorno's notion of purposelessness can be infused with questions pertaining to the cultural capital of the curator, and I appreciate their shift away from "prestige seeker" toward that of the "connoisseur." This shift fathoms the highly stylized consumer and producer practice of the creative individual.

Curating brings the labor that the reader is to perform into proximity with art. In this sense, curatorial labor also elevates the objects at hand from "mere comic books" or "mere computer games" to an artistic vision or a unique, idiosyncratic experience. But what happens to the distinguishing markers of high art and mass culture—and their supposed purposelessness à la Horkheimer and Adorno today? In *Post-Postmodernism* Jeffrey Nealon points out that coordinates of culture have become interchangeable and marketable, similar to an industry product. Nealon suggests a flattening out among commodities: "in the twenty-first century, it's very hard indeed to suggest that knowing a lot about the Beatles is different in kind (or somehow more 'authentic') than knowing a lot about the various styles at Abercrombie & Fitch. In contemporary parlance, they both allow you to be a quintessential 'prosumer,' that consumer who produces him- or herself through consumption" (Nealon 2012, 64). Nealon evokes the prosumer back on the plane, whom we have met before as a reader (and curator) of planned confusion—who, ultimately, bestows a sense of self through consumption onto herself.

But Nealon is also interested in questions regarding authenticity, which he relegates toward niche capitalism. He writes that the

> rock 'n' roll style of rebellious, existential individuality, largely unassimilable under the mass-production dictates of midcentury Fordism has become the engine of post-Fordist, niche-market consumption capitalism. Authenticity is these days wholly territorialized on choice, rebellion, being yourself, freedom, fun; and these, what one might call the "values" of classic rock, today hold for your choices in music as for your choices in cars . . ., computers . . ., and virtually every bother commodity you can think of. (Nealon 2012, 57–58)

Nealon brings the idea of post-Fordism and fragmentation back into conversation, and we detect parallels to the way we assemble our commodities—but how we are also able to distinguish the flattened out hierarchies between the Beatles and Abercrombie & Fitch, Beck Hansen and Topshop. The connoisseur whose "attention . . . used to be reserved for wonking your favorite bands has made its way all the way up to the board room—where innovation and rebellion are touted as necessary to any healthy business model—and all the way down to the ever-changing minutiae of cell-phone applications and ring tones" (Nealon 2012, 64). This intersecting of purposelessness and connoisseurship outlines a slippery slope: the positioning of the curator as a connoisseur and expert of the material at hand is comparatively less institutionalized and therefore often more precarious than that of the artist or author. Again, curation connotes something different than "cleaning up" or "bringing into order"; much rather, it signifies implementing an artistic, creative vision, a *Gesamtkunstwerk* of an artist—thus elevating the "mere" commodity into the esoteric spheres of art.

Hip competence

The curator accentuates (elevates?) the fragmentary work not only by bringing order into planned confusion but also by creating new hierarchies among cultural objects. Texts like *Building Stories* or *Kentucky Route Zero* presuppose a reader who is willing and able to implement an artistic (and purchasable!) vision that is not her own. As a connoisseur and curator, she is to perform "good work" with the preset components made available. She signals that she is in the know: as Horkheimer and Adorno have pointed out in the previous section, one simply "has to" read the new Ware novel or one "has to" listen to the new Beck Hansen album to be among the flock attuned to the latest fads in the folds of obscure and esoteric American (pop) culture. Hence, to implement is to be in the know, to be part of the pleasure and culture industry of the twenty-first century. Otherwise the album would remain mute, the building would remain unfinished, the computer game would not move forward: this reward and demand (or, rather, compulsion and pleasure) of interaction is one crux of curatorial labor.

To elucidate, let me slightly tilt an argument made by Jen Harvie on participatory theater and flexible spectatorship. As much as Harvie makes an argument about theater and the active involvement of *stand-ins* in a theater, we can relay what she claims about "labor" performed on stage toward the multifarious roles the reader is ascribed to. Harvie's argument conjures up a de-skilled and alienated stand-in performer in performance art who is summoned onto stage to perform menial labor, like carrying swords or sitting in a café as a fill-in to the scene. This can function as foil to the objects, for they do something decidedly different, and I posit that the texts (i) blossom in niches for a *narrow* audience and (ii) facilitate highly skilled, highly specific reading practices. In contrast, these texts "know" their participants. Harvie's notion of participatory labor "deskills its participants. Because this labour rarely 'knows' its participant/workers but recruits them all equally, it casts them to perform in usually quite basic ways" (Harvie 2013, 47). Who are the key players, then? The object, the reader, or the author?[20]

Curatorial labor is not de-skilled. Much on the contrary, the readership learns how the text has to be read and handled. The reader performs highly specialized (and idiosyncratic! For no reading experience will be comparable to that of another reader) labor, ranging from playing the guitar to gluing together parts to selecting options in a database. For these activities fall under the category of reading, it gives us an image of cultural productions

---

[20] Harvie writes that the participants who fill the scene

> create the spectacle and help concentrate the focus on the key players. Whatever skills an audience member might actually have ... these are very unlikely to be either called on or effectively permitted in the immersive performance. ... The audience member as worker in this flexible art and performance economy is rendered, in many ways, insecure, deskilled and alienated. (Harvie 2013, 47)

This echoes Ulrich Beck's assertion of the multi-activity societies. In *Brave New World of Work* Ulrich Beck sees the transition from "work society" to "multi-activity society" take place. This shift can dilute one seemingly very simple question: What *is* work? Beck allocates activities such as "family work, parental work, work for oneself, voluntary work or political activity" within this fold (Beck 2000, 58). Further, Beck fathoms the implications of why new ways of distributing work are necessary (i.e., shorter hours with full pay, of flexibilization).

that fundamentally "naturalize"[21] the leisure/work dichotomy. In this sense, these texts seek out a specific target/niche audience who is, always and already, attuned to their aesthetic and poetic affordances. Contrary to Jen Harvie's idea about the de-skilled spectatorship, I suggest that the texts know and find their audience. The question of curation as highly specialized labor turns out to be among the strategies to produce and consume markers of distinction. Taste and "niche labor" conjure up the necessity to prove *competent* in working the stories out (i.e., "being in the know"). This idea exceeds technological or dexterous competence. It taps into questions of predilection, fandom, and taste.

Based on these assumptions, we can delve deeper into the tension between author and reader. As a first gesture toward this, let me extrapolate on how ideas of quality and legitimation unfold. Undoubtedly, "quality," idiosyncrasy, and uniqueness are leitmotifs in Western consumer culture of the twenty-first century: artisanal coffee, personalized sneakers, one-of-a-kind adventure vacations to far-off places, hand-tailored clothes, tasteful online interior blogs and other "singularities," as Andreas Reckwitz via Igor Kopytoff[22] calls them, speak to this idea. Quality and purchasing power are seemingly what makes the individual an, well, individual—unique and distinguishable *through* consumer options. No surprise, then, that the ever-new, ever-changing shape of a graphic narrative, album, or point-and-click adventure game taps right into this zeitgeist: they presuppose artful *selection* and *choice* with every reading. Within this logic, stories become singularities, too, that mirror the taste (and the competence!) of the reader who is on the one hand hip enough to recognize a Ware comics book, and also competent enough to implement

---

[21] Jen Harvie writes about naturalization vis-à-vis performance art how the audience is enticed to participate in stage performances to help naturalize their work patterns. She writes that

> it is . . . possible to argue that this art and performance practice effectively *naturalizes* capitalism's desire for and reliance on workers' flexibility in what [Richard] Sennett . . . refers to as the "unstable, fragmentary social conditions" of the era. In helping *audiences to rehearse their flexibility at work*, these art and performance practices manage workers' expectations about using—or, rather, not using—their skills and enhance workers' flexibility with both tasks and co-workers in ways that the new capitalism precisely desires to ensure its own profitability. (Harvie 2013, 49, emphasis mine)

[22] Igor Kopytoff is invested in what he calls the cultural biography of *things*. Kopytoff describes how we "accept that every person has many biographies—psychological, professional, political, familial, economic and so forth—each of which selects some aspects of the life history and discards others. Biographies of things cannot but be similarly partial" (Kopytoff 1986, 68). He suggests thinking about objects having culturally informed economic biographies and how the biography of things in complex societies lies within the uncertainty of their identity. My question is, Where is the final resting place for a thing or object that changes its shape?

and "play" it. In this sense, the curator cannot just tell *any* story, but she must tell *the* story of *Building Stories* or *Kentucky Route Zero*, and this story should rather be good.

This quest for quality unfolds into different directions. It is a way to legitimize the text's intrinsic value and its significance in our cultural moment. ("That object is interesting, and my interest validates its significance.") Secondly, the reader must be competent enough to navigate the text's structures. ("I understand this text, for I know how to read it and engage with it in all its complexity.") As Igor Kopytoff suggests, "In the homogenized world of commodities, an eventful biography of a thing becomes the story of the various singularizations of it, of classifications and reclassifications in an uncertain world of categories whose importance shifts with every minor change in context. As with persons, the drama here lies in the uncertainties of valuation and of identity" (Kopytoff 1986, 90). I appreciate Kopytoff's "drama," which here indexes the processes of legitimization and of value that individuals (and objects!) are subjected to. In regard to legitimatization processes, then, there is always pressure on the fan and zealot to tell (build, manage, create, play) a good, "right" ("the") story in order to legitimize the text *and* herself (see Kelleter and Stein 2012, 277–78).[23]

These tensions between skilled and unskilled readerships, the idea of being "in the know" and seeking out creative endeavors gives us an idea of Bourdieuian (art) competence. The reader understands the many different categories that art/pop culture/artisanal coffee/sneakers entail. In Bourdieuian terms, the reader is "competent" to navigate categories, as she would be able/competent to point out Impressionist paintings, a McSweeney's publication, or a Beck song. Derek Robbins explains, "The highest level of art competence involves the recognition that the object of apprehension, whether a Cézanne

---

[23] There is no English translation available for this text, and Frank Kelleter and Daniel Stein write about such legitimization processes vis-à-vis serialization, and it is worth quoting at length here:

> Letztlich beschleunigen die hierdurch forcierten Identifikationskonflikte einen Prozess kreativer Proliferation, der oft unabhängig von (und sogar in Opposition zu) den Absichten und Zielen der Personen ablaufen kann, die er einbezieht. Statt von Interessen und Identitäten gesteuert zu werden, bringt er Interessen zur Anwendung und lässt Identitäten sich selbst erkennen. Autorisierungskonflikte sind demnach immer auch eine Arena populärkultureller Selbstbeobachtungen: ein experimentelles Feld, auf dem serielle Erzählungen die Möglichkeit und Mittel ihrer Fortsetzung erproben. Vielleicht lässt sich solche Rekursivität am besten als evolutionärer Prozess beschreiben, der sich ein beispiellos großen Anzahl von Spielern und Produkten, Ambitionen und Bindungen, ideologischen Zugehörigkeiten und sexuellen Präferenzen bedient, um immer weitere Variationen und Mutation (glückliche Zufälle) für künftigen Einsatz und rückwirkende Mobilisierung zu schaffen. (Kelleter and Stein 2012, 278)

painting or a U2 concert, is a self-referential system which demands to be appreciated in on own terms" (Robbins 2000, 58). The mastery of these codes is a significant part of obtaining such art competence: "It is possible to differentiate sociologically between the codes which people deploy and, according to Bourdieu, equally possible to differentiate sociologically within codes. The degree of mastery of any code is measurable independent and supposed hierarchical status of that code" (Robbins 2000, 58). The reader must be able to *recognize* the special niche into which the body of work taps. At the same time, she is validated about her own status of being in the know, of being able to categorize and distinguish and demarcate these texts from other similar texts (i.e., knowing the difference between a Chris Ware comic strip and a Daniel Clowes comic strip; knowing it is Beck Hansen and not Thurston Moore; knowing it is not a LucasArts game, but one programmed by Cardboard Computer).

This means that the texts presuppose an audience that "knows where to look" and that can traverse the less mainstream waters of contemporary American pop-culture. As Pierre Bourdieu posits, "The readability of a work of art for a particular individual varies according to the divergence between the more or less complex and subtle code required by the work, and the competence of the individual, as defined by the degree to which the social code, itself more or less complex and subtle, is mastered" (Bourdieu 1993, 224). This can be regarded, similar to "being busy," as yet another "status symbol" in contemporary consumer culture, for other readers might not be attuned to the texts' subtleties. Note, though, that the commodity character of the work of art allows for this position to emerge and flourish. Caroline Hamilton explains how knowledge of "certain subjects, or the possession of certain objects, has symbolic value in particular social circles and this value is conferred upon the owner. This 'cultural capital' can, just like money, be accumulated and 'spent' in interactions where the same cultural currency is recognized" (Hamilton 2010, 20). While hip, cultural capital, unfortunately, can hardly pay the rent for apartments in Greenpoint (or Neukölln), as Caroline Hamilton jests, it nonetheless "gives one an inordinate amount of legitimacy and authenticity" (Hamilton 2010, 20). This double bind of "creative integrity and appreciation for art that goes beyond monetary value the artist makes the market appear irrelevant; what matters is cultural capital—a currency possessed in large quantities by the 'right readers'" (Hamilton 2010, 21). And this "right reader" is a highly skilled connoisseur who "recognizes" the complexity and the niche status of the texts to attain such cultural capital. Yet, the competences *Kentucky Route Zero* presupposes differ from *Building Stories* competence. The texts find the target niche groups they "want" (and need!) and turn them into curiosity seekers. This nudges the objects into hipster culture and its notions of commercialized, commodified, institutionalized geekiness.[24]

But what happens if I just don't get it? Bourdieu writes how individuals possess a definite and limited capacity for

> apprehending the "information" suggested by the work, a capacity which depends on their knowledge of the generic code for the type of message concerned, be it the painting as a whole, or the painting of a particular period, school, or author. When the message exceed the possibilities of apprehension, or, to be more precise, when the code of the work exceeds in subtlety and complexity to code of the beholders, the latter lose interest in what appears to them to be a medley without rhyme or reason, or a completely unnecessary set of sounds or colours [sic]. In other words, when placed before a message which is too rich, or "overwhelming" ... they feel completely "out of their depth." (Bourdieu 1993, 225)

If the labor predetermined by the work of art is too esoteric[25] or overwhelming, the reader just cannot keep up. This flipside of highly specialized

---

[24] In the article "Race, Sex, and Nerds: From Black Geeks to Asian American Hipsters" Ron Eglash traces the intertwining of technology (tinkering, radio hobbyists of the early twentieth century) with masculinity. He subsumes in his article that there "exists the racist stereotype of Africans as oversexual and Asians as undersexual, with "whiteness" portrayed as the perfect balance between these two extremes. Given these associations, it is no coincidence that many Americans have a stereotype of Asians as nerds and of African Americans as anti-nerd hipsters" (Eglash 2002, 52). Eglash's article was published in 2002, and the visibility of the nonwhite nerd has increased and gained momentum in the 2010s: Donald Glover's series *Atlanta* (FX) performs similar cultural work and portrays a young African American Princeton drop out at odds with his surroundings. In American literature, the nonwhite nerd has gained a platform particular in Junot Díaz's writing, specifically in *The Brief Wondrous Life of Oscar Wao*, for which he won the Pulitzer Prize for Fiction in 2008. His novel chronicles the brief, if wondrous life of Oscar Wao, an overweight Dominican boy who grows up in Paterson, NJ. He surrounds himself with comic books and sci-fi and fantasy literature. Notably, predecessors of hipsterdom can be traced back to jazz, where the word "hep" described people who were in the know. Gender and racial dynamics are highly visible, and texts such as Norman Mailer's "The White Negro" delineated mid-century hipness.

[25] Notice here that Wolfgang Iser postulates something similar from a hermeneutical perspective. I am enticed to take his words at face value:

> The reader's enjoyment begins when he himself becomes productive, i.e., when the text allows him to bring his own faculties into play. There are, of course, limits to the reader's willingness to participate, and these will be exceeded if the text makes things too clear or, on the other hand, too obscure: boredom and overstrain represent the two poles of tolerance, and in either case the reader is likely to opt out of the game. (Iser 1986, 108)

work would turn *Song Reader* into an album only for professional musicians. Likewise, a text like *Building Stories* would only be approachable and tantalizing for an editor of comic books, or somebody who is a comic book author herself, looking up to Chris Ware's genius layout design or meticulous lettering. *Kentucky Route Zero*, ultimately, would be a game for gamers and for data analysts. This identifies the other end of Jen Harvie's notion of the de-skilled laborer, for if the tasks are *too* specialized, the audience is alienated and confused by the work they are to perform.[26]

What a möbius strip: through her engagement, the reader legitimizes the work of art *and* her proficiency and fluency in niches. She is able to engage with and work out the material and is eager to teach herself to build Ware's graphic narratives, play Beck Hansen's songs, or click through *Kentucky Route Zero*'s dystopian, dream-like landscapes. She "gets it," but she will never be among artists like Beck Hansen, Chris Ware, or the team behind *Kentucky Route Zero*. Put differently, it seems as if the texts *need* a curating, careful reader to attain such levels of quality and legitimization. Even if the outcome seems amateurish, the *experience* of tasteful curating and displaying to be "in the know" is what is privileged and what shows privilege. This helps unpack in what way the question of legitimation can be approached from another angle: Even within her geeky erudite position ("Yeah . . . I *totally* get this text"), the reader remains in an inferior position vis-à-vis the author. The engagement with the text, I argue, similarly legitimizes the *author's* position, and more pressingly, in turn, creates what Pierre Bourdieu would call a proletaroid intelligentsia.[27]

The failing author

The curator is held at bay through a rhetorics of failure. For the authors, to maintain an elevated positioning toward the reader means to fail. Chris Ware and Beck Hansen hide behind a smoke screen of obscurity. And this indexes yet another möbius strip of failure and implementation:

Both strands mark the "overstraining" and boredom as two poles between the readers oscillate.

[26] Notably, Marxist ideas of the worker's alienation from the act of production *and* consumption shine through here—not through yielding wages but through the lens of being distanced from author, object, social status, and the work of art.

[27] The proletaroid intelligentsia is to "experience the contradiction between aesthetic and political position-takings stemming from their inferior position in the field of production and the objectively conservative functions of the products of their activity" (Bourdieu 1993, 131).

self-deprecation on the side of the author and self-legitimization (i.e., being "in the know") on the side of the curator. In his article "Chris Ware's Failures," David M. Ball traces a long history of self-deprecating rhetoric within the American literary tradition, reaching back well into the nineteenth century. (Ball discusses the self-positioning of authors like Herman Melville and Nathaniel Hawthorne.) Failure (and not the *successful* text!), Ball suggests, becomes an artistic vision for the (male) author who are, in turn, "celebrated failures."[28] This is an apt term to frame in what way success is viewed as antithetical (or not trustworthy!) to artistry. Failure *is* the artistic vision here, for the author, not for the curator. The rhetorical gesture inherent in apologizing[29] unsettles the author as authority, for they remain elusive through insufficiencies. The author refuses to see the texts as complete or fulfilled, but merely as a failure[30] or as a "bad" example. Chris Ware, for example, oftentimes refers to himself as merely a cartoonist.[31] On its "dust jacket" *Building Stories* is

---

[28] David M. Ball writes,

> Understanding this larger literary historical treatment of celebrated failures, where success is viewed as antithetical to artistic aims, allows us to better understand the counterintuitive thrust of Chris Ware's omnipresent rhetoric of failure. . . . Rather than senseless self-deprecation or morbid fascination, failure becomes a kind of artistic vision, part of a larger tradition of American authors' persistent invocations of the rhetoric of failure to convey their highest aspirations for literary success. From Herman Melville's claim that "failure is the true test of greatness" to Henry Adams's self-identification with the "mortifying failure in [his] long education" and William Faulkner's eagerness to be judged by his "splendid failure to do the impossible," such rhetorical gestures have occupied the center of canonical claims to American authorship and authority. (Ball 2010, 53).

[29] In relation to this, Simon Willis points out it in his article: "[Ware] apologises a lot, and you needn't even meet him to know it. On the back of the 20th volume of the ACME Novelty Library . . . is an ISBN sticker with a short explanatory note. It ends 'apologies and deep regrets.'" In a booklet to accompany an exhibition of his work in Lincoln, Nebraska, he wrote an essay entitled "Apologies, etc." At the back of the booklet he thanked the exhibition's sponsor, Todd Duncan: "We hope it proved an effective tax shelter" (Willis 2013, n.p.). Ivan Brunetti, a friend of Ware's, sees him as "almost aggressively self-deprecating" (Willis 2013, n.p.).

[30] What if we are not creative, but refuse to engage, remain passive, or are overwhelmed with the demands posed upon us? The pitfalls are explored in *Kreation and Depression—Freiheit im gegenwärtigen Kapitalismus*, edited by Christoph Menke and Juliane Rebentisch. Particularly Diedrich Diederichsen's aforementioned essay in context with playbour in this collection "Kreative Arbeit und Selbstverwirklichung" is illuminating.

[31] The penultimate chapter of Douglas Wolk's book *Reading Comics* is entitled "Why Does Chris Ware Hate Fun?" and focuses on the means how Ware "systematically dismembers the idea of light entertainment" (Wolk 2007, 347).

advertised as "never-before-published" work that was deemed to obtuse for a respectable publication (Ware 2012b, n.p.).

In the same vein, it is only an artist like Beck Hansen or Chris Ware[32] who can "afford" to release a fragmentary text. But Ware's self-deprecation stands in stark contrast with the highbrow media outlets that publish and review his work. His interviews and comic strips appear in prestigious magazines like *The Paris Review* or the *New Yorker*. Through this self-positioning, he seeks proximity to a specific audience of such media outlets, and, say, not to a readership tending toward a magazine like *Entertainment Weekly*. Likewise, Beck Hansen hardly gave any interviews for *Song Reader* but decisively remained in the background. In combination with the release of *Song Reader* in 2012, McSweeney's merely released a long interview with Beck Hansen on the website. Other interviews were published in outlets such as *The New York Times*. *Kentucky Route Zero* seems to be more accessible: coverage ranges from pop-culture websites to Christian gaming websites (they exist!). Nonetheless, the production company is called "Cardboard Computer," suggesting that the coding of the game happened on a makeshift computer.

These rhetoric gestures toward self-deprecation indicate a strange, bizarre game of distinction that is outsourced toward the individual reader: failure and self-deprecation embedded in an American literary tradition to validate and legitimate Chris Ware, Beck Hansen, and *Kentucky Route Zero* versus the Reckwitzian dispositif of creativity imposed on the reader to tell a creative story and "make" her life(style) one of singularities. What emerges is a dichotomy between a successfully implemented text and the elusive, fragmentary material that affords failure as *modus operandi*. In a similar gesture, the *reader* is figured as somebody who cannot attain the level of mastery. Crudely put, the reader cannot afford to fail. The authors, on the other hand, are "celebrated failures" who have established their positioning through self-deprecation and ironic winks (and failure as artistic vision certainly goes contrary to the neoliberal ethos). Now it is creativity *and* a failing artistic vision that can be purchased. This accentuates the curator's

---

[32] Pertaining to failure and idling around, David Ball maintains that Chris Ware's
    rhetoric of failure appears both paratextually—in places such as dust jackets, publication information, and author biographies that customarily codify and reinforce the text's value as a signifying tool—as well as narratively, in stories that routinely revolve around themes of anomie, humiliation, and despair. For some, this abnegation is nothing more than the outward manifestation of a self-effacing author, part and parcel of comics artists' carefully constructed personae as neglected outsiders in a harsh and uncaring world. (Ball 2010, 46)

precarious situation even stronger—and makes possible gender divisions even more prevalent.

There seems to be a curiously gendered feedback loop at play that caters to debates revolving around legitimization, failure, visibility, and invisibility. Self-deprecation and nerdiness are inherent in all of my case studies. But notice how the texts (by male artists) reproduce pastimes that are highly gendered—historically, ideas of collecting, making parlor music, or even coding are connoted as feminine, domestic activities. Jane Tompkins in *Sensational Designs* urges that most of twentieth-century literary criticism taught readers to equate domesticity with triviality (failure?) and implicitly, with "womanly inferiority" (Tompkins 1985, 123). She refers to the female (sentimental)[33] novelistic tradition of the nineteenth century, whose mission represented a "monumental effort to reorganize culture from the woman's point of view" (Tompkins 1985, 124). Her point can be extended toward efforts of domestic, predominantly female activities (what we would now call hobbies or pastimes) that my case studies replicate. I am particularly intrigued by Tompkins's idea of triviality and the way domestic, inferior pastimes in the nineteenth century mirror the distinct rhetoric of self-deprecation (and elusive, unattainable genius!) in the twenty-first century of the male authors. At second glance, this fact makes a project such as Beck Hansen's *Song Reader* peculiar and peculiarly precarious, for he relocates a predominantly female pastime (playing sheet music) allocated within the private sphere (within the context of the parlor) into the public realm. Beck Hansen sheds sheet music from its "trivial," female connotation and shifts it toward predominantly male (public!) spaces (I discuss this idea further in my chapter on *Song Reader*).

This conversation between domestic activities of the nineteenth century and niche activities pertaining to hipness in the twenty-first century may begin to unravel shifts in media interaction (and self-reflexivity of media), which will help me segue into the last section of this chapter. Lisa Gitelman outlines in *Always Already New* how the phonograph, for instance, became an intelligible medium of home entertainment. By using the phonograph

---

[33] Likewise, David Monod's book *The Soul of Pleasure* on the rise of mass entertainment in the nineteenth century illuminates how public spaces of entertainment, like the theater, were predominantly male-connoted spaces—at some point in history, it was disrespectable for women to even be seen in theaters—what can be subsumed is that female entertainment was located in private spaces. David Monod's work recognizes even earlier moments of gendered practices in the entertainment industry, for he turns to theater spaces in the nineteenth century and the uneasy gender dynamics between male spectators and female waitresses who could banter and flirt freely (see Monod 2016, 123–42).

as her case study, Gitelman reconstructs the changing media landscape of the nineteenth century and in what way it was highly gendered:[34] "Women helped engender a new mutual logic for media and public life" (Gitelman 2008, 15). The phonograph[35] as mass medium was defined deeply by women and negotiated the home and public, "constructions that relied centrally... on changing roles for women, and further, changing experiences of gender and cultural difference," and this new medium was "shaped by potently gendered constructions of work and leisure as well as of production and consumption" (Gitelman 2008, 15). Likewise cultural historians, such as Miriam Hansen,[36] explore what kind of sociocultural changes occurred that made gender lines porous, like going to the movies.

Yet the objects I take as case studies do not aim at forming a consensus of any "reading public" or "media public"—rather they stratify and distinguish, creating hierarchies of competence and "being in the know" to a specific niche. Likewise, they shun any politization of their DIY status (i.e., DIY being deeply engrained in punk). Rather, I believe that enfolded within these inquiries is the emergence of a "new" creative middle class of the twenty-first century—Andreas Reckwitz argues along similar lines in *Die Gesellschaft*

---

[34] Gitelman explains, likewise (if differently), "telephones, monthly magazines, and motion pictures" also changed these experiences of gender and cultural difference (Gitelman 2008, 15).

[35] The phonograph, as a medium, "preserves ghosts that would otherwise be evanescent," as John Durham Peters points out in his history on the idea of communication *Speaking Into the Air* (Peters 1999, 160). What else, he argues, does a phonograph do but inscribe? (Does it inscribe gender practices, too?) Peters adds that in the end, mediated communication is "ultimately indistinguishable from communication with the dead" (Peters 1999, 276). This is an interesting idea when turning to questions of media archaeology and "communicating" with "dead" and obsolete media by way of contemporary media.

[36] Miriam Hansen's work pertains to theater spaces in the nineteenth century as a "shared" experience that enabled audiences (and immigrants and women in particular here) to negotiate and subvert modes of production and distribution. This we must understand as a subversive gesture toward the consensus of the nineteenth century, according to Miriam Hansen. Her work turns to early cinema, and she underlines how going to the movies marked "significant changes in the patterns of working-class culture itself— changes, specifically, from an ethnically separatist, inward-looking public sphere to a more inclusive, multiethnic one, and from a gender-segregated public sphere (like the male domain of the nineteenth-century saloons) to a heterosocial one in which women of all ages and marital status could move in relative freedom from family and social control" (Hansen 1991, 62). She connects these ideas to the emergence of publics of spectatorship in the nineteenth and early twentieth centuries—particularly through the emergence of the cinema as mass entertainment.

der Singularitäten.[37] Reckwitz goes as far as to suggest a *degendering* of (professional) skills and abilities[38]—he underlines that even if gender differences are not done away with entirely in late modernist societies, they nevertheless do maintain a different status/fulfill a different role. In his view, and I do not fully agree here, the "gender culture" of late capitalism rather offers a "portfolio" of gender-accessories that can be adapted to, tried on, and discarded—he sees it as a repertoire of gender stereotypes that can be combined and played with (see Reckwitz 2017a, 339f). This might be able to unravel the dynamics between male authors, female pastimes, and singularities of the twenty-first century. In the final section, I would like to elaborate on the idea of media practices and understand how media are now turned into experiences and processes. The ghosts of media past preserved (and the female pastimes replicated) in mass-produced graphic narratives or sheet music albums are out to haunt a nerdy[39] individual who both might or might not be oblivious to this flirting with the past while, fallaciously, cater to ideas of newness, innovation, and the avant-garde. Thus the material desire evoked by these objects may open a tomb of old, forgotten forms and examine media interaction by way of fragmentation.

---

[37] Reckwitz enumerates several key elements for this lifestyle of singularities: food, living/apartments, travelling, the body, school and education, as well as work-life balance, urbanity, juvenilization, degendering, and new liberalism (see Reckwitz 2017a, 308–42). Particularly questions pertaining to juvenilization (i.e., *Song Reader* and Beck Hansen's persona of the eternal man-child) and degendering come to the fore within the case studies my project turns to. Likewise, and not quite unironically, they also negotiate work-life balance.

[38] Andreas Reckwitz underlines a certain gender neutrality in the designing of pastimes, the realization of the self, the investment into the status and professional skills: "*Degendering* bedeutet also, dass die zentral beruflichen Fähigkeiten (etwa Unternehmergeist, soziale Kompetenz oder Intelligenz) als geschlechtsneutral angenommen werden. Dies gilt auch für den Lebensstil in der Freizeit und das generelle Ziel der subjektiven Selbstverwirklichung und der Statusinvestition" (Reckwitz 2017a, 339). I do not fully agree with Reckwitz's notions here, for (my) life is by no means gender-neutral in all the opportunities and privileges that I enjoy as a young, white woman living in one of the most affluent countries in the world. But we can begin thinking with his ideas about a gender-neutral design of free time and hobbies. This would gesture toward the merging of female pastimes and male niche coolness that my case studies are invested in, if maybe only implicitly.

[39] Nerdy or geeky has been increasingly connoted with cool. In response to geeks and nerds in the contemporary American imagery, Judith Kohlenberger argues that "recent popular cultural representations of (techno)science in mainstream American film and television are increasingly informed by a prominent focus on cool as an aesthetic and affective, rather than cognitive or ethical form of scientific legitimation. . . . Cool thereby acts as a novel and popular form of legitimation, challenging and potentially replacing traditional cognitive and/or ethical justifications" (Kohlenberger 2015, 13).

From product to process

Those failing authors certainly were busy for a long time: It took Beck Hansen about fifteen years to conceptualize and finalize *Song Reader*; Chris Ware began publishing *Building Stories*' stories in several print outlets and his ACME publication series in the early 2000s before he released it as a keepsake box in 2012; Cardboard Computer's developing team took its time with the release of the fourth act of *Kentucky Route Zero*, much to the chagrin of their fans (as of writing this, the last act is still to be released). These are works in *and* of progress.[40] It is here where the fragmental nature of the texts and their bricolage aesthetics undermine expectations toward an album, graphic narrative, or computer game. But let's not forget that they also ask questions toward the history of their *matter* and *materiality*,[41] and in what way the fragment or the single unit stands in relation to the whole. Steve Tomasula ascribes contemporary fiction akin to the objects I turn to as "innovative literature" that takes its "own medium as part of its subject matter . . . [or works] out of assumptions, including those about literature, other than those of the status quo of the mainstream" (Tomasula 2010, 217). I appreciate this assessment, and fragmenting and collaging media helps acknowledging the negotiation of future and past forms of media as its own subject matter.

I borrow the idea "from product to process" from Kathleen Fitzpatrick who in her book *Planned Obsolescence* inquires into the flows and processes

---

[40] The idea of how the texts privilege the *experience* of being built/read/rehearsed over the end product relates back to Reckwitz's idea of the aestheticization of the singularity, and as my discussion has shown thus far, this experience might just carry out neoliberal logics inherent in the experience—reproducing the paradoxes and paradigms of capitalist labor that the material, at first sight, seem to have shunned. Of course, Horkheimer and Adorno's notion of purposelessness shine through here once again: the singular experience of engaging with a work of art versus the "Montagecharakter der Kulturindustrie" that alludes to both Fordist mass production as well as a critique of modernist art toward mass consumption.

[41] N. Katherine Hayles writes of materiality that it is as an

> emergent property, materiality depends on how the work mobilizes its resources as a physical artifact as well as the user's interactions with the work and the interpretive strategies she develops—strategies that include physical manipulations as well as conceptual frameworks. In the broadest sense, materiality emerges from the dynamic interplay between the richness of a physically robust world and human intelligence as it crafts this physicality to create meaning. (Hayles 2002, 33)

I find this useful to carve out haptic interaction in relation to the more conceptual questions the works in progress I look at inquire upon. As an "emergent" property, materiality also acknowledges *changing* properties—materiality is evoked anew with every reading.

of academic writing and versioning in the online spheres[42] (see Fitzpatrick 2011, 66–70). Versioning, Fitzpatrick writes, must be understood by way how (academic) texts are no longer

> discrete or static, but live and develop as part of a network of other such texts, among which ideas flow. Of these features, however, versioning may in some ways be the most disconcerting for traditional authors, including academics, whose work lives have been organized around writing conceived not as an ongoing action but rather as an act of completing discrete projects. (Fitzpatrick 2011, 67)

Open access and creative commons platforms such as media-commons.org advertise "open scholarship in open formats," inviting readers to comment and give feedback on scholarly texts. Likewise, the German cultural critic Dirk von Gehlen in *Eine neue Version ist verfügbar—Update: Wie die Digitalisierung Kunst und Kultur verändert* explores how versioning changes the form (and industries!) of texts, music, and film. His focus lies rather on business models and how companies adopt to the ever-changing and quick turnover in the culture industry. The digital moment, von Gehlen outlines, infuses established roles attained by authors, audience as well as publishing houses with new possibilities (see von Gehlen 2013, 11). Both Fitzpatrick's and von Gehlen's inquiries point toward the porous contours around established divisions and acknowledge that the "body of work" has indeed been rendered fragmentary, particularly by way of digitization processes (i.e., open source). The academic text that can now be crowd-sourced challenges the notion of who and what an author and collaborator is and in what ways interventions into an existing body of work can be performed.

What about the arts? Already in *The Open Work*, Umberto Eco sought to understand how modern artworks can be rendered open by their author and further completed by the performer/viewer/reader/audience. Eco uses Karlheinz Stockhausen as an example of a modern composer who created

---

[42] In *Planned Obsolescence* Kathleen Fitzpatrick pays particular attention to the idea of versioning as an academic practice. In conjecture with versioning as a current writing feature of "open-source" and interactive writing, there is
> another factor, however, one perhaps peculiar to academic authorship, that puts additional pressure on completion as the most significant moment in the writing process. Only at the point of completion, after all, can our projects at last attain their final purpose: the entry of a new item on the CV. This emphasis on the academic version of the bottom line—evidence of scholarly 'productivity' that must be demonstrated in order to obtain and maintain a professorial appointment—brings a distinctly Fordist, functionalist mode of thinking to bear on our work as writers. (Fitzpatrick 2011, 67)

"open" music. A single music sheet with a series of groupings was presented, and the performer was given the freedom to perform the sequence of musical units in the order she chose. So Stockhausen's piece could assume a variety of forms by different performers. We can assume to say that this piece has unlimited interpretations. But Umberto Eco stresses that Stockhausen indeed remains the author of the piece and is responsible for both its constraints and openness. *The Open Work* ultimately outlines that this "openness" does not mean "infinite possibility" or complete freedom of reception (Eco 1989, 6). Rather for Eco these types of contemporary works are "works in movement" that depend on an author's intention and a performer who chooses among options. As Eco explains, these works in movement consist of unplanned or "physically incomplete structural units" (Eco 1989, 12). An artwork like one of Alexander Calder's mobiles constantly "creates their own space and the shapes to fill it" (Eco 1989, 12). Calder's lovely filigree art stands in opposition with the bulky box that *Building Stories* is; still, both explore "dynamic structures" from different vantage points (see Eco 1989, 13).

The works I examine can therefore certainly be thought along the lines of Eco's assumptions, but they also take Eco's notion of "openness" and Fitzpatrick's idea of "versioning" into new terrain. These concepts—be it versioning or the open work—refine the premises of buzz words like "participatory culture," "open source," and other keywords that define online modes of interaction. In particular, the *haptic* affordances exceed what Eco describes of modernist works. They demand practices that seem counterintuitive or exhausting in the digital age and make clear that these processes do not spring out of the digital era. These are *objects* as much as they are *stories*, they want to be built, maintained. This conjures up an idea that traversing the storyworlds and the materials that *Building Stories*, *Song Reader*, and *Kentucky Route Zero* present depends on technological fluency of the reader.

Building Stories, *Song Reader*, and *Kentucky Route Zero* are all playful, colorful, beautiful *objects* that tell stories; they interrogate a different form of digitality, for they are haptic. They guide fingers away from touchscreens to perform fiction dexterously. *Song Reader* cannot be instantly accessible or streamed on spotify; *Building Stories* cannot be swiped through; *Kentucky Route Zero* does not offer access to single levels, but has to be played from the beginning on, every single time. Caroline Hamilton concurs: "Books become mysterious lost objects, gateways to worlds of wonder, steadfast friends in one's darkest hour. In a culture dominated by LCD screens and digital devices McSweeney's is reassuringly tactile, crafted. These are literary works designed not only to be read, but to be collected—and displayed"

(Hamilton 2010, 22). What are "collection" and "display" here, if not readerly practices of engaging with a particular form of openness? To extrapolate from Hamilton's arguments on McSweeney's toward the objects of my inquiry: they rely on their tongue-in-cheek reference to the history of their respective genres (graphic narrative, music album, computer game) and, simultaneously, underline their "mysterious" aura that serves as gateways to worlds and stories of wonder.

By eschewing to be embedded within conventional digital media and by rethinking "digitality" as a haptic experience, the objects scrutinize digital processes that have come to orchestrate the anxieties of daily life in the twenty-first century (i.e., the failing of the database in *Song Reader*'s case, or *Kentucky Route Zero*'s broken computer, *Building Stories*' themes of alienation by way of technology). This is where we can approach them, in Caroline Hamilton's parlance, as mysterious things. In this sense, Bill Brown writes how

> current interest in object agency, animate matter, panpsychism, and the mystery of objects—these can be read as symptoms of significant changes in the material culture of our present: new robotic technologies, drones, an expanding field of nonconscious cognition, the *Internet of Things*, etc. It's not so much that we've never been modern (as Latour once put it) but that we're inhabiting some newly unmodern (or differently modern) world. (Brown 2016, 12)

I appreciate Bill Brown's question about a contemporary, "unmodern" world that signals significant shifts in the work that materials perform—historically, culturally, and undoubtedly also economically. The objects I turn to can say something about their respective medium's history, and in turn reveal how we come to be "unmodern" in our highly digital, technological moment. Their genre and medium labellings deserve parentheses and a skeptical second glance: Is *Building Stories* really a graphic novel? Can Beck Hansen's sheet music collection really be seen as an album? And in what way does *Kentucky Route Zero* blur the boundaries between game and novel and is maybe more a clickable novel than a readable game?[43]

---

[43] Digitization underwrites the status of the medium (and, likewise, demonstrates the flexibilities inherent within), and Mark Hansen suggests how

> transforming media from forms of actual inscription of "reality" into variable interfaces for rendering the raw data of reality—then not only can the medium no longer be said to be "motivated," in the sense of having an elective affinity with the concrete reality it presents, but the very task of *deciding* what medial form a given rendering shall take no longer follows from the inherent differences between media. (Hansen 2004, 21)

Here, recent work in media studies has demonstrated that shifting from media history to media *archaeology* may give new insights in a work's openness. I find this distinction useful, in particular for the way media archaeology allows to see not where a medium comes from, but rather what old forms inhere in the new. Wolfgang Ernst's idea of media archaeology,[44] for example, outlines that it is less about telling stories or even counterhistories than it is about *how* stories and objects are recorded, in what kind of media, through which kinds of processes. Such a media-archeological approach allows to contour how an MP3 album might contain within it traces not only of the vinyl record but also of the jukebox and sheet music. We can thus identify them as self-referential, as metamedia.[45] They make available a process-oriented outlook on their materiality: In this way, they interrogate "challenges of digitization in creative and often unlikely ways"—as mysterious things (Starre 2015, 7). Texts such as *Building Stories*, *Song Reader*, and *Kentucky Route Zero* enter the "debate on the future of the book as active social agents that perform cultural work not merely as discursive, but also as material interventions" (Starre 2015, 23–24). In addition to being *material*, as Starre says, they are also curiously interactive and manipulable—this conjures up an image of archaeology in the most literal sense. But this comes with a twist: What can a graphic narrative tell us about the medium when it is not a "graphic narrative" in the traditional sense? Why can Beck Hansen's album tell us more about the medium of the music album in the twenty-first century? And how can *Kentucky Route Zero* reflect on the way we have been using computers over decades and how they have come to shape our everyday life?

The texts urge the reader to reflect on their mediality and their materiality, and by engaging in them, this interaction conjures up a set of skills that seems to be counterintuitive in our digital moment—subverting notions of contemporary consumer practices. Media demand relentless attention, and yet, sometimes, they are in some ways invisible, because media "become pervasive and ubiquitous, forming the building blocks for our constant remix of the categories of everyday life (the public and the private, the local and the global, the individual and the collective), they become invisible . . . we

---

[44] See here Wolfgang Ernst's work *Digital Memory and the Archive* (2013), Parikka (2012), and Erkki Huhtamo's volume which he co-edited with Parikka (2011).

[45] Alexander Starre's *Metamedia* examines McSweeney's playful materialities in its quarterly magazine, Mark Z. Danielewski's novel *House of Leaves* or Jonathan Safran Foer's experimental novel *Tree of Codes*, among other contemporary objects, and it investigates what Jessica Pressman has coined the "bookishness" of literature in the twenty-first century.

become blind to that which shapes our lives the most" (Deuze 2011, 137). As Zara Dinnen puts it,

> When a medium is working, it disappears from view. Books work best when we forget they are there: if a book is too heavy, our arms get tired and we disengage; if we drop a book in the bath, its paperiness becomes an obstacle to our reading. As new media theorists have long argued, 'the digital' is a reification of the effacing condition of all media. (Dinnen 2018, 4)

Building Stories, *Song Reader*, and *Kentucky Route Zero* counterbalance this very "invisibility"[46] by staging their own materiality as an integral part of their material and narrative strategies (i.e., taking their own medium as subject matter, as Tomasula posits).

So, what is it exactly that is being made visible? And who is made invisible? What is being made "new" here?[47] What practices do these texts remix? I have already shown how they intertwine materiality and mediality with a reading positioning that is to unearth older practices

---

[46] By making repetition part of their mode, they similarly comment on media practices and the way media become invisible through routine. Wendy Chun in *Updating to Remain the Same—Habitual New Media* turns to habits in twenty-first-century media usage and postulates that by

> revealing that our media matter most when they seem not to matter at all, that is, when they have moved from the new to the habitual. Search engines are hardly new or exciting, but they have become the default mode of knowledge acquisition. Smart phones no longer amaze, but they increasingly structure and monitor the lives of their so-called owners. Further, sites that have long since disappeared or which "we" think have, such as Friendster. com (as of 2015, it was mainly a South Asian gaming site), live on in our clicks and our habitual actions, such as "friending." Whether or not a virus spreads depends on habits, from the regular washing of hands to practicing safe sex. Through habits users become their machines: they stream, update, capture, upload, share, grind, link, verify, map, save, trash, and troll. Repetition breeds expertise, even as it breeds boredom. (Chun 2016, 1)

[47] Mark Hansen's *New Philosophy for New Media* is invested in this question. He asks,

> For almost every claim advanced in support of the "newness" of new media, it seems that an exception can readily be found, some earlier cultural or artistic practice that already displays the specific characteristic under issue. This situation has tended to polarize the discourse on new media art between two (in my opinion) equally problematic positions: those who feel that new media have changed everything and those who remain skeptical that there is anything at all about new media that is, in the end, truly new. (Hansen 2004, 20)

Later he warns that the "reinvention" of the medium does not suffice to "theorize new media art" (Hansen 2004, 23). Hansen turns to affective, phenomenological notions and evokes thinkers such as Brian Massumi and Gilles Deleuze; he is invested in hybrid techniques (such as cinema-digital-video) and how they expose the viewer to "minute shifts in affective tonality well beyond what is visible to natural perception" (Lenoir 2004, xxv).

within the new—a reader, basically, flirts with the past, maybe knowingly or unknowingly. This reveals the processes of reading that might be most salient in our increasingly digital lives: any user of the internet understands "surfing" and "browsing" as practices of clicking more or less haphazardly through a sea of links. The experience of navigating the internet often feels aimless, endless, open-ended. And yet, we know that our path, however random, is predetermined by the websites we frequent, with cookies and browsing history merging the future with the past. Despite being delineated and predetermined, the internet seduces us with fantasies of infinity and boundlessness and permanence. Endless storage, cloud services, all-encompassing archives—these technologies represent a certain desire to transcend the limits we associate with media themselves.

Curation, then, in this context frequently entails repetition, interaction with given components, and the mastery of unusual, context-specific skills. Whether they themselves are digital objects or not, these texts are symptomatic of the "versionings" of the self we have learned to inhabit and curate online. If these works do not just mirror or replicate such online practices, but in fact comment on them in some meaningful way, this might paradoxically happen because of their finitude. The texts evoke the experience of openness while also making visible the hand of their authors and the closedness of the work. The reader may use the same skills that she has honed online, but instead of perceiving her task as endless, she more often negotiates the openness of the reading process with the tightly controlled nature of the work. The reader is a curator; the collection is finite. Frank Kelleter stresses that even the "most open" artwork must end at some point and find a place for itself. "To exist as an artwork at all, it must find a place (perhaps distrusted but always identifiable) between two book covers or in a catalogue raisonné, under a unified title, credited to one or more human creators" (Kelleter 2017, 7). Similarly, Umberto Eco concurs that works in movement "circulate imperceptibly until they are adopted and justified as cultural data which have to be organically integrated into the panorama of a whole period" (Eco 1989, 13). They signal that they *will*, at some point, be brought to a conclusion, even if at times, that conclusion seems unimaginable.

This tension between open reading and the author's inescapable authority (even if it is connoted with failure and self-deprecation) often results in aesthetic strategies of deferral. Ironically, these aesthetic strategies that contribute to the texts' impression of openness may in fact be understood to relate to their endings. But what are we to make of their endings? The "final resting place" that Frank Kelleter identifies (or even Igor Kopytoff) is, in these cases, itself open to question.[48] And Eco reminds us that openness does not mean "infinite possibility." One option is to stop: we stop assembling Ware's text, we grow tired of Beck Hansen's sheet music, we log off Cardboard Computer's game. Do the texts continue without us or do they require their readers? Though scholars have asked such questions of novels for some time, they assume a different urgency here. "Game over," after all, is something different than "the end."

---

[48] To refer back to Fitzpatrick, she identifies the academic's CV as the final resting place. A paper held at a conference or an article written for a publication are ultimately put to rest and buried on the CV, an achievement tally sheet in PDF format.

2

A Tale of Two Buildings: Chris Ware's *Building Stories*

Chris Ware's *Building Stories* is a curious curiosity. Sold in an oversized keepsake box, it is so much more than what its fourteen discrete, loosely connected pamphlets, accordion books, brochures, foldout game boards, broadsheets, children's booklets, newspapers, and linen-bound booklets suggest at first glance. The sum of all its parts paints an incomplete picture of a life lived—episodes left inconclusive, vignettes going nowhere. With every reading, the reader combines the booklets anew and pours over the contents like a puzzle or a Rubik's Cube. *Building Stories* can be, mathematically speaking, read in 87178291200 different ways, and its interactive tasks stand in proximity with a readerly practice of selecting, combining, and remembering, arranging, caring for the material at hand. The reader, here, is to be an accomplice and collaborator to build and maintain *Building Stories*. The box, the weight of the booklets, the texture of the paper, or the picking and choosing of the next booklet are just as much an integral element to the reading experience as to *what* is being told. Because of the strong emphasis of the intersecting of material and narrative, *Building Stories* comments on digitization processes in ways that hardly any other contemporary text is capable of in scope and design. It magnifies the idea of interactive art in the digital age—negotiated here through printed ephemera and obsolete media. The reader has to examine the way *Building Stories*' poetics, its "story building," operates in, through, and around its different (material) accoutrements and strategies.

Through its idiosyncratic format (see Figures 2.1 and 2.2) *Building Stories* suggests that life is woven out of nonlinear and contingent memories and episodes that, when combined, unite to a mere *sense* of completion. David L. Ulin of the *L.A. Times* points out in his review how the graphic narrative has to do with "loneliness, with disconnection, which is why the open structure works so well. Ware's point is that we drift through existence, suspended between past and future, the present often empty, comprised in equal part of anticipation and loss" (Ulin 2012, n.p.). Ware's employing of what Ulin appropriately calls the "open structure" emphasizes a feeling of merely

Figure 2.1 *Building Stories*—author's own image.

Figure 2.2 *Building Stories*—author's own image.

floating through the story like drifting through life. While one booklet might meticulously chronicle the protagonist's routines (going to work or to the supermarket, performing household chores, reading and drawing, paying bills), another one might contrast these daily motions with scenes of the protagonist's aimlessness and bouts of anxiety and depression. David L. Ulin's choice of words of course also echoes Umberto Eco's conceptualization of the open work, who assumes that efforts such as *Building Stories* "reject the definitive, concluded message and multiply the formal possibilities of the distribution of their elements. They appeal to the initiative of the individual performer, and hence they offer themselves not as finite works which prescribe specific repetition along given structural coordinates" (Eco 1989, 3). This brings about a mere sense of an ending the reader experiences on an "aesthetic plane" (Eco 1989, 3). And, to argue more forcefully, Ware's open structure intertwines this aesthetic plane with the material plane. This is not an easy convergence, for the ready-made collection does not ever indicate whether it is even ever completely "performed" and maintained. The contingency and precariousness experienced toward and felt for the narrative and the material while browsing through *Building Stories* drives at exactly this pleasure and uncertainty.

What is it that the reader builds? I could say that the novel is about an unnamed woman in her twenties and thirties and chronicles her living by herself in an apartment building to moving to the suburbs of Chicago with her husband and daughter in the first two decades of the twenty-first century.[1] That is only half of the story,[2] but what we can subsume is that *Building Stories* functions as an elusive twenty-first-century *Bildungsroman* in which Ware expresses the sufferings of the dwindling middle class[3] and the "corrosive sarcasm of youth to the sickening earnestness of maturity" (Ware 2012b, n.p.). The young woman studies art in Chicago and then drifts in and out of jobs (she works as a nanny for a rich suburban family; she helps out in a flower shop) up until she starts her own flower business later in her life. Her life is told in episodes that encompass the protagonist "wondering if she'll ever move from the rented close quarters of lonely young adulthood to the mortgaged expanse of love and marriage" (Ware 2012b, n.p.). Ware pays particular attention on the protagonist's artistic aspirations and resulting

---

[1] Though a timeline it never explicitly established, *Building Stories* is set in the late 1990s to the early 2010s. Chris Ware marginally places cultural references, such as allusions to Barack Obama's presidency, the rise of the popular online streaming service *Netflix*, the changing designs of computers and cellphones, and small talk about gentrification, to determine the time span of the story of the protagonist. There are some diagrams on the internet that place the booklets into the correct chronological order.

[2] The other half of the story focuses on the talking house; a bee family living next door to that house; the house's landlady and her regrets and missed connections in life; a couple that fell out of love living in the second-floor apartment.

[3] Ariela Freedman traces the intertextual references to what she calls the "high" canon of literature within *Building Stories*. She compares the protagonist to Gustave Flaubert's Emma Bovary, for "she allows [Ware] to explore the suffocating world of the middle class, to develop his own mode of ironic realism, and to represent romance and marriage through the perspective of a woman" (Freedman 2015, 342). It thus can be seen as an experimental, and nonlinear twenty-first-century *Bildungsroman*. But if a *Bildungsroman* suggests progress through time, *Building Stories* places emphasis on the *process* of being read and being made sense of in *space*, spread out on the reader's floor.

self-doubts; she goes to art school, she writes and draws, she attends a creative writing class, and she composes little stories for her daughter. Yet a feeling remains that she does not "have it in her." The protagonist yearns for a more unconventional, creative kind of life.[4] She carries within a sense of incompleteness; a life not lived to its fullest potential. Interwoven with this twenty-first-century vision of life in the United States before the Age of Trump are glimpses backward to previous times and forward to future possibilities. Horse carriages and milk men are bookended by futuristic, gentrified visions of urban life in Chicago. The bucolic is brought into proximity with huge skyscrapers, frequented by people wearing sensory space suits that transmit sexual stimuli.

Much of *Building Stories* is predicated—and maybe even controlled—by the different formats of its booklets. The heartbreaking tale of how the protagonist loses both her cat and her best friend on the same day is chronicled in the large-scale newspaper—a subtle material irony unfolds how the most depressing and devastating moments in life have nothing to do in the most sensational format. It does not sit comfortably. Ware also includes smaller formats, such as a *Little Golden Book* children's book or literal comic strips. The children's booklet minutely chronicles one day—*September 23rd, 2000*—an ordinary Sunday that the protagonist spends at home, drawing and idling around. Later that day, she goes to a dinner party and meets her future husband, Phil. Unlike the newspaper, which will eventually tear or be tossed out tomorrow, the sturdy children's book may be kept out of sheer sentimental reasons. Ware consciously plays with the reader's (unconscious) affective responses to the booklets—how "touching" they are. The reading experience is predicated by how the reader remembers the stories haptically, how she remembers a story by the weight of a booklet or by the unhandiness of it. She may even wonder about the story behind the booklets she holds in her hands, scaling the weight, brushing over the texture of the paper with her fingertips, imagining chaotic traces of a felt-tip pen on the children's book. Ultimately, she might not remember where exactly one scene took place, but she might be able to recall the weight or size of the booklet where she read it. Ware hereby underlines the interlinking of memories and tactility, lost on the surfaces of digital devices.

It is here where Ware's impeccable style and control of the page comes into play. His work emphasizes craftsmanship and highlights the history of

---

[4] At one point of the story, the reader learns that the protagonist throws out all of her writing. She kept it in a box in a closet and is frustrated by her naive take on the world. This is an important detail that will figure as an important aspect to the grander poetics of *Building Stories*.

the comics medium.⁵ His books are extraordinary feats of printing, layout, design, and marketing. They self-reflexively underline what Martha Kuhlman calls an "artistic seriousness" of the medium (Kuhlman 2010, 80). Douglas Wolk calls Ware "a technical and formal wizard" (Wolk 2007, 347). Ware is particularly renowned for his use of diagrams to visualize the complicated interrelations between people, objects, history. Thierry Groensteen sees Chris Ware's diagrams and meticulous page layouts as "the foundation for his poetics" (Groensteen 2011, 48). These diagrams beg the question where image begins and text ends, or, even more to the point, where style begins and character ends: the "flat, simplified cartooning style that characterizes most of Ware's mature work, in which many objects and even characters nearly resemble pictographs or ideograms" (Cates 2010, 96). Isaac Cates underlines the openness of the visual forms, examining Ware's "flat fields of color, and the simplification of organic background elements like trees and bushes until they resemble symbols on an architect's plan: all of these elements of Ware's style are engineered to approach this Bushmiller-like (or Gould-like) immediacy, a kind of stylistic transparency. And yet, Ware's comics are, as a general rule, anything but easy to read" (Cates 2010, 97). While the diagrams make his cartoons seem arguably "transparent," they are likewise juxtaposed by the complicated layouts and "central characters whose main attributes are emotional paralysis or painful awkwardness" (Cates 2010, 97).

His meticulous layout seems to counterbalance the protagonist's disappointment in life and the emptiness she often feels inside. Her inner struggle and battles with loneliness and depression remain in between the lines; in their proximity to the diagram, these emotions are rationalized, quantified, made visually navigable. Similarly, Ware's detailed, precise depiction of high-end technology, his crafting of beautiful cityscapes, and his keen eye for architectural structures stand in contrast to the characters' inscrutability and shapelessness. They have no sharp edges, no idiosyncratic features, no quirky hairdos. The characters are drawn in a round and homey manner. They look like soft toys, or, rather, like marshmallow Matryoshak dolls induced with life. Their bodies are smooth and soft—lovely figurines living in neat and stylish, yet eerily empty apartments, staring at phones and television sets. *Building Stories*' veneer is cute, adorable, sweet, a little quirky, but what is happening on the inside of the box is something else entirely. To further explore this

---

⁵ Academic discourse on the medium of graphic narrative has arisen particularly since, but not exclusively because Art Spiegelman's *Maus* won the Pulitzer Prize in 1992. For more on the medium, see Chute (2010), Eisner (2008), Frahm (2010), Groensteen (2007, 2011), McCloud (1993, 2000), Versaci (2007), Wolk (2007), and Chute and Jagoda (2014).

tension, Ware employs a distinct palette of warm, coordinated colors for his spreads, creating coherence on the page, but likewise disguises the emotional detachment and precariousness of his characters. Their cute veneer and their flailing emotional energy are juxtaposed through Ware's tight artistic control. Unlike what Isaac Cates calls a "stylistic transparency" of Ware's craft, the characters' inner turmoil remain opaque, hidden behind Ware's thick veneer of style and craftsmanship. The anxiety and depression the protagonist feels is subdued by the page's layout, the color-coordination schemes of spreads, or minute gestures (like shooing away a fly or picking up a glass of water are elongated over four panels) in slow panel progressions.[6]

The convoluted design hints at the subduing of the emotional make-up of the characters. This might even suggest that the most beautiful things can trigger the most awful memories, for Ware's style invokes an "optical discomfort" or "visual discomfort" (Cates 2010, 98). I would like to argue more forcefully here to say that it creates not only (visual, optical, *and* material) discomfort, but that these are *trompe d'oeils*. They exceed a sense of discomfort to a more precarious discomfort regarding ambiguity, memory, and trauma that remains hidden and unspoken, just like Matryoshka dolls, neatly stacked into one another. For in interviews over the years, Ware has likened his style to how memory works:

> Cognitive research apparently implies that we're constantly rewriting our memories, and when we think we're remembering something, we're actually pulling sense memories and concepts from various places and simply putting them together, theater-manager style. Interestingly, this process is something along the lines of what goes into drawing comics; everything the cartoonist puts on the page is from his or her memory, the exception being the use of photo reference, but even that eventually filters through some hierarchy of memory, fusion, language, and life to coalesce into what that particular artist thinks is important, which I guess is what we call style. (Ware 2012c, n.p.)

Following Ware's claim, we can approach his work as an attempt to create a memory map and a narrative network at the same time. Ware's style—the amalgamation of what he calls memory, language, and life—expresses what is right in front of our eyes might not be what the picture wants to say. In the following, I argue for memory/remembering and recollecting as predominant modes of the narrative and material of *Building Stories*. Building

---

[6] The aesthetic category of slowness will be discussed in Chapter 4, via *Kentucky Route Zero*.

up on my introductory remarks, allow me to first explore the tension between collection and consumer item and the positioning of the reader toward the fake collection.

The collection and practical memory

"I need to collect myself real quick": To sort through thoughts, to regain composure, to pull oneself together—uttered usually in a rush or when out of breath. It indicates how collecting is an essential feature of the human condition: being and collecting are deeply intertwined with one another. Collecting, Mieke Bal argues, "originates in the need to tell stories, but for which there are neither words nor other conventional narrative modes. Hence, collecting is a story, and everyone needs to tell it. Yet, it is obvious that not every human being is, or can afford to be, a collector. The essentializing gesture obscures the class privilege that is thereby projected on the human species as a whole" (Bal 1994, 103). Bal intriguingly links the urge to collect to the notion of narrative, the need to tell stories through collecting to make sense of the self. Through the collection, self and objects can be reshuffled and curated continuously, offering ever-new combinations of the same material and components. Also Jean Baudrillard sees a promise of a sense of self in collecting, hunting down, accumulating:

> The singular object never impedes the process of narcissistic projection, which ranges over an indefinite number of objects: on the contrary, it encourages such multiplication, thus associating itself with a mechanism whereby the image of the self is extended to the very limits of the collection. Here . . . lies the whole miracle of collecting. For it is invariably oneself that one collects. (Baudrillard 1994, 12)

But to collect oneself implies more than just to hold on for a second and reorganize one's thoughts: the possible multitudes contained within the self can be expressed in the myriad ways of reassembly, as "one becomes conscious of one's self, one becomes a conscious collector of identity, projecting one's being onto the objects one chooses to live with. Taste, the collector's taste, is a mirror of self" (Elsner and Cardinal 1994, 3).

Each reading of *Building Stories* opens up to the reader multiple possibilities to build her own stories and arrange "her" collectables anew—it is a shapeshifter in the truest sense. Yet the reader of *Building Stories* must play a game of "fake collecting" here, for she has never collected these accumulated booklets herself. Instead, she is to sift through a loose, ready-made collection whose aleatory structure leaves plotlines dangling and incomplete. Through *Building Stories*' design of a colorful variation of fourteen "distinctively discrete Books, Booklets, Magazines, Newspapers, and Pamphlets"—to quote from self-description on the bottom of the box—Ware amplifies the notion of accidental, haphazard collections that just come to *be* in the course of time (Ware 2012b, n.p.). Jean Baudrillard's notion of collection being the ideal mirror for the collector to look into is articulated here: "For the images it reflects succeed one another while never contradicting one another. Moreover, it is ideal in that it reflects images not of what is real, but only of what is desirable" (Baudrillard 1994, 11). And it is imperative to underline that to collect and to remember is tightly linked to the unsteady meanings of consuming (i.e., time-consuming shopping). The box toys exactly with this: a game of memory (one of the booklets could be bought randomly at a bookstore, for example, while another pamphlet was maybe picked up at a gallery opening, yet another one is a children's book held onto as a keepsake, a souvenir from childhood), a game of desire for a vague sense of an ending, and a game of make-believe consumption (i.e., pretending to have collected the collection).

Building Stories draws a connection between collecting and remembering, for they are activities both predicated and structured by contingencies and happenstance, not primarily on spending power. Chris Ware relates in an interview with Tavi Gevinson,

> I wanted to make a book that had no beginning or end, and . . . to try and get at the three-dimensionality of memories and stories—how we're able to tell them starting at this or that point depending on the circumstance, and to take them apart and put them back together, whether to actually try and make sense of our lives or simply to tell reassuring lies to ourselves. (Ware 2012f, n.p.)

What, if not the practice of collecting, echoes in Ware's words? Here Chris Ware expresses how remembering and collecting congeal in narrative, material, and visual manifestations, and how they become available as "a form of sensation and state of consciousness" (Sattler 2010, 207). *Building Stories* makes available an *experience*—a contorted and convoluted one, no doubt—that simultaneously teaches its readership how it wants to be read—how it wants to be consumed and how it wants to be remembered.

Only by engaging with Ware's work can the reader learn how to collect, preserve, handle, and fondle the objects in the box, building and destroying the story with every reading. Collecting, thus, becomes a multifaceted experience that equates reading with remembering and curating. As a collector of both comic books and memories, then, the reader experiences a form of what Walter Benjamin coins in his *Arcades Project* "practical memory" (Benjamin 1999, 205). Benjamin continues in a section fittingly called "The Collector": "But this is the way things are for the great collector. They strike him. How he himself pursues and encounters them, what changes in the ensemble of items are effected by a newly supervening item—all this shows him his affairs in constant flux" (Benjamin 1999, 205). Benjamin's quote speaks directly to *Building Stories* and how it seems to also always be in flux—no reading experience resembles the other, and with every reading (and every new object), something new might "strike" the reader as particularly noteworthy, for she might have overlooked a detail the other time(s) before.

This idea of practical memory finds expression in the souvenir, which is, according to Susan Stewart, capable to *distinguish* experiences, yet displaces attention toward the past (i.e., the golden booklets as a souvenir from our childhood). Stewart writes that we

> do not need or desire souvenirs of events that are repeatable. Rather we need and desire souvenirs of events that are reportable, events whose materiality has escaped us, events that thereby exist only through the invention of narrative. Through narrative the souvenir substitutes a context of perpetual consumption for its context of origin. It represents not the lived experience of its maker but the "secondhand" experience of its possessor/owner. (Stewart 1993, 135)

The focus here is again on *experience*—be it secondhand or practical, unrepeatable and unique (but ironically, *Building Stories* builds upon its "repeatability"). This implication of experience exceeds one of hermeneutical potential and manifests itself within the material contingencies. Particularly Stewart's remarks on the souvenir—the mementos we keep—that rely on a reiteration of the invention of narrative is particularly striking. This signals a shift from maker to possessor, from reader to performer, who is now struck "by the confusion, by the scatter in which the things of the world are found" (Benjamin 1999, 211). No wonder that Ware chose a keepsake box that catalogues the leftovers of a life lived, a life experienced, as an adequate medium for this experience.

Practical or experimental memory invokes as a physical, bodily event, a *"feeling* of remembering, the phenomenology of memory itself. . . . It is linked, that is, to the process of optically navigating the comics page as well as the activity of consolidating that page in one's mind" (Sattler 2010, 210, emphasis mine). The outcome is, again to borrow from Benjamin, in flux, for it is, as Sattler points out, a "fluid experiential boundary between insides and outsides, between the experience of imagining a world and the experience of seeing it. The medium 'calls up' one's memories but does so in a way that makes those memories visible, that allows those memories to be encountered—not objectively, but as a matter of feeling—within the external world, on the page" (Sattler 2010, 213). I find it noteworthy in what way Sattler's idea of an affective response echoes the "optical navigating" of the comics page (i.e., Ware's tightly controlled ideograms and layouts) and the subduing of affect within the story through its counterbalancing with Ware's design choices.

There is also a commentary enfolded within *Building Stories* regarding the history of collecting comics. With the keepsake box, Ware draws attention to the obsession of comic book readers who carefully catalog and possess every issue of their favored publications and series. The comic book nerd and the curator might not be too far apart from one another—both are extremely knowledgeable in their field of expertise and aim at preserving its artifacts. Ware intensifies this further: he presents a collection that never *was* in the first place—it is a ready-made, a fake collection that the reader never collected herself, but can be purchased in a "complete" way in a bookstore or online. Jared Gardner widens the term of a collection toward that of the "archival database." Comics collections, Gardner continues, "are archives in the loosest, messiest sense of the word—archives of the forgotten artifacts and ephemera of American popular culture, items that were never meant to be collected" (Gardner 2012b, 150). The idea that these media were never meant to be collected in the first placed—but are, as Gardner says, forgotten artifacts and ephemera of American popular culture—makes for a tricky positioning in modern consumer culture and mass media.

This fact—"their ephemeral nature, their quality of waste products of modern mass media and consumer culture"—might constitute, according to Gardner,

> perverse pleasures of those who collect, organize, and fetishize them. These are collections organized by invisible grids, by individual desires, by the accident of geography or inheritance. And yet, these archives are far from the random gleanings of the packrat or the hoarder. Their exploration and the disciplines and skills required lie somewhere between "data mining" and "dumpster diving," between analysis and scavenging. (Gardner 2012b, 150)

I am intrigued by Gardner's terminology, for collecting comics does not subdue affect (compared to *Building Stories*' inscrutable characters), but brings about "perverse pleasures," "fetishism," and "desires." Yet *Building Stories* is a comics collection that was never meant to be collected in the first place, for the reader herself never collected it. That means that Ware creates a proxy for a reader who is aware, say, of the history of the medium, who curates the story by taking care of the object, who expresses taste and a literal "feeling" for the object (Desire! Fetish! Pleasure!), but who also dives into dumpsters to find her fetishized object of desire. The curating collector turns into an obsessive geek.

This indexes a bag of mixed, contradictory affects pertaining to the object (and the self that tells itself through collecting). Hunting down and neatly cataloging comics books is affective labor in its own right: we take care of *Building Stories* by archiving it—by taking the booklets out of circulation (or the dumpster) and re-embedding them into a private, individualized logic of a (fake) collection. Precariously ephemeral, prone to tear and be lost, delicate as narrative, inhabited by characters who need love and support, the labor poured into *Building Stories* can be thought along the lines of Sianne Ngai's inquiries regarding cute as a contemporary aesthetic category.[7] Remember the tension between the diagrams and the marshmellow-y characters. Here, we can turn to Ngai who postulates that cute is a weakened aesthetic category (and judgment!), namely, "a demand for care that women in particular often feel addressed or interpellated by" which suggests that cute "designates not just the site of a static power differential but also the site of a surprisingly complex power struggle" (Ngai 2012b, 11). Oh how *cute*: diminutive, weak, and subordinate, a category that evokes both affection and aggression, indexing an intimate, *sensuous* relationship with an object that is based on these oftentimes contradicting emotions (see Ngai 2012b, 54).

Her reading of this aesthetic category pertains particularly to twentieth-century poetry, yet Ngai highlights how cuteness is linked to commodity fetishism (i.e., see Gardner's choice of words regarding the dumpster-diving comics geek). The "subset of 'minor' aesthetic categories seems markedly salient for the historical account of the rise of consumer aesthetics in the postwar United States and Europe" (Ngai 2012b, 58). Cute becomes an emergent consumer option, arising out of the "marriage of modernism and mass culture"—Ngai argues persuasively that "these aesthetic categories [are] based on milder or equivocal feelings make explicit" and that it is "the continuousness and everydayness of our aesthetic relation to the often artfully designed, packaged, and advertised merchandise that surrounds us in our homes, in our workplaces, and on the street" (Ngai 2012b, 58). Her assertion can be productively interlinked with Ware's strategies in *Building*

---

[7] The aesthetics categories of cute, zany, and interesting are markers "grasping how aesthetic experience has been transformed by the hypercommodified, information-saturated, performance-driven conditions of late capitalism" (Ngai 2012b, 1).

Stories: the marriage of high modernism[8] and mass culture, offering a twist to the collection of small, diminutive objects and stories. What is cuter (as in, culturally diminutive) than the sorrows of one unnamed woman told through beautiful comics books?

The reader, again and again, stumbles over "cute things" in *Building Stories* (not only on the material level!) that express a peculiar ambivalence between caring for and the potential for an aggressive response: the daughter in a princess dress—lovely to look at, but laying out her possible heteronormative gender destiny; the landlady as a dress-up doll—conflating her being a toy with (social, gendered) immobility and shyness that stymied her throughout life; Branford Bee, the bee from the neighboring lot—a children's story that deals with the bee's sexual instincts that it cannot control (i.e., culturally coded as "sex addiction"); the sort-of "cute" guy the woman on the second floor falls for, who starts abusing her physically and emotionally. This affection-aggression further unpacks the *material*[9] of the graphic narrative—the commodity aesthetic of the object at hand—for this ambivalence of caring for and aggression comes to the fore in the means of interacting. It equally caters to protection and care as well as a staging toward the assimilation and commodification of (social) difference (see Ngai 2012b, 60). This interlinking of the considerations toward cuteness and collecting helps unravel how the gendered notion of the collector emerges: by making available gendered activities (caring, collecting, dumpster-diving), Ware interrogates the crux between male comic book nerd and female consumer, care-giver and care-taker for the incomplete collection. So, "whether you're feeling alone by

---

[8] For more on Ware's gestures toward modernism in *Building Stories*, see Daniel Worden's highly illuminating article "On Modernism's Ruins: The Architecture of 'Building Stories' and *Lost Buildings*." He argues that Ware's *Building Stories* "contrasts the possibilities embedded within architectural space in the early twentieth century with the archival fantasies about the same space that provide comfort in late twentieth-century America" (Worden 2010, 108).

[9] To take this idea even one step further, we can turn to Donna Haraway's ideas in regard to the feminization of work in *A Cyborg Manifesto*:

> To be feminized means to be made extremely vulnerable; able to be disassembled, reassembled, exploited as a reverse labour force; seen less as workers than as servers; subjected to time arrangements on and off the paid job that make a mockery of a limited work day; leading an existence that always borders on being obscene, out of place, and reducible to sex. (Haraway 2000, 304)

I am drawn to this quote because of the challenges of being disassembled, reassembled, and exploited (as a woman! As a body!), just like the object that *Building Stories* is. If we understand this correlation to the feminized object and the indexation of it as female, we can ask a different set of questions pertaining to curatorial labor and its interrogation of gender as a social construct that sorts human bodies (and books!) into binary "categories in order to assign labor, responsibilities, moral attributes, and emotional styles" (Halberstam 2007, 118).

yourself or alone with someone else, this book is sure to sympathize with the crushing sense of life wasted, opportunities missed and creative dreams dashed which afflict the middle- and upper-class literary public (and which can return to them in somewhat damaged form during REM sleep)" (Ware 2012b, n.p.).

The boxed dilemma: Browsing *Building Stories*

Let's lift the lid and peak inside this dream: The comic spread "Browsing" helps untangle the intricate layers of meaning enfolded within the keepsake box. Set in a moment in the unspecified future, unrelated to any other story line in the graphic narrative, the reader learns that the box appeared to the unnamed protagonist in a dream (i.e., in "damaged form during REM sleep"). In her dream she is in a bookstore, "browsing" the shelves. One book catches her attention because of its odd format—it turns out it is *her* book. It is a box, containing her writings that she threw away a long time ago. The protagonist marvels at how it had *"everything* in it" (emphasis in original). She sits in a café with her daughter, who is now grown up, and she continues to relate her dream to her:

> My diaries, the stories from my writing classes, even stuff I didn't know I'd written. . . . Everything I'd forgotten . . . abandoned or thrown out. . . . All of the illustrations (and there were a lot of them—there seemed to be more and more the more I looked) were so precise and clean it was like an architect had drawn them. . . . They were to colorful and intricate.

But what is most striking about her dream is the way she relates the format of the book:

> It wasn't—I dunno—it wasn't really a *book*, either—it was in . . . *pieces*, like, books falling apart out of a carton, maybe. . . but it was . . . *beautiful* . . . it made sense." The daughter replies off-handedly: "Your dreams are always so *retarded*, mom . . . c'mon . . . it's so *obvious* . . . an *architect*?

The protagonist wipes away a tear as her daughter laughs it off as just a dream about her mother's (now apparently ex-) husband, Phil (who works as an architect). But there is more to this spread than just some "retarded" dream work or how bookstores went out of business because of our consumption habits of "browsing" the internet. In "Browsing" lies the Rosetta stone of

Building Stories—the collector learns that *Building Stories* is indeed a dream book.

Walter Benjamin posits that a collection echoes in us like a dream, and "we may say, the collector lives a piece of dream life. For in the dream, too, the rhythm of perception and experience is altered in such a way that everything—even the seemingly most neutral—comes to strike us; everything concerns us" (Benjamin 1999, 205–06). What is this "everything" if life is incomplete? (The book had everything in it, though.) Is it the crushing sense of life wasted and opportunities missed and creative dreams dashed? Ultimately, the reader realizes that the stories included in the *Building Stories* box are the accumulation of her (failed) creative output, which the protagonist created (and discarded) throughout her life (speaking of affection and aggression toward things!). It turns out that the booklets in the box are the protagonist's creative writing tasks; she wrote stories about her neighbors, the landlady, Branford Bee, and the unhappy couple living one floor beneath the protagonist.

Ware does not make this fact too obvious, but he merely leaves little clues and allusions throughout the graphic narrative on how the material compiled in the box is indeed that of the protagonist. Chris Ware points out in an interview with Calvin Reid of *Publisher Weekly* that "the idea behind that is supposed to be that the main character is doing these stories for a creative writing class and those stories are part of the stories she's written for the class" (Ware 2012a, n.p.). This revelation contorts the material and narrative planes of *Building Stories*, for Ware plays a confusing meta-game here between the protagonist, the reader, and himself. He challenges the boundaries between the fictional and the material levels of the book. What does it even mean when the protagonist, the author, and the reader suddenly read (and build) the same book? How can we hold a dream in our hands? Is this book a dream and how does this fact reconstitute the relationship between object, narrative, and the curatorial tasks at hand?

The spread "Browsing" encapsulates these questions and acknowledges the bizarre idea of collections and dreams as narrativizing tools—unpredictable, composed of unconscious impulses, nonlinear, "damaged," and haphazard. The *protagonist* now too enters the realm of the fictional arena as a curator (both as reader and consumer!), curating her own abandoned, forgotten collection. This shortens the distance between the protagonist and the reader, because they are engaged in the same task—presumably unknowingly so. It also leads us back to the commodification of *Building Stories* and the artistic vision behind the collection (to collect is to consume, no less). The protagonist's most private writings are now a commercialized good for readers to sift through and buy. Making her box and therefore her past as well as her dreams available for purchase seems to trigger all of the protagonist's anxieties and self-doubts—for she never thought her artistic work would be good enough for a broader audience (or, similarly, in his self-deprecating tone, Ware's for *his* audience). Her collection, the physical object the reader now holds in *her* hand, does not only contain notions of the self but shows her what could have been, but never was. Katherine Roeder fittingly relates that it is the poring "over the box's contents [that] makes you reflect on the unpredictable nature of memory, as certain events take on more significance as the back story reveals itself" (Roeder 2012, n.p.). For the protagonist finds everything she had "forgotten . . . abandoned or thrown out."

What Ware might suggest here is that memories as commercialized goods and objects trigger regret and nostalgia for times past that infiltrate present and future. But when looking more closely at the spread, there is something peculiar going on. From panel to panel, her missing leg changes its form—first it is a rather rudimentary prosthesis, then a more sophisticated one, until then, finally, it turns into a book.[10] But a book and a leg hardly follow the same function? What is being propped up here? The book the protagonist stumbles upon in the bookstore and her body come to conflate, dazzling her with what she has created "in her mind" to make it part of her body. Her leg stands in for both a prosthesis and a metaphor for the book itself: It is crowbar *and* prosthesis, dream work *and* a consumer product. *Building Stories* occurs to her in a dream, but the reader also holds the book with her discarded writings in her hand.

Let us look a little closer at the design of the cover of the (dream) box. What is it that caught her (and our!) attention? The cover design relates the box to a building: a brick wall, window ornaments, morning shadows on the wall, a door, the house, the sound of "ding dong" (of *Building Stories*) when ringing the doorbell, the protagonist curled up in bed—these images foreshadow major plotlines. On the back of the bottom part of the box, we see the blueprint of the protagonist's house in Oak Park into which she moves in her thirties with her family. It is a map to the places in her house where the protagonist left the booklets lying around. The blueprint is a suggestion

---

[10] Many of Chris Ware's characters have bodily ailments. Some are obese, some walk on crutches, others come to terms with their changing bodies during puberty. What is oftentimes conspicuously missing in reviews and plot summaries (and also in the self-descriptive synopsis on the "dust jacket") is any indication of the physical disability of the protagonist. She lost her leg in a boating accident and has worn different artificial limbs throughout her life. Susan Squier's assertion that the graphic narratives *Epilecptic* by David B. or *The Ride Together* by Paul Karasik and Judy Karasik are able to "unsettle conventional notions of normalcy and disability" can help understand the means of how the medium unveils potentials toward the interlacing of form and story (Squier 2008, 71).

"made as to appropriate places to set down, forget or completely lose any number of [the box's] contents within the walls of an average well-appointed home" (Ware 2012b, n.p.). The newspaper, for instance, lies underneath the couch table in the reading room; the board game sits in a dusty corner next to the sofa in the living room; the leaflet with the red mask on it lies on the kitchen counter. This intertwines the unsorted arrangement of the keepsake box not only with the orderly layout of a house but also with our handling of paper in domestic spaces. Who of the reading middle- and upper-class public has not left leaflets or books strewn around in disarray in private? Further, we can subsume how this interlinking leads to the architectural spaces in and of *Building Stories* and their interactions with books, bodies, and memory—and how we lose and forget things in our own four walls.

At one point in the story, the protagonist ponders where and how memories are stored in the human body, and she concludes it must be the head and the mind. Here, she draws the parallel to the layout of a building: "Why is it always the attic where we banish our past? Is it because since it's always above us, it feels analogous to our minds? You know "looking up" whenever we're trying to remember something." (And, of course, one "looks up" information on the internet.) Chris Ware emphasizes how memories (and dreams) are an architectural construct, a blueprint, a scaffold for lives lived. This offers a slight detour to answer our inquiries into the boxed dilemma, yet we should acknowledge the way Ware has been interested all through his career in the architectural spaces[11] of cities and the lives of houses. *Building Stories* has probably become most famous for one rather peculiar character, namely, the narrating house, an old, ramshackle apartment building owned by an elderly lady in Chicago. The protagonist "used the building as a character itself and its sort of this self-conscious way for her to get inside of it. I left it very vague" (Ware 2012a, n.p.).

Ware offers analogies to the way memory is structured via the house: a messy dream and an architectural structure. The narrating house might serve as a greater metaphor for the comics medium as a contested space for memory construction and also its fallacies. Daniel Raeburn draws on Art Spiegelman's idea of how the word "story" descends from "the medieval Latin

---

[11] A good example is Ware's cooperation with Ira Glass on *Lost Buildings*, a mixed-media story (Glass did the narration, Ware the drawings, and it was published on a DVD which was included in a little book) about a boy who is obsessed with Louis Sullivan's buildings during the 1960s and 1970s, when they were torn down in Chicago to make room for newer buildings. Further, the family of the unnamed protagonist moves to Oak Park, a suburb in Chicago, which was architecturally shaped by Frank Lloyd Wright. In some of the panels in *Building Stories*, that is, when the protagonist goes for a run around the neighborhood, she scoffs at tourists who marvel at Lloyd's prairie style houses.

'historia', which meant 'picture' as well as the horizontal division of a building. Latin users derived this conflation from the medieval practice of placing a picture in each window of a building, especially in churches. . . . A storey is a row of colored pictures/windows" (Spiegelman in Raeburn 2004, 26). The stories, then, are also the floors of the house.[12] It would be Building *Stories*, for "the house furnishes us dispersed images and a body of images at the same time" (Bachelard 1994, 3). We can draw analogies from the dispersed image to the collectible in the collection. Gaston Bachelard offers a suitable meditation on the house as a space for daydreaming[13] and memory, which can be intertwined with *Building Stories*' spaces of archives and collections. This helps interlink the metaphor of the house with the architecture of Ware's graphic narrative. Yet understanding Ware's design and the keepsake box as an interpretation and visualization of recollecting serves to acknowledge its constant reorganization; comic panels, like memories, resemble frozen images, compartmentalized into single panels, arranged in a rigid sequence. In contrast, *Building Stories* presses its own material flexibility. Subsequently, panels are like adjacent rooms, (to be) filled with stories. But a house will be rigid forever, for rooms cannot be shuffled. In keepsake boxes or in buildings is where we store, reassess, and reassemble our memories.

Building Stories allows to "browse" through memories in the most literal sense. I'd like to return to the challenges that the box as a spatial (if not architectural) metaphor for memory and collecting enables. I wonder what the role of the implied reader as architect is here, the one that the protagonist dreamed about. We must assume that we browse through *Building Stories* and that we "look up" memories that are banned on the attic. But memory is messy and confusing. It hits us when we least expect it. Here, Ware's interest in palpable, experimental memory comes to the fore again and overlaps with a wonky interactivity that leaves the reader

---

[12] *Asterios Polyp* by David Mazzucchelli beautifully investigates how architectural styles mirror personal styles. The graphic narrative tells the story of Polyp, an architect and professor at Cornell, who tries to change his life after he lost his partner and a lightning strike hit his apartment.

[13] Gaston Bachelard writes:

> If I were asked to name the chief benefit of the house, I should say: the house shelters day dreaming, the house protects the dreamer, the house allows one to dream in peace. Thought and experience are not the only things that sanction human values. The values that belong to daydreaming mark humanity in its depths. Daydreaming even has a privilege of autovalorization. It derives direct pleasure from its own being. Therefore, the places in which we have experienced daydreaming reconstitute themselves in a new daydream, and it is because our memories of former dwelling-places are relived as daydreams that these dwelling-places of the past remain in us for all time. (Bachelard 1994, 6)

second-guessing. The title of the spread, "Browsing," remains imperative, for she keeps on shifting and shuffling through the elements of the box. I would now like to turn to the objects that are stored within the keepsake box and think further about what it is that we keep in these boxes, anyway. In the course of *Building Stories*, Ware tries out different vehicles through which we recollect and remember our lives, and we see the characters write in diaries, take photographs, talk to buildings and rooms, or stalk Facebook profiles in order to remember. None of these strategies make the spontaneity and unpredictability of memory as palpable as what I come to call *centerpieces*. These objects allow us to go deeper into the rabbit holes of recollecting and rearranging memories.

The centerpieces

Oftentimes in the booklets rigidly designed pages of what we could call "visual comfort"—neatly aligned, color-coordinated, symmetrical—are disrupted by large double page spreads that are chaotic and convoluted. One singular object floats at the center of these pages, and little vignettes and episodes "cloud" around it. I suggest calling these objects "centerpieces," and I ascribe incredible hermeneutic potential to them. *Building Stories* teaches its readers how to think *around* objects: These centerpieces[14] are loosely related to the grander narrative of the spread, all the while they are discreet and independent from the rest of *Building Stories*. They arrest the flow of the reading experience and amount to an unclear, overwhelming, and sometimes frustrating engagement with the pages that can only be amended by scrutiny and patience. This indexes a shift from visual comfort to visual discomfort: The spreads take the readers and the protagonist out of the "now" into the vortex of memories—messy, convoluted, weird. Both Sattler's and Benjamin's notions of experimental memory come to the fore, and the centerpieces continue to blur the lines between author, reader, and protagonist. These

---

[14] Ware uses twenty-six centerpieces, which are eight photographs of people and perspectives on (empty) rooms; one empty diary with a pen tucked to the corner; one artsy Ben-Day stylized dot printing of a vagina; one edgy painting of a vagina by an art student with the phrase "Fuck Me Harder" painted onto it; one delicate orchid; one comic "BOOM" cloud; one $1 bill with a dog ear in its upper-right corner; the front and back of a mask of a blonde woman; six faces/one mirror (the old lady as a young woman, the unhappy couple of the house, the protagonist's daughter, and the protagonist herself, with both her face and the red "inside" of her face); two birth control pill packs, one full and then used; the protagonist's daughter as a baby; one rose brooch; and the hands of the unhappy neighbors.

are the objects the protagonist writes stories about for her creative writing assignments, but likewise, these could also be tchotchkes that a collector puts into a keepsake box.

The centerpieces encapsulate Ware's endeavors regarding how memories and stories interrogate one another. Ware shows what we collect over the course of a lifetime and how these stories amount to our life story, putting emphasis on the mundane and everyday. The centerpiece is employed as a symbol and placeholder for a bigger, overarching theme for the double page spread and takes on new significations throughout the reading experience. This happens through *remembering*: an orchid flower, for example, becomes a symbol for the protagonist's sexuality; a blank page of a notebook is a symbol for the protagonist's stymied creativity; a stylized comic *BOOM* cloud and a $1 bill are symbols for the 2008 economic recession and the housing crisis;[15] the protagonist's daughter's face turns into a placeholder for the protagonist's hopes in the future; a coin is a token that reminds the protagonist of her abortion, since the fetus was just the size of a dime when she had the procedure. These visual clues first have to be "unlocked" by the reader to revel in the hidden layers beneath the story that run through *Building Stories* like a strong, if silent undercurrent. Ware finds an "object language" that reveals hidden layers to the story that the reader must learn and remember.

The centerpiece takes up the role of a narrative, a visual, *and* a material placeholder on the page—it is an object, a collectable, as well as a symbol that sutures together the spread. Bluntly speaking, we could understand a centerpiece as a magnet for memories. Let's look at one object to understand and untangle its significance as narrative, visual, and material conceit: the brooch in the center of what I call the "rose lapel spread" can direct the *narrative* progression and the *layout* of the spread. More importantly, it unsettles the notion of who is writing whom here (the dilemma of the box outlined above: a book that came to the protagonist in a dream). In the course of *Building Stories* the reader learns that the protagonist's landlady once gave a rose lapel pin to her sick mother as a Christmas present. According to her, it was a "really cruel gift, really, as she couldn't go out." The rose brooch stands in as a symbol for the burdens the landlady had to carry throughout her life: taking care of her bed-ridden mother; doing chores around the apartment building, like renovations and renting apartments out; her waifish and shy demeanor.

---

[15] In light of the housing market and its collapse in 2008, it seems like it is no coincidence that *Building Stories* was published in its wake. It is almost as if Ware shifts *Building Stories*' focus willfully onto the discussion of how houses are not only commodities or status symbols that bring fortune or ruin and how they may function as subjective spaces of affective and memory *investments*.

Neither mother nor daughter had any occasion to wear it. The expectations the landlady had toward life were never fulfilled but dreamed away.

The rose is timeless while time passes around her. The page combines the history and present of the landlady: we see old snapshots, renovations and building maintenance, today and yesterday blurring together. Also notice the color coordination. The lettering and coloring of the page is adjusted to the centerpiece: the page is dominated by red, gray, green, and mud colors. These different strata coexist on one page, brought together by the brooch, with no hierarchy ascribed to them. The spread also complicates the fiction of *Building Stories*, for the rose pin "pops up" at another point in the story, in somebody else's hands, namely, the protagonist's. The rose lapel helps unravel the fiction of the box, for we learn that the protagonist once had a mortifying experience in a creative writing class where one of her short stories was harshly criticized. In that spread, the reader only hears the last words of the protagonist's (bad) story, and, notably, these words are indeed uttered by the landlady at another point in *Building Stories*. A fellow (male) class member advises her not to write about "everyday life" (huh!) but to go into a thrift store and buy old photo albums to invent stories around pictures of people long lost and forgotten. Despite her embarrassment, the protagonist promptly follows suit to try out this method to write about vintage secondhand objects. While browsing through old photo albums for sale, she happens upon a small rose lapel pin on display and buys it on a whim. We must wonder: Can this be the same brooch that the landlady gave to her mother? Or is it possible that the protagonist made up the story of the brooch? Is she writing fiction not only about people in photographs but also about objects, like vintage jewelry?

We can take Ware's explanation of the stories being included in the box as assignments for that creative writing class at face value to delve deeper into the multilayered fictions folded into the centerpieces. Both the reader and the protagonist pore over the box's contents, looking at the objects one by one, and the distance between these two instances—reader and protagonist—conflates. The protagonist writes about ordinary life, and the reader builds ordinary life out of her fragmented writings. Peter Sattler points out how the protagonist is the imagined author of a book

> she did not or could not create. These fragments, *Building Stories* tells us, are something like the memories (or dreams) of what one woman *might* have made, the books and drawing that she might have created. And this story, as a whole, is as much a fiction of the person she might have been as it is the fictional recreation of people she, through memory and imagination, has tried to understand. (Sattler 2012, n.p.)

Sattler's remark resonates in the protagonist's dream of finding her diaries in a bookstore, and, more importantly, *Building Stories*' continuous emphasis on the sheer endlessness of possibilities to rearrange the fragments. We might wonder what could have happened, what might have happened if we had a different "reading route." The reader is caught in a web of fictions created by three instances: the protagonist, Chris Ware, and herself, the reader, in a bizarre, coauthored effort that conflates the feeling of memory integral to *Building Stories*. The reader's recollections become the protagonist's recollections about the objects. Chris Ware chips in, too: "Nonetheless, it remains an odd feeling to find one's own memories completely realigned and re-collected. Without warning, all *my* memories were now those of our narrator too" (Ware in Sattler 2012, n.p.).

This complicates the function of the centerpiece, specifically if we pay closer attention to its location—the gutter, which negotiates hermeneutical potentiality in comics. By being located in the space between two adjacent panels, the centerpieces take on a temporal and spatial independence from the rest of the page. Panels and gutters make up the basic grammar of the comics to indicate that time and space are being divided on the comic's page. Time in comics can be bent. It is not necessarily linear but "infinitely weirder," as Scott McCloud points out (McCloud 1993, 94). On one single page, past, present, and future are "real and visible and all around us. Wherever your eyes are focused, that's now. But at the same time your eyes take in the surrounding landscape of past and future" (McCloud 1993, 104). With past, present, and future swirling around the reader, panels and gutters can set a rhythm to the weird temporal and spatial experience reading a comics might be (echoing the weird temporal and spatial experience of remembering *and* collecting!). At first sight the space of the gutter seems to be nothing but an empty, white no man's land between two panels. But they can spatialize time and temporize space: "The few centimeters which transport us from second to second in one sequence could take us a hundred million years in another. So, as readers, we're left with only a vague sense that as our eyes are moving through space, they're also moving through time—we just don't know by how much" (McCloud 1993, 100). Each panel represents one moment in time of which the reader is not sure how long it lasts. As insignificant as it may be in itself as a naked space created haphazardly as a by-product, its emptiness is rich of causality that the reader needs to establish herself. A comics is, after all, a "story that is full of holes" that the reader has to fill herself—again, just like memory (Groensteen 2007, 10).

The gutter therefore becomes the joint of the panels; it is just as an essential part of the story as the panel. It is a space to create meaning and reveals itself to be the site of "semantic articulation, a logical conversion, that of a series of utterables (the panels) in a statement that is unique and coherent (the story)" (Groensteen 2007, 114). Without this hermeneutical investment, the panels would otherwise just be framed pictures hanging next to one another, like Spiegelman's idea of the adjacent rooms in a house. Thierry Groensteen explains, "The intericonic gutter also marks the semantic solidarity of continuous panels above all, both working through the codes of narrative and sequential drawings. Between the polysemic images, the polysyntactic gutter is the site of a reciprocal determination, and it is in this dialectic interaction that meaning is constructed, not without the active participation of the reader" (Groensteen 2007, 115). Thus, the gutter has enormous hermeneutic potential for the reader of comic books in general—and for *Building Stories* in particular. We can subsume that the centerpiece is panel-less, unbound and unframed, lingering in the very center of the page. It seems to be floating aloof from the action yet is still in the center of everything.

The free-floating, "frozen" centerpiece compromises the freedom of the reader; neither anchored in nor separated from the page, it stands isolated from the story in both time and space. The centerpiece defies integration into the linear narrative of the panels surrounding it—yet by being panel-less, it can also radiate its signification into the sheltered grid of the gutters. Here, it is able to dominate the page and the hermeneutic intervention of the reader with its idiosyncratic meaning. It is still the main influence of the double page spread, orchestrating and subjugating everything around and between it. The centerpiece stands within and outside of the story, allowing for memories to randomly pop up and attach themselves to the object. My reading of the centerpieces, the box, and the gutters in *Building Stories* thus hinges upon how the centerpiece becomes a paradox: on the one hand the centerpiece amplifies the gutters, making visible and hence underlining the importance of the reader's participation within the rearranging of the booklets. But then again, it is an object she never bought herself.

To argue more forcefully, it is the experience of *memory* that takes place in the gutters. By neither being confined within a panel, nor being anchored to one single moment in time, a centerpiece can defy temporal and spatial categorizations. Scott McCloud notes how most of us

> are so used to the standard rectangular format that a "borderless" panel . . . can take on a timeless quality. When the content of a silent panel offers no clues, as to its duration, it can also produce a sense of timelessness. Because of its unresolved nature, such a panel may linger in the reader's mind. And its presence may be felt in the panels which follow it. (McCloud 1993, 102)

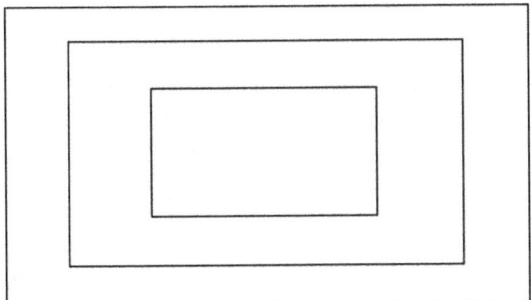

Figure 2.3 Overlapping panels or inset panels—author's own image.

Through the panel-less, silent centerpiece, then, time is "no longer contained by the familiar icon of the closed panel, but instead hemorrhages and escapes into timeless space. . . . Such images can set the mood or a sense of place for whole scenes through their lingering timeless presence" (McCloud 1993, 103). The effect that Ware's centerpieces have is that they give no indication in terms of their duration or even their precise timing in the narrative: the rose lapel pin will forever be in bloom.

Eric Berlatsky's concept of overlapping panels, or "inset panels" is imperative to think further about what he calls "vertical embedding" seen in the different narrative frames of Mary Shelley's *Frankenstein*. I would like to borrow his idea and underline that what is crucial is the spatial (overlap) and temporal (overlay, like an overlay at an airport) aspect of vertical embedding (Figure 2.3), and he links these narrative frames back to the panels/frames and gutters of comics. In the inset panels the frames "overlap" and "overlay" with one another, and consequently the space of the gutter is nil. No "fresh" meaning can be created here. Berlatsky's analysis of the mediation, layering, and framing function of inset panels in *Frankenstein*[16] translates to the medium of comics: the

---

[16] It is worth quoting Berlatsky's analysis of the inset panels in *Frankenstein* at length here to get at the gist of his idea:

> The "vertical embedding" seen in Frankenstein . . . is different . . . because the reader never gets a narrative from Victor that is not mediated and re-presented by Walton, while these two narrators also mediate the Creature's narrative. In some ways, then, the Creature never speaks, his voice always being enclosed by Victor's and Walton's. In other ways, however, the reader can easily lose sight of this fact, since the Creature's narrative is long, self-contained, and rarely interrupted. The method of transmission of inset panels in comics is similar. . . . In *Frankenstein* as published (1818 or 1831), we never know if we receive the Creature's "actual" words since Victor (and/or Walton) may be shading or changing things to fit his own motives. The Creature's narrative is independent and dependent in a manner similar to an inset panel. (Berlatsky 2009, 178)

reader can focus solely on the interior panel, viewing and reviewing the picture and words within it in their independence and totality. A shift in perspective allows him or her to see that the panel is within another, however. Never quite independent or univocal, it depends on the larger panel for its meaning, just as it acts as part of the compositional meaning of that surrounding picture. (Berlatsky 2009, 178)

He draws out a reciprocal relationship here; the inset panel does not speak for itself without being "filtered" and mediated through other instances and voices, but it can very well dominate the story: "[The] two frames can never be completely competitive since the interior panel is always a constitutive part of the larger picture" (Berlatsky 2009, 178). We can transfer this idea onto Ware's centerpieces: While the centerpiece is not confined in another panel, it operates on the same principles as an inset panel. Ware enables a different, "private" story, detached from *and* dependent on the rest of the page.

These stories do not compete but constitute one another; they not only speak for each other but also remain silent and temporally and spatially unspecific. If each panel is a frozen image of a memory, it is, as Ware postulates, experience and activity, the glue between palimpsestic still lifes. Even when centering the story on static, mute objects, Ware gives centerpieces the power to subjugate the panels swirling around them. This makes the temporal and structural arrangement of the centerpiece both beautiful and complicated. Its openness and timelessness, a piece inside *and* outside of the narrative, relates the centerpiece to the narrative and organizational systems of a collection. After all, a collectable is an item taken out of temporal and spatial order, reintegrated into a collection, bestowed with an altered, idiosyncratic meaning by its collector. *Building Stories* draws out the centerpieces as a collection around which memories and stories are built—and bestows commonplace objects like a brooch or a coin with idiosyncratic meaning established by Ware. This ties in with Ware's reassessment of what can happen in the gutters: a move out of the comic book toward the curio cabinet, from the page into the hand of the reader toward a tangible collection.

Curio cabinets and cut outs

I would like to linger a little bit longer in and on Ware's weird gutters. He has already made use of a completely different, yet comparable idea to the centerpieces in his earlier work, namely, the inclusion of what I call *cut outs*. Particularly in *Jimmy Corrigan—The Smartest Kid on Earth* cut out paper sculptures play an instrumental role and must be seen as part of the narrative progression that the reader *has* to build and "collect." The story would otherwise remain incomplete if the cut out instructions remained merely on the page. This brings us back to the idea of thinking *around* an object, as he points out in an interview with Christopher Irving and Seth Kushner:

> As for the paper sculptures, they're something of a joke on memory, how we reconstruct things from our senses, literally rebuilding the world in our minds. . . . But mostly, it's because I just love those sorts of things; I love paper cutouts and books that have things in them that are unexpected or promise some sort of magic, for lack of a less queasy word. It's another way of looking at a story, of thinking around a story, or of thinking around a memory. (Ware 2012c, n.p.)

To think around a memory, the cut outs become story by taking on narrative and material significance. They illuminate on how the story in the graphic narrative is, quite literally, constructed and *built*. Ware thus presses the interplay between page and object, and also between author, character, and reader by means of elevating the manual of a barn or zoetrope into a haptic, tactile experience.

In *Jimmy Corrigan*, the eponymous protagonist tries to construct a paper zoetrope while embarking on a journey to meet his long-lost father. Sitting on a bumpy flight, Jimmy labors to build a little toy that animates a robot on crutches, only to fall asleep and wake up as said robot. At first sight, the zoetrope manual seems to deliberately disrupt the story. Jimmy is never shown building this cut out zoetrope. Instead, it is the reader who emulates Jimmy's position to build this odd, outdated entertainment device. The cut out now "literally interrupt[s] the sequence of panels; where the ordinary comics panels that precede the cut [out] function normatively as images or representations of the events narrated, the zoetrope (at least potentially) stands as the thing itself: the reader can literally cut it out, construct it, spin it, and even watch the proto-film that would result" (Bredehoft 2006, 870). Both the reader and the character are engaged in the same activity, which minimizes their distance to each other. It brings the reader closer to the socially awkward and isolated comic books collector Jimmy (after all, they both do the same thing: building a zoetrope and watching the robot walk). And the reader herself creates an outdated film apparatus out of the gutters of the page she can now put on her shelf.

Since Ware never shows Jimmy building the zoetrope, the reader needs to fill in this narrative gap through dexterous labor and tinkering over the assembly instruction. What seemed disruptive or gimmicky at first now turns into a necessary device (pun intended!) to complete the scene on the airplane. The reader renders an "invisible" plot visible, the building of said zoetrope, by engaging in and embodying it herself. In the same instance, the resulting zoetrope turns into an object pertaining to and independent from the narrative progression of *Jimmy Corrigan*. Hence, the robot zoetrope is equally a story within a story as well as a meta-textual device to allude to the architecture of Ware's comics. Relating back to Scott McCloud's assertions, the panels can be seen as still life palimpsests to be "animated" by the reader within the gutters. Ware's tender irony comes to the fore by replacing the reader with a zoetrope to animate what happens between the still lifes of the early film roll.

The robot zoetrope (see Figure 2.4) is a toy made out of paper, showing a machine walking on crutches, just like Jimmy in the graphic narrative. Human and machine conflate—Susan Stewart points out that

> mechanisms do not feel or tire, they simply work or do not work. As part of the general inversion that the world of the dead represents, the inanimate comes to life in the service of the dead awakened. The theme of animation is itself a kind of allegory of memory, and of the role willed memory plays in re-awakening the obdurate material world given the passage of time. (Stewart 1994, 205)

Figure 2.4 The zoetrope in *Jimmy Corrigan*—author's own image.

This zoetrope cut out awakens memories stored on paper, and by doing so, it asks, Can paper tire? Does time go in a cycle, stuck in a loop? Do *we* go in cycles in our memories, always returning to the beginning? After all, it is the reader's task to bestow life on the inanimate—the panel counts as still life and the gutter as joint; and the turning of the zoetrope is to render the robot's movement fluid. As an allegory for memory, this mechanical/paper toy hybrid zoetrope transcends the world of the living but is also linked to that of the dead, the inanimate, to "the end of organic growth and the onset of inaccessibility to the living" (Stewart 1994, 204).

Ware's zoetrope facilitates this transition from death to life for the reader, yet draws attention to their overlap. The reader has to bestow life (she builds and she animates) while her own agency collapses in the same breath. She herself becomes inanimate by operating the zoetrope with a flick of her finger, being replaced by a machine (of her own making!) that gives the illusion of life of a machine, no less. Thomas Bredehoft calls attention to this:

> It is certainly intended to function at least as powerfully as a comment on the problems inherent in the construction not of a model, but of a narrative, or a book. It may be the case that such issues could, in fact, be raised without the use of a three-dimensional narrative intervention, but in *Jimmy Corrigan*, there is a thematic link between the three-dimensionality of the models and the narratively thematized issues of construction and recollection. (Bredehoft 2006, 883)

The mechanical toy hence alludes to processes of "mere" reading versus "active" building and collecting of the book as such. The zoetrope bridges two "stillnesses": it renders fluent the proto-film in its machinery, but also the comics medium that is static and two-dimensional, bound to the page. Now the comics medium breaks out into three-dimensionality by inducing movement, life, and death with the zoetrope.

This brings forth a tension of static to active, of reading and building: the zoetrope not only "stores" information about a broken robot but also channels Jimmy's emotions about meeting his father. Affect and technology converge; while (digital) data arguably does not degrade or fail or *feel*, the zoetrope is fickle, it can tear, break, and crumble, just like the distressed Jimmy. Once torn, all information and memory is lost and rendered illegible. Subsequently, the zoetrope can convert and store dreams or unconscious impulses; they become available as light entertainment for everybody who Xeroxes the zoetrope manual out of the book (similar to the commercialization of the keepsake box in the protagonist's dream). On the other hand, though, Jimmy builds the robot zoetrope to forget about his feelings—the entertainment device should make dreams and emotions go away and replace them with a little gadget Jimmy could nervously fidget with. The zoetrope thus enables a string of contradictions: the robot wants to emancipate itself from its medium; Jimmy builds the apparatus to ignore his dreams and longings and feelings; and the reader facilitates this by her "manual work" but struggles with being replaced by the zoetrope to animate the gutters; and ultimately the comics medium, which is stuck in two-dimensionality and discovers its translation into and interaction with another, interactive medium.

Chris Ware has admitted to finding cut outs useful when composing his stories, as Daniel Raeburn points out: "In prose a writer can describe one setting in infinite ways, but in naturalistic comics a writer has to ensure that he draws his setting exactly the same, time after time, from many perspectives. Ware built [a model of the Corrigan's house] to help him keep his facts straight" (Raeburn 2004, 73). In another temporal strand in *Jimmy Corrigan*, set during the Chicago World's Fair of 1893, Ware interrupts an episode of children playing hide-and-seek with a cut out of a barn. And keeping the facts straight is necessary here. The barn cut out is a companion piece to a sequence of twelve symmetrical panels. It is a temporal and spatial jigsaw puzzle; the reader is one step behind in knowing where and when the gutter will catapult her next. A Native American on a horse and an Italian immigrant boy meet in one panel; in the next, Jimmy's grandfather, who is then still a young boy, hides behind a beam of the house, while the other panels show the house already finished and fully constructed.

Chronology and causality are both explicitly contradicted, representing "only the narrative line, and failing to represent chronology" (Bredehoft 2006, 880). The paper cut out may now help with each jump in between the panels to adjust more quickly or more conveniently to the warped time and space zones that Ware juggles with in the spread. It is to be turned in the hands of the reader, over and over again, trying to find the right beginning. The manual labels the barn as a "miniature paper construction offered as an activity to those for whom experience in matters of the flesh is not necessarily a defining personal characteristic" (Ware 1999, n.p.). It ultimately is a "handy virtual reference guide to the psychological setting rendered within the pages of the offered chapter. Though too small to be constructed with any degree of satisfaction, a pantographic reproduction of the primary shapes and careful study of the construction principia will reward the concerted craftsman with a model of relative uselessness" (Ware 2001, n.p.). Even though it is not "necessary" to complete these tasks, and Ware's self-deprecating lingo comes to the fore here again. The cut out mirrors a state of being forever a blueprint for the house memories are always being constructed anew.

In the instructions Ware relates that "those wishing a more fully-developed sense of the events related within these pages may find some diversion by crafting the attached, as it allows a simulated maneuverability about the spaces described, and may, at the very least, prove a lightening influence upon a Sunday afternoon's weakened heart" (Ware 2001, n.p.). Esther Claudio argues how the cut outs arrest the flow of narration and "challenge the semiotics and architecture of [*Jimmy Corrigan*]. They are, in the end, metafiction, devices that self-consciously address the work, exposing its narrative strategies bare" (Claudio 2011, n.p.). The cut out exposes narrative strategies on a meta-textual level and draws attention to "meta-material" ideas of paper enduring time and space in the hands of the reader. The reader *has* to start this collection of curiosities (zoetrope, the Rubik's Cube house) to get a grasp of the story; she has to also prove dexterous enough (and patient enough!) to make these hidden stories visible through craftsmanship. Space and time hence become maneuverable, but a "weakened heart" might taint both.

Maybe she will put the model of "relative uselessness" into a collection, put on display in a cabinet hanging on a wall or in a box full of magazines and photographs, like *Building Stories*, sheltered against dust and sunlight. By being extracted from the narrative progression of the story and thus being able to defy the spatial and temporal progression of *Jimmy Corrigan*, the home-made cut out turns into an object that can linger in the present of the reader-turned-collector (hopefully a little longer than the papier-mâché buildings in the White City). The physical paper object is both part of the story and removed from the story. Ware's cut outs oscillate within this spectrum of being both a collectible and a photocopy, of being a rare original and a mass-produced toy. The cut out prompts the reader to think about the object's inherent economic value, for they are impossible to build with merely one *Jimmy Corrigan* copy alone. The manual instructions are printed on the other side of the page, and the reader destroys her *Jimmy Corrigan* edition (and diminishes its collector's value!) by cutting out the model. She needs to either photocopy the pages or buy two copies. But as a photocopy the cut out might lose its "authenticity" as a unique object coming straight out of a Ware book. This is the conundrum that Ware toys with, for the reader destroys one collectable (the comics book) to retrieve another (a zoetrope, a model house). Ware hooks the reader into a circle of questions pertaining to value, "collectability," and her own agency within the story construction.

Two aspects strike me as important. It is the thinking *around* a memory, of circumventing it (i.e., expressing trauma and the unutterable), that is expressed through the objects. In case of the cut outs, the reader has to give up "her" space of the gutter to produce these objects, making the way "around" the memory palpable. Both the reading progression and the space of the gutter in between panels are, quite literally, destroyed by dexterous labor to excavate a hidden plot. Her space of possibility in the gutter makes way for a guided, directed reading controlled by Ware. He encourages the weakened-hearted reader to hold the model in her hands to "keep the facts straight" but collapses the realm of agency altogether. The effect of the paper cut out narrative (i.e., the story told in the manual of the zoetrope, but also the story the reader invents for and around the collectables) within the greater narrative is that there might be a different, invisible story going on in the gutters that could function independently from the rest of the story. The "invisible art" of comics and of hermeneutic investment gain a palpable gestalt within this object. As Thomas Bredehoft posits, "Ware's two- and three-dimensional narrative interventions are put to the same kinds of ends as other contemporary challenges or responses to traditional narrative linearity. But the reclamation of three dimensions operative in these examples does even more, presenting a challenge to the pervasive metaphor that links time to space in the first place" (Bredehoft 2006, 885). It remains imperative that these paper-structures are mobile and movable, to be turned around in the reader's hand or spun like a wheel, handheld predecessors to digital light entertainment in the twenty-first century. No less, Ware draws parallels to light entertainment by way of the hollowed in Chicago's White City, whose buildings were constructed out of nothing sturdier but papier-mâché.

By subtracting it from the page and placing the object on display, Ware makes a move away from a two-dimensional, linear progression on the page to a three-dimensional, nonlinear jumbled collection to mark memories as experience. By destroying the gutters with a pair of scissors and mutilating her space of interpretation, the reader creates meta-perspectives and meta-materialities. The cut out of the house is a Rubik's Cube not only to keep the story straight but also to address these tensions of authorship and artistry.[17] There is no straying off Ware's predetermined path, and this minimizes the character-reader distance as well as the writer-reader distance immensely. The cut outs "clearly open the door for a compromised or collapsed distinction between author/artist and narrator" (Bredehoft 2006, 881). Jared Gardner points out, it is, in the end,

> collaborative work on the part of the reader that accounts at least in part for the deeply personal, prideful relationship that many collectors have

---

[17] To gesture toward the question of authority of the author *and* reader, Frank Kelleter and Daniel Stein posit conflicts of ownership, hierarchies, responsibilities, and authorization as a central dynamic of serialized popular culture, what they coin "Eigentums- und Zuständigkeitskonflikte" (Kelleter and Stein 2012, 282).

for the comics they hold in their possession—and the desperate longing they have for those pieces that remain forever out of their grasp. These are not simply artifacts they own but texts they have helped to make meaningful. (Gardner 2006, 800)

Gardner continues that the drive to collect comics is "a forge for the (always uneasy) collaboration between reader and writer that is central to the comics form" (Gardner 2006, 800). Yet, neither Ware nor the reader can be understood as the authors of the barn or the zoetrope. Ware has undoubtedly designed it, but can he be labeled as the author of it, if he himself needs it to keep his own story straight? Does the object, then, and not the reader/author, negotiate these conflicts of ownership and responsibility? Is this why Ware figures his readers as collectors of ephemera and copies? Who is architect and who is author?

By interlacing the building of gadgets with precarious memories and precarious objects, curation emerges as a reading practice that oscillates between mending and breaking the narrative (building the cut outs, finding the read thread between the objects). No matter how dissimilar the cut outs of *Jimmy Corrigan* or even the centerpieces and books in and of *Building Stories* are, they operate within the same logic—they are part of the reader's collection that could tear or break. She must maintain, expand, and care for the objects at hand (or, well, build them first). Curating turns into a practice that blurs the lines not only of authorship but also of fact and fiction: the artistic vision of Ware's work is transferred onto the reader, whose role is tightly controlled by Ware's visual style and the protagonist's fiction games.

Impossible collections

How to build a Chris Ware collection, if his oeuvre is light entertainment for weakened hearts, predicated on Xeroxed cut outs and daydreams?[18] The

---

[18] While there is an increase of academic interest on collecting comics in general, articles on collecting Chris Ware's work specifically are scarce. Jared Gardner makes gestures toward collecting Ware's work and the difficulties it brings along in *Projections*; Aaron Mauro's highly illuminating article "'Mosaic Thresholds': Manifesting the Collection and Production of Comics in the Works of Chris Ware" and parts of Emma Tinker's doctoral thesis *Identity and Form in Alternative Comics 1967–2007* analyze Chris Ware in particular. Many interviewers ask Chris Ware about his own, personal habits of collecting, drawing attention to his admiration of the American artist Joseph Cornell. His house in Oak Park is said to be filled with curiosities and carefully preserved collectables.

curious publishing history of *Building Stories* accentuates Ware's investigation in market crazes and the collector's value of comics. Many of the *Building Stories*' stories were first published from 2002 onward in print outlets such as the *Chicago Reader*, the *McSweeney's* iPad app, *The New York Times Magazine* or the *New Yorker*. Ware then published the comics in his serial publication *The Acme Novelty Library* (issues 16–18 include parts of *Building Stories* and "Branford Bee"). After having his work run through these initial publication phases, Ware reworked some of the strips, added new stories, and compiled them within the *Building Stories* keepsake box in 2012. *Building Stories* "collects a decade's worth of work, with dozens of 'never-before published' pages (i.e., those deemed too obtuse, filthy or just plain incoherent to offer to a respectable periodical)" (Ware 2012b, n.p.). Of course this begs the question: Whose writing? The protagonist's attempts or Ware's writing, that of reputation and renown?

The definite boxed *Building Stories* publication promptly earned Ware four Eisner Awards and a Harvey Award for "Excellence in Presentation," among many other accolades. This long and selective process of publishing stands in conversation with *Building Stories* being a tedious and detail-oriented (if fictional) process of collecting of comics strips that might be too filthy or obtuse to print. Ware left his comics like breadcrumbs in American and British print publications for readers to find and collect. The stories included in *Building Stories* are not cut outs, but what one could coin fictitious *tear outs* from magazines, now stored in a keepsake box. No doubt, today's newspaper, the old read-through *The New York Times Magazine* issue, or that pulp comic book will be tossed out tomorrow. But Ware toys with this in *Building Stories*, for the ephemeral prints are now neatly archived (and highly sought after). They have turned from waste paper into collectable ephemera, from ugly ducklings of consumer culture into swans of hipsterdom.

The gutters can function as a metaphor for the publication history of *Building Stories*. Scott McCloud's following description can be transferred onto what happens in between the publication of *Building Stories* issues (also called the serial gap) and objects of a collection: "No matter how dissimilar one image may be to another, there is a kind of—alchemy at work in the space between panels which can help us find meaning or resonance in even the most jarring of combinations. Such transitions may not make 'sense' in any traditional way, but still a relationship of some sort will inevitably develop. . . . However different they had been, they now belong to a single

---

For Ware as a collector and his how his admiration for Joseph Cornell influences his aesthetics, see Benjamin Widiss's article "Comics on Non-Sequential Art—Chris Ware's Joseph Cornell."

organism" (McCloud 1993, 73). Transferred onto Ware's strategies, it is not of concern how dissimilar the publications are compared to one another or the uncertainty of how the comic strips might relate to one another. They depend on the invisible made visible, on the *alchemy* at work between panels, issues, objects, and print outlets. This very alchemy turns *Building Stories* into a collection, first on a narrative level (i.e., by employing centerpieces to juxtapose the tension between coherence and fragmentation, employing reoccurring motifs and having a fixed set of characters), and then on the material level by combining the booklets and pamphlets in the keepsake box as such tear outs. And of course, Ware is well aware of who his readership is and hence caters to the reading habits of the middle- and upper-class (as he points out on the back of the *Building Stories* keepsake box). He chooses prestigious outlets such as *The Guardian* or *McSweeney's* for his readership to find him.

Ware encourages these middle- and upper-class readers to become compulsive combers of "archives, warehouses, and dumpsters" to find either what the protagonist threw out, what Ware deemed unprintable, or what the bourgeois intelligentsia tossed out with recycling waste (Gardner 2006, 799). The reader's (make-believe) hunting grounds are not the gutters of the comics anymore, but they now have shifted to the serial gap in between issues of magazines and newspapers, waiting for the next installment to pop up somewhere else. This is tightly linked to a more material idea of fickleness and incompleteness that is inherent within the medium of comics. Jared Gardner relates: "The desire to possess comics—to hunt down every stray work by a favorite creator, to contain and reassemble the scattered pieces of a fragmentary comics universe—is a familiar one for many readers.... It is the compulsive need to fill in the gaps, to make connections between issues ... that drives the "collector" in search of missing issues" (Gardner 2006, 800). Collecting *Building Stories* "as is" remains close to impossible, given its geographical and temporal impossibilities. It enhances the reader's precarious positioning within the overall project to establish an alchemy between two issues that are merely loosely related and temporally (one story published in 2003, another one in 2007), geographically (one was published in Great Britain, another one in the United States), and medially disparate (one strip published in the print outlet of the *New Yorker*, another one in the *McSweeney's* app). In this fiction game of hunting and gathering, the reader must wonder if she missed an issue or a comic strip somewhere in (print) media, in space, in time. And of course the narrative gives no indication as of when the collection of the nonlinear and fragmented stories can ever be deemed complete.

Oh, the "anxiety, the interruptions, the long gaps not knowing"—Jared Gardner sees the uncertainty of the serial gap (is the story complete? Where will it be continued?) as a pleasurable experience for the audience to make assumptions about the protagonist's life and how the story lines come to interweave in the end (Gardner 2012b, 36). Susan Stewart's writing on the souvenir comes back to mind, for she sees that the "place of origin [of the souvenir] must remain unavailable in order for desire to be generated" (Stewart 1993, 151). Unavailable—like a forgotten dream or a newspaper thrown out, half-remembered and half-forgotten. This imbues the geographical and temporal precariousness of *Building Stories* with desire and longing to complete the collection (this, of course, leads us back to the unconscious impulses and dreamwork seen in "Browsing" that Ware interlocks with capitalist activity). To bridge the gap, Ware elevates the (printed) ephemera into a permanent, purchasable collection, and, hence, into a commodity—an artful, beautiful object that readers do not find in dumpsters but in boutique shops and indie bookstores. The *Building Stories* tear out widens the range of activities of the reader from seeking out the magazine to dumpster diving to tearing out the page and putting it into a plastic bag for preservation and protection. But, ultimately, all she might do in the end is touch "Buy Now" on her cellphone screen.

But let us indulge in the fiction that these collectables are found in the trash—they are waste paper. Surprisingly, this fiction shortens the distance between the protagonist and the reader, because it is her writing she threw out that the collector now retrieves out of the protagonist's trash. Both protagonist and collector/reader/curator are confronted with the impossible collection within the keepsake box. They occur as dreamwork in the protagonist's psyche and as comic strips in *The Guardian* or *The New York Times*. The protagonist's dream becomes the reader's dream, as much as Jimmy's zoetrope is a foil to the reader's engagement with *Jimmy Corrigan*. Ware's interest in these overlaps between reader and character and author enables the curator to be now a performer of the narrative—and this brings us back to experimental memory in the vein of Walter Benjamin and Peter Sattler. Sattler explains, "As a 'performer' of the comic composition, the reader moves among and connects the episodic/visual and narrative/textual memories, and that activity of reading creates its own experiential rhythms, its own sense of time, and its own set of feelings" (Sattler 2010, 210). The terms Sattler's quote evokes, such as rhythms, sense of time, and feeling, sequence, bring us back to ideas of curation: that *Building Stories* needs to be performed as much as it has to be read.

These interconnections of the serial gap and the performer of memories lead us back to the house, which figures the reader as curator and *architect*. By publishing *Multi-Story Building Model*, Ware allows the collector/reader to fill it with her own life and to start from scratch. The *Multi-Story Building Model* accompanied *Building Stories*' official release in the summer of 2012 (Ware calls it an "artificial satellite"): promoted, in Ware's self-deprecating lingo, as an "unnecessary addendum" to the "already-unmanageable" *Building Stories* graphic narrative, *Multi-Story Building Model* is an "outrageously expensive signed limited edition print [which] will find few interested parties or adherents to its demanding, labor-intensive brand of rainy day leisure" (Ware 2012e, n.p.). In no way is the model house to "violate the reader's experience of that work, nor to confuse the art appreciator into feeling the or she absolutely need to procure it towards a fuller familiarity with the aforementioned" (Ware 2012e, n.p.) Shrink-wrapped, serially numbered, and first sold at an exhibition of Chris Ware's work in 2012 (and now up for auction on eBay for $150 and more), *Multi-Story Building Model* (Figure 2.5) serves the "discriminating" and "unsocialized" reader/collector as a plastic reference model of the narrating house.

Figure 2.5 *The Multi-Story Building Model.* © used with permission by Drawn and Quarterly.

Its title, *Multi-Story Building Model*, suggests nothing more and little less than an architectural model for a generic multi-story house. It contains "90 pieces of paper replica, facsimile and simulacrum concreting the below pictured female protagonist's misreminiscences and inaccurate recollections of the midwestern rental space inhabited during the last years of the twentieth century" (Ware 2012e, n.p.). The detailed kit includes everything ranging from clothes items to a toilet, a fully equipped miniature kitchen with tiny cereal boxes, a cut-out computer and "one-sided conversations and even false memories" to be stored in the upper-level apartment, the protagonist's home during her 20s (Ware 2012e, n.p.). Ware promises that *Multi-Story Building Model* will one day surely be a "collector's item when flammable tinder is at a premium," so "be prepared to start your post-apocalyptic campfire now with this 13 sheet collection of dry technical drawings, paper thin walls and cramped psychological spaces" (Ware 2012e, n.p.). In his ironic shtick, Ware undersells this achievement as a dry pastime. But here memory becomes an architectural structure that must be cut out and glued together in order to be experienced and performed. Similarly to the barn cut out or the zoetrope, the house gives gestalt to memories to reveal a hidden plot—not in the gutter, but in the serial gap.

Ware writes that any "student of the history of the neighborhood in question will note that the reconstruction presented here is not without its inconsistencies; based, as it is, upon reminiscence and fragmentary recollection, some details reproduced may possibly contradict and/or overlap one another" (Ware 2012e, n.p.). The cut out of the building can do little else than create memories that are not "right" or accurate. Ware underlines how "care should be taken when projecting any of this aid's details temporally forward or backward, as some street names have changed, vegetation has developed, and those personalities concerned with the area have either moved away, perished, or their relative sense of the scale of the world has changed" (Ware 2012e, n.p.). The house, therefore, remains atemporal, unless we decide to take it out of its shrink-wrap and build it (and diminishing its market value dramatically). This affords, again, affection and aggression that Sianne Ngai postulates. Should we "care" for the building and leave it unbuilt or should we be aggressive toward it and build it—or set fire to our post-apocalyptical campfire with it?

The curator does *maintenance*: building maintenance, collection maintenance, and memory maintenance. It is a slippery slope that illuminates the set of interactive practices that Ware's work in *Jimmy Corrigan*, *Building Stories*, or the *Multi-Story Building Model* presupposes as self-reflexive and recursive. Curatorial labor in Ware's oeuvre is predicated on *building*—it is engaging with the printed page and making it three-dimensional. In this way, Ware's work interrogates a self-reflexive performance of the analog—demanding reader interaction and reflecting upon the nature of digital technologies that have come to define our contemporary moment, of acknowledging that the flat screen of the computer has a three-dimensional haptic predecessor. On closer scrutiny, it comes to reveal practices of digitality—Ware's strategies underline the diverse modalities of digitality before and after its everyday implementation with and through the internet. Pages of a book can be converted into new "information" and a blueprint cut out give the reader space for projections. The last section of this chapter shall gesture toward this.

Analog memories

My discussion has shown that Ware draws attention to the translation and interaction of different media,[19] and we shall wonder what centerpieces, cut outs, tear outs, and fake collections can tell us about memory in the twenty-first century. Ware's paper-based strategies to explore questions of digitality comment on the way memory is stored and constructed online— rerouted through manual labor and patience. *Building Stories'* design points toward how a finished, definite, correct arrangement of storylines is indeed inadequate to narrate life in the twenty-first century. Rather, it is the act and process of weaving the webs that make life (and story!) what it is. A sense of closure, *the* essential driving force in comics grammar, is eschewed for the idea of endless possibilities and recombination. Yet a merging of modern-day internet lingo with *Building Stories'* strategies seems inevitable. Notice how Gardner earlier evoked the database—one of "association, assumptions, memories, icons and signs with which the reader works to activate the comic," and whether or not these are false or fake might not be of greater importance (Gardner 2012a, n.p.). *Building Stories* evokes such a feeling of tapping into this cultural database[20] to make the collection come alive.

Life portrayed in *Building Stories* relies on WiFi signals, text messages, and Facebook updates. In the protagonist's case, ex-boyfriends suddenly come

---

[19] An overview on digital comics today give Lukas R. A. Wilde, "Distinguishing Mediality: The Problem of Identifying Forms and Features of Digital Comics" and Jared Gardner's *Projections*, particularly the "Coda: Comics, Film, and the Future of Twenty-First-Century Storytelling."
[20] Kara Schoonmaker points out in regard to databases that the information "stays the same, but the way it is viewed, interpreted, and interacted with changes constantly. Given this shifting nature, hyper-organization is an ideal means of organizing information: it offers access that is as fluid and flexible, as in-depth or as shallow, as specific or as broad, as its user wants it to be" (Schoonmaker 2007, n.p.). This invites us to think further about the preset number of modules and components of *Building Stories* within digital spheres.

back from the dead as "suggested friends," Netflix suggests even more movies that she might like depending on her preferences and user history, and she delves into obsessive rants about conspiracy theories about oil she read about online. Her deceased Stephanie lives on through her posts on Facebook and through the emails she once sent; accessible immediately and everywhere, the protagonist obsessively scrutinizes each and every post Stephanie ever made. Likewise, Ware shows us how digital devices isolate users from each another (there are many instances in the story where the protagonist and her husband just sit quietly next to one another, both immersed in their devices) and underlines how these activities have come to construct a significant portion—routines—of contemporary life (and fiction[21]). Ware explained that he "lingered on those moments when they're staring down into their little glowing pits and not really experiencing the moment (which is simply a technological high jacking of what adults are apt to do anyway). Lately, I'm flabbergasted at the number of times I'll find myself in the exact same circumstance with my wife. Maybe there's an 'app' for this" (Ware 2012d, n.p.). *Building Stories* showcases several different ways of visualizations and materializations of remembering—how we remember, through what means we recollect experiences, when and why memory hits us. The characters space out and daydream about yesterday, about lost connections and things that never happened.

Maybe *Building Stories* can here be seen as a database that allows the reader to "explore the potentials inherent in the complexity of industrialized societies" (Thurtle and Mitchell 2007, 267). I find this shift of terminology instructive here, and it leads us back to Jimmy's construction of the zoetrope. Remembering becomes a mechanism and an algorithm—compulsion and programming and routine. Ware's zoetrope animates the inanimate and the dead come back to remind us how mechanisms do not tire, nor do memories ever vanish. These cut outs are thus hybrid structures that not only bring alive the comic's page and render the narrative in a three-dimensional fashion but also enable translations of the medium of comics into more participatory, interactive arenas. Yet, what is made participatory and interactive here is key, for Ware makes present something that might be lost (the collection of writing) or unutterable (the trauma of an abortion or the death of a friend). None of these experiences that are part and parcel of industrialized societies can be adequately represented on Google or on Facebook, but, as Ware suggests, primarily in dreams and keepsake boxes and obsolete media.

---

[21] In *The Digital Banal* Zara Dinnen explores the effacing of digital routines in contemporary American culture. Some of her examples include David Fincher's movies and Jennifer Egan's novel *A Visit from the Goon Squad*.

In this regard, I find Wolfgang Ernst's challenges toward memory and the internet[22] imperative here regarding Ware's methods: "If there is memory, it operates as a radical constructivism: always just situationally built, with no enduring storage" (Ernst 2013, 138). Ernst's quote reminds us of the random situations when and where memory hits the protagonist (i.e., over a plate of Trader Joe's pasta). Ernst's assessment also illuminates the meta-material strategies of Ware's work that are simultaneously self-reflexive performance of the analog (i.e., the zoetrope) but likewise situationally built (the reader may ask, Which booklet to read next?). Yet the affective labor that is poured into the recalcitrant, overwhelming graphic narrative speaks to a certain type of interaction that might seem foreign or cumbersome in the digital age—it asks us where to store memory, affect, and story and what kind of devices we deem fit to hold these kind of "information." So is this the curator's task? To bring order in the chaos and handle the delicate ephemera and its experimental memory? To shelter memories from the post-apocalyptic campfire that is likely to eradicate the medium of the book in the twenty-first century?

We can subsume that curation indexes a set of interactive practices that include collecting, cutting up and rearranging, and, interestingly, misremembering. We can easily think back at "browsing" and "looking up" here, for these terms evoke the curatorial practices that *Building Stories* facilitates.

---

[22] Certainly, *Building Stories*' convoluted format draws attention to printing culture in the twenty-first century and asks the question of how to collect and archive digital and analog media accordingly. These questions of memory and collecting hence extend to the caring for the art of bookmaking and the individual's experience with the book-as-object vis-à-vis twenty-first-century print-capitalism and print-consumerism. The supposed recent demise of the book through digital services is counterbalanced by innovative publications such as *Timothy McSweeney's Quarterly Concern* or contemporary experimental novels that play with form (such as *S*, *House of Leaves*, or *Tree of Codes*). Take McSweeney's as an example: The layout and content of the respective issues, which come in the design of a human head or junk mail, defy the notion of routine or stability. There is no single, consistent reading experience in *McSweeney's Quarterly Concern*, because there is no consistent *layout*. Instead, there is a heterogeneous form that requires new and intensified forms of reading labor. To put it more simply, the act of reading *McSweeney's Quarterly Concern* is an individualized one because it does not create a narrative of constancy in which one reader can clearly imagine the reading experience of a fellow subscriber. Instead, McSweeney's depends upon a singular grappling with dynamic and sometimes obdurate form: an affective negotiation that stresses the reader–text or reader–object relationship over reader–reader one. But I am equally inclined to posit the opposite claim that readers are connected to fellow subscribers by the labor required to work through the layout and content. While the experience of this unpacking, understanding, and unfolding the issues is a private one, a reader is assured that thousands of others stumble through the same difficulties, reaching different conclusions and insights. These publications hence celebrate means of experimentation and eccentricity within the boundaries of the print medium, seeking out proximity to the online realm to undermine its dominance in cultural productions in the same breath.

They simultaneously encapsulate the practice of *reading* as well as the practice of *remembering*, of dreaming, of getting lost in reverie. Yet the reading experience of *Building Stories* cannot be replicated online, for its material quiddities are such integral elements of the experience—the touching, the shuffling, the building, and maintenance of the text. The booklets, the material may help us remember a certain passage or a panel, for we might remember how the booklet felt in our hands while we read it. We might remember the weight of the newspaper, but an iPad has the same weight and texture, no matter what we read.[23] But Ware borrows digital techniques in the composition of his panels: conceptually, then, the aesthetics that a text such as *Building Stories* incorporates does feature aesthetics like zooming or the interlinkings and nodes and networks. By reshuffling and resorting, by zooming in and out, the reader encounters the same elements from different angles, read in a new string of possibilities, with new plotlines unearthed. Hence this incorporation of digital aesthetics into a distinctly analog text makes *Building Stories* so intriguing.

Chris Ware's latest, retro-fitted digital "graphic novella," *The Last Saturday*, reroutes these assumptions of digital memory spaces in dialogue with analog reading practices. His novella has been published episodically online on *The Guardian* website (as well as in the Saturday edition of the newspaper) and is created wholly for a virtual online experience in an "outdated" way (i.e., weekly installments, it being labeled a newspaper comic strip, its "retro" feel of the 1970s). Supervised by *The Guardian*'s interactive team, the graphic novella is a highly reflexive work that draws on its own constructedness and medium conventions. Set in 1970s suburban Michigan, it chronicles the everyday life of Putnam, a ten-year-old geeky boy. In his self-deprecating and shoe-gazing *modus operandi*, Ware suggests that *The Last Saturday* is nothing but a waste of paper and must therefore be a digital graphic novella: the last installment "as inscrutable and patient-testing as this saw print on actual paper was 1.3798×10^{10} years into the contraction/expansion cycle of the prior spacetime continuum, or $10 \times 10^{100.976}$ years ago. . . . The strip was not appreciated by its reader(s) and ended almost immediately following its inaugural appearance" (Ware 2014, n.p.).

---

[23] One of the comics strips in *Building Stories* was previously released on the *McSweeney's* iPad app called *Touch Sensitive*. During a panel discussion along with Daniel Clowes, Charles Burns, Seth, hosted by Hillary Chute, Chris Ware expresses his disappointment with the translation of his strip onto the interactive medium: "I did a stupid e-thing version of this for the iPad, trying to use the touch interface of an iPad to somehow connect with the idea of physical contact in a relationship and how it changes—a very pretentious idea. After I did it, though, I just thought: I really like the paper better" (Chute 2014, 158).

Drawing from my own experience when reading *The Last Saturday* on the iPad, my fingers took the same routes on the screen, over and over again. The further I progressed, the more the experience of reading Putnam's story became a routine than an experience (but maybe routines *are* the experience of digital life?). At one point, my fingertips got a little sore from gliding over the surface of the iPad, because something was missing: the tactility of turning a page and the texture of a piece of paper.[24] Maybe because the graphic novella is set in the 1970s, with flare jeans and ocher color schemes, reading it on the iPad feels weirdly anachronistic. This innovative story designed for an iPad is devoid of twenty-first-century technology, and it showcases how communication between kids is based on tiny written notes in class and not on text messages, where playing Twister, and not browsing on Facebook, can fill up an entire afternoon. This stands in stark contrast to *Building Stories*' characters, whose eyes are glued to screens and tablets even in the most intimate moments. Putnam's question on life echoes our questions toward our collections:

> What if every single one of the particles that constitute a particular organism could somehow be copied and arranged to make an exact replica, of, say, *me* . . . would that exact replica *also* have all the same thoughts, memories, fears, loves, and secrets that *I* seem to have? . . . or more likely, would it simply be an empty, lifeless and unfeeling husk? (Ware 2014, n.p.)

To extend his train of thought, how can they endure during time? Again, Putnam seems to have the answer to this question:

> Time sure does *pass* . . . well . . . *actually* . . . as we have already seen, time does not "pass" at all, but persists as a static medium through which *we* pass . . . all forming frozen, eternal shape of life itself. Yet one question uncomfortably lingers: Do our thoughts and memories exist as part *of*, or apart *from*, this continuum? And if the latter, then . . . *where*?" (Ware 2014, n.p.)

---

[24] In relation to this, Hillary Chute and Marianne DeKoven underline how the medium of the graphic narrative itself is a "form that also always refuses a problematic transparency, through an explicit awareness of its own surfaces. Because of this foregrounding of the work of the hand, graphic narrative is an autographic form in which the mark of handwriting is an important part of the rich extra-semantic information a reader receives" (Chute and DeKoven 2006, 767).

Isn't this what the collection does? The things we collect are frozen, eternal elements that give shape and meaning to a life. As Putnam contemplates, objects are never to be done away with, because we create ever-new spaces for them to exist—it is only that *we* vanish. Expressing the crux between cute pastime, obsessiveness, and market value logics, Ware's strategies echo the collector's latent desire to make her collection a world of her own in which past or lost versions as well as future versions of the self may coexist—it depends on how much she cares.

3

The Broken Record: Beck Hansen's *Song Reader*

What, or, more precisely, who is a *Song Reader*? Hardly any other contemporary pop-cultural object investigates the role of the fan and her perseverance and stamina to be a fan in such diverse and manifold ways as Beck Hansen's *Song Reader*. Beck's[1] colorful collection of sheet music songs comes to terms with what strategies a music album can unfold when handed over to the reader at her own disposal. The reader, in turn, is invited to slip into the role of a sheet music historian, of an aficionada, of a collector and curator, of a musician and a self-promoting, self-taught fan. *Song Reader*, which was released in 2012 as a self-proclaimed "album" with twenty new songs by Beck, can hardly be labeled a "Beck album," or maybe only in the widest, most contorted sense. While Beck is the officially credited songwriter of songs such as "Old Shanghai," "Don't Act Your Heart Isn't Hard," "Do We? We Do," "Title of This Song," and "Saint Dude," it is his fans who bring these songs to life. These reversed roles test the fan's investment (and commitment!) as well as the boundaries of Beck's authorship. Central to the success of the project is that the reader and fan needs to appropriate a subject position and consumer practice that should be termed "song reader."[2]

This song reader interacts with the album on myriad levels, and she is deliberately hooked in a circle of legitimation and competence: without her, the project seems to fail and remain inaudible, all while Beck's status as rock star and songwriter is manifested and further bolstered. This song reader position interweaves and transgresses important focal points to a successful implementation of *Song Reader*. Further, the intermingling of online and offline spheres interrogate the questions of work and leisure/play (also of playing along), of endurance and curating. To align *Song Reader* back to back

---

[1] In this chapter, I will refer to the musician Beck Hansen as Beck. In other chapters, to avoid confusion with cultural historian Miriam Hansen, media historian Mark Hansen, or sociologist Ulrich Beck, rock star Beck will be called by his full name, Beck Hansen.
[2] While I will refer to the object of the sheet music collection as *Song Reader* (capitalized and in italics), the subject position of the Beck fan will be referred to as song reader.

with *Building Stories* offers a productive continuation of questions pertaining to authorship and nostalgia for old and forgotten forms that simultaneously undermine contemporary digital incarnations (the digital iPad novella and the YouTube clip, respectively). Both are stylish and stylish-ly similar (twee, colorful, retro, yet slightly overwhelming) and cater to a nerdy audience of people "in the know," who do not eschew challenging and grandiose concept "books." Bringing *Building Stories* and *Song Reader* in conversation with one another offers nuances to curatorial labor, for Beck's music project challenges the investment of a fan that pertains to the means of how creativity unfolds in digital spaces. Both of them interrogate similar questions toward a creative subject position the reader adopts in order to make the object work out (or, at least, continue and go on).

Yet, here are different degrees of "competences" sought in the reader: when reading *Building Stories*, the graphic narrative gradually teaches its readership how it wants to be read and remembered. While it takes diligence to navigate the overwhelming page layout and to connect the dots in between the booklets, the reader slowly sees coherence behind the collection on a narrative and material level. *Song Reader*, on the other hand, already presupposes specific competences in playing a musical instrument, being able to read sheet music, or even knowing who Beck is and what kind of style his music has—"competences" following different paradigms that intertwine with issues relating to fandom, digitization, and nostalgia. *Building Stories*' collectables already have a place to be stored again, for they will be neatly put back into their keepsake box. But at the core of the *Song Reader* project lies a question of to whom these songs belong in the twenty-first century and what media an ephemeral pop song presupposes—into which (digital) spaces these Beck songs should be sent to and how they should be remembered (an *Ohrwurm* won't do here).

Fans and academics have begun to increasingly encounter pop musicians in intellectual debates, in exhibitions, on bestseller lists, or in MA classes taught at the university. A Bob Dylan archive will be built in Tulsa for self-proclaimed "Dylanologists" to peruse Dylan's enigmatic notes, doodles, song fragments, and scribbles to further interpret the imagery of the elusive rock star's lyrics; Patti Smith's *Just Kids* has been received to universal acclaim and won the National Book Award in 2010 for best nonfiction book; the University of Liverpool offers a Master of Arts program called *The Beatles, Popular Music, and Society* to embed the Beatles into academic discussions and show their wider cultural significance in the twentieth and twenty-first centuries; curatorial efforts about rock stars and their careers are growing in legitimacy, such as the "David Bowie Is . . . ." exhibition which has been traveling around the world for the last years, showcasing David Bowie's stage costumes or other memorabilia in Toronto, Berlin, Brooklyn, or

Groningen. These instances show how rock music merges with other media and spaces (i.e., the museum, the university, the bestseller list) and becomes institutionalized, canonized. These shifts signal a need to approach and visualize creativity and ingenuity of contemporary (musical) geniuses from both academic and curatorial standpoints. The displaying and archiving of music's many different materialities will undoubtedly become an important point of discussion in the years to come—for music seems to vanish from our hands. It is here where this chapter on Beck Hansen's *Song Reader* will mediate issues about the rock star persona and interrogate from a media standpoint what kind of shapes music takes up and how rock music will come to last.

Yet Beck takes up a curious (counter)-position: he himself canonizes his project as a self-proclaimed new American Song Book, bringing his songs to his fans as a ready-made sheet music collection that can be purchased for $30. Releasing his project with the publishing house McSweeney's in 2012, Beck drew inspiration for *Song Reader* at an earlier point of his career. He had been sent a sheet music book of one of his previous albums (presumably his 1996 hit album *Odelay*) and was surprised to find in what way the chaotic, noisy, and contingent elements of his songs were translated back into sheet music—thus into language and musical symbols, ordered according to a logical system of notes: "Someone had transcribed [the album] for piano and voice. The album itself was full of noises, beats, bent sounds, feedback—it had a lot of sonic ideas that were meant to be heard, as a recording. Seeing those songs reduced down to piano parts made me feel like they'd become abstractions" (Hansen 2012a, n.p.). These sonic contingencies made it obvious to Beck that "most of the songs weren't intended to work that way," but actually that his music albums relied on improvisation and haphazardness (Hansen 2012c, n.p.). This fact is contrasted with *Song Reader*'s larger project mission, for its songs are intended to work exactly the other way around. The printed, "fixed" sheet music becomes an ephemeral song again through rehearsal, allowing for bents and breaks to happen. While the songs are stripped bare of noise (but are fixed/legitimized/institutionalized through the officiated release with McSweeney's), Beck's sheet music functions as the inaudible copy of a non-existing original.

It is the song reader's obligation to make the printed songs ephemeral again and to infuse them with her own vision of how the songs should sound like. It reverses this process that Beck took as inspiration: *Song Reader* intends the reader to interpret and fill the skeleton songs with bents and beats herself to mingle Beck's and her own voice. This loop speaks to the grander implications of the album: Beck stresses how the *Song Reader* songs are

> meant to be pulled apart and reshaped. The idea of them being played by choirs, brass bands, string ensembles, anything outside of traditional

rock-band constructs—it's interesting because it's outside of where my songs normally exist. I thought a lot about making these songs playable and approachable, but still musically interesting. I think some of the best covers will reimagine the chord structure, take liberties with the melodies, the phrasing, even the lyrics themselves. There are no rules in interpretation. (Hansen 2012a, n.p.)

Because there is no original version of a song that could be covered in the first place, the songs rely on Beck's "brand"—his status as rock star is both a prerequisite *and* amplified through the fan's implementation of *Song Reader*. Beck's audience pulls the songs apart and reshapes them. On the other hand, Beck himself seems to function as a ventriloquist, as an enabler for this certain kind of creative labor to emerge in the blurry boundaries between online and offline. *Song Reader* caters to and challenges phenomena of the digital age—plagiarism, pirating, torrenting—and interlaces these prevalent themes of media usage and consumption of the twenty-first century with traditions of covering and creativity. It comes as no surprise that Beck aligns his project with the Great American Songbook of the nineteenth century and uses the concept of canonization as a prism to reflect the role of the rock star in the digital age.

Beck examines twenty-first-century "participatory culture" through the lens of nineteenth-century participatory culture by way of the medium of sheet music (see Figure 3.1). Let me stress how the "old" is incorporated

Figure 3.1 *Song Reader* © author's own image.

within the "new" and how earlier forms evoke practices that are still prevalent today. It is here where I trace how *Song Reader* replicates practices that feel foreign but indeed speak to media practices of today's online world. The dusty page of sheet music suddenly is able of posing questions toward the digital spheres and how processes of creation and adaptation, of "borrowed authorship" and ventriloquism are negotiated online. To put it crudely, *Song Reader* tests the boundaries of what a music album and a fan are and must do in the twenty-first century in most bizarre ways. It challenges issues like authorship and plagiarism while, simultaneously, encouraging them. The process of making the cover songs accessible to a broader audience unveils the work of affinities and alliances in the digital age. *Song Reader* therefore stages a dialogic relation between the conceptual and the consumer, between the fan and the artist, with an emphasis on contemporary ideas/ideals of participatory culture online. Here, this subject position of the song reader unfolds, for distant spectator and fan are congruent, both invited to participate, maybe even in a slightly duplicitous way, with the possibility of failure already built in.

Hipster marionette and ventriloquist: Beck and the indie rock field

Beck Hansen's commercial breakthrough came in 1994 with his song "Loser," which has been hailed as the slacker anthem and tapped into a certain American post-Grunge pop-culture zeitgeist. First treated as a mysterious coffeehouse open-mike artist, then marketed as a voice of a generation (and dismissed as a one-hit-wonder) or ageless man-child, Beck is now regarded as one of the more eclectic artists of the last twenty-five years. He has managed to reinvent himself as one the most multifaceted and renowned musicians and producers in the indie rock world. Always attempting to shun genre conventions, Beck's music oscillates between "every musical genre imaginable: the blues, rap, country, punk, funk, folk, soul, bluegrass, techno, metal, free jazz, jangle pop, salsa, slow jams, spoken word, Southern-fried rock. Beck . . . [is] a classicist, a MoMA curator with two turntables and a microphone" (Gordinier 2008, 28). His singer-songwriter album *Mutations*, for example, is bookended by the experimental albums *Odelay* and *Midnite Vultures*. In Beck's own words,

> I think I gave indications early on that [my career] wasn't just going to be a commercial, er, career. If that were the case, then the first record would

have been 10 versions of "Loser." I always thought it would be interesting if there was no such thing as gold and platinum records, or record deals, and people were just making music. What would the music sound like? (Hansen 2002, n.p.)

During the peak of his commercial success and public exposure in the late 1990s and early 2000s, one eccentricity followed the next, making Beck's next artistic step unpredictable.[3] In the last couple of years, Beck's career has focused more on producing than recording, but, to much surprise, he won the 2015 Grammy Award for Album of the Year[4] for his album *Morning Phase*, which aligns itself with his more introspective albums *Sea Change* and *One Foot in the Grave*. His most recent album *Colors*, released in fall 2017, is again more akin to his more experimental albums, like *The Information* or *Guero*.

Beck was brought up in artistic and countercultural circles: his grandfather was the fluxus artist Al Hansen; his mother, Bibbe Hansen, frequented Andy Warhol's Factory in the 1960s; his father, David Campbell, is a Canadian composer and conductor; Beck's brother Channing Hansen is an artist; and his wife Marissa Ribisi is an actress and fashion designer. Throughout his career he has collaborated with the French-British singer and actress Charlotte Gainsbourg and produced records for Thurston Moore (Sonic Youth's former frontman) and Stephen Malkmus (Pavement's lead singer); he models for the luxury label Saint Laurent Paris and is friends with its former creative director, Hedi Slimane; the filmmaker Spike Jonze and the writer Dave Eggers appear on the track[5] "The Horrible Fanfare/

---

[3] Other music artists such as Madonna and David Bowie have been considered as postmodern artists whose aim is to reimagine themselves with every album release. Particularly Madonna has been read as a feminist postmodern icon to explore feminist identity politics in flux.

[4] Beck Hansen also won two other Grammy Awards for *Morning Phase* that year, in the categories Best Engineered Album, Non-Classical, and Best Rock Album. In both 1997 and 2000, Beck won the Grammy Award for Best Alternative Music album for his albums *Odelay* and *Mutations*, respectively.

[5] Beck relates how their collaboration on the track was to be seen as a meta commentary to the production of a song:

> We brought [Jonze and Eggers] in, and we were going to have a commentary going through the whole album, almost like the two old men in *The Muppets*. It was hilarious. A heavy beat would kick in and they would go, "Shit! Listen to that beat! That drummer is so confident!" But we couldn't fit it all in. I asked them, "What would the ultimate record that ever could possibly be made sound like?" That's what they're going on about. They're saying it would be like an illuminated manuscript, handmade by monks. Or it would be a record that changed every time you listened to it. It was a great conversation. (Hansen in Salmon 2016, n.p.)

This gives us an idea of *Song Reader*, which is a record that changes every time you play it.

Landslide/Exoskeleton" from his 2006 album *The Information*; Beck has remixed songs for artists ranging from Björk to Philip Glass; he recorded music for a Dior runway show and for the computer game *Sound Shapes*; he founded the now defunct *Record Club* on his website to cover rock albums (i.e., The Velvet Underground's debut *The Velvet Underground & Nico* and Leonard Cohen's debut *Songs of Leonard Cohen*) with other artists such as St. Vincent, Devendra Banhart, Wilco, and Feist. Alongside these "indie" endeavors, Beck also appeared on stage alongside with Annie Clark of St. Vincent at a Taylor Swift concert in 2015, co-wrote the song "Dancin' in Circles" with Lady Gaga for her album *Joanne* in 2016, contributed music to the *Twilight* soundtrack in 2010, and made a cameo in the film adaptation of Dave Eggers's novel *The Circle* (2017). He collaborated with brands like Apple for a special-edition Beck iPod model and with Martin Guitars for a custom-made signature guitar. These many collaborations and his movement between indie and mainstream channels give insight how Beck is capable of and invested in transcending markets that often remain separate.

 To contrast his high visibility in the indie rock field, Beck has repeatedly underlined in interviews the importance of remaining somehow inaccessible and elusive to the wider public. He consciously subverts the role of the rock star in his stage performances. Not only does he remain opaque through his nonsensical lyrics, but he acknowledges how fallacious or superficial the rock star persona can be: unlike other celebrities, Beck does not maintain an Instagram account, nor does he tweet or give many interviews anymore. In an earlier interview Beck points out that a "rock star conjures up something like a mystic: someone who has the key to the secret that people want to know. The cliché of what a rock star is—there's something elitist about it. I never related to that. I'm an entertainer. I think of it as, you're performing for people. It's not a self-glorifying thing" (Hansen 1997, n.p.). Beck's conscious stance against elitism in his line of profession draws a parallel to Chris Ware's self-deprecating rhetoric. While Chris Ware maintains that he is merely a cartoonist, Beck calls himself an entertainer who toys with the tried and tested poses of rock stardom.

 In an attempt to break the conventions of the rock star image and of the rock stage, Beck "reimagined" David Bowie's song "Sound and Vision" for the Los Angeles Philharmonic Lincoln Center in 2013, where he performed the song with a 157-piece orchestra. Beck stood on a rotating stage, alone with an acoustic guitar, wearing a sequin suit and his trademark fedora. The performance was taped and is now available for an online immersive interactive experience in which the user can manipulate the camera angles.

In a short piece on the *Rolling Stone* website, Beck explains that it "was an experiment and an opportunity to try something completely irrational. . . . I attempted to conjure some scenario that could only exist in this kind of space for a one-time performance. It's doing something you could never do on a tour. I was thinking a lot about Busby Berkeley films and multiples of musicians and dancers" (Hansen in Appleford 2013, n.p.). Jeff Gordinier's off-hand comment on Beck being a "MoMA curator with two turntables and a microphone" is indicative, for Beck fuses high and low culture and explores the outer limits of what indie rock can be. By paying homage to David Bowie at a philharmonic, Beck collages technology, pop music, and classical music into one interactive online experience that does not seem irrational or over-the-top, but something only an artist like Beck could "pull off."

The tour for his album *The Information* (2006–07) featured a mise-en-abyme mini-stage on stage, on which marionettes played alongside the band (see Figure 3.2). This marionette band also appears in an alternate music video for "Nausea," one of the singles of the album, to perform the rock song in lieu of Beck. Again, this can be understood as a self-deprecating gesture in the vein of Chris Ware toward stardom and the figure of the rock star, but it can also be read as a twee and ironic gesture toward stage performances and cliché rock star poses. In a concert review in *Rolling Stone*, Kevin O'Donnell

Figure 3.2 Beck Hansen and his puppet doppelgänger at a concert in September 2006. Usage under creative commons license, photo credit: Scott Beale/Laughing Squid; laughingsquid.com.

writes how "hipster marionettes lend charm to the troubadour's dazzling live show":

> When Beck and his crew of merry pranksters strolled onto the stage, it became clear that the tiny puppets were outfitted in hipster duds matching the band's outfits perfectly. For the duration of the stellar show, the mini-band played their own tiny instruments in perfect time to the music. Beck's puppet-double even strummed a miniature version of his junk-shop Silvertone guitar, opening its mouth to lipsynch whenever Beck sang. The spectacle created a goofy, playful hall-of-mirrors effect. (O'Donnell 2006, n.p.)

Beck's "rock and roll puppet show" (to borrow from O'Donnell's concert review) illuminates this self-deprecating, playful hall-of-mirrors effect of the marionette rock star persona.

Both the "Sound and Vision" art performance and the marionette show on stage pose questions about laissez-faire and slackerish coolness. Why can Beck afford to shrink himself to a puppet-caricature of himself? Carrie Brownstein, the guitarist and singer of the (all-female) rock band Sleater-Kinney, offers a nuanced perspective on the male-dominated field of rock in her memoir *Hunger Makes Me a Modern Girl*. Brownstein writes about blasé, detached indie boy slackers in 1990s rock scene, and it is worth quoting at length here:

> In the '90s the term "slacker" was applied to a certain kind of breezy, laid-back male artist: Beck, Stephen Malkmus of Pavement, Rivers Cuomo of Weezer. These guys were understated, sneaker-wearing; they acted like they couldn't be bothered and had a tossed-of coolness. Lyrics seemed to pour out of their mouths in profound, poetic drips. They made it look causal, like the stakes were low or nonexistent. I admired and listened to the music, and I think the perception and reception were different from their intent. But I also thought about what a privilege it must be to feel—or to affect—that entitlement; to be onstage, to play music, to get up in front of people and appear not to care.
>
> [...]
>
> Though the term "slacker music" (not one that these musicians put upon themselves, I should stress) has since disappeared, certainly the affectlessness remains, the gutlessness, in many bands and artists that have come since. Entitlement is a precarious place from which to create or perform—it projects the idea that you have nothing to prove, nothing to claim, nothing to show but self-satisfaction, a smug boredom. It breeds ambivalence. It's as if instead of having to prove they are something, these musicians prove they aren't anything. It's an inverted dynamic, one

that sets performers up to fail, but also gives them a false sense of having already arrived. (Brownstein 2015, 191–92)

She reflects on important aspects of entitlement and cool detachment within rock that resonate strongly in light of the discussion of Beck's public persona and his artistic agenda both as an indie rock fixture and as the author of *Song Reader*. Brownstein draws out an important gender divide and the habitus of male rock star *sprezzatura*: the effortless, smug coolness that really has no agenda or political message,[6] but which is brilliant and innovative nonetheless. This stance insists that making music is not a job, but a calling and "way of life."

Brownstein underlines the privilege and entitlement of the male rock star, which speaks indirectly to the warped, gendered dimensions of Beck's *Song Reader*. The project encourages the fan to emulate a privileged, *male* position of smugness and disinterest. Unlike the affective labor that the collector pours into *Building Stories*, *Song Reader* performs an obverse, ironic operation that, on first glance, does away with a caring for the performance or the outcome of the song. It bolsters a breezy, aloof stance toward the project. While *Song Reader* is, on the one hand, to be understood as an ironic wink at what shape a record (and a rock star) can take up in the twenty-first century, to engage with *Song Reader* nevertheless reinforces Beck's image as the affectively and stylistically cool male rock star. *Song Reader* offers a DIY kit for tentative approaches toward this bored rock star(dom), yet it is *still* labor that the song reader must perform to reach the pinnacle of smug boredom. This indexes the tension between Beck (i.e., hipster marionettes and rock star *sprezzatura*) who adds bents and breaks to the rock star habitus and, on the other hand, the song reader, who "plays" by the rules to implement the elusive creative vision of Beck's project.

Only an artist like Beck has the cultural capital and "aura" to subvert rock star expectations, to cover David Bowie in a philharmonic or to release an album in sheet music form, while shunning the elitism of rock stardom completely. The fan, on the other hand, must display competence and "be in the know" to navigate the sheet music album. Then again, Beck presents his fans naive, playful, and almost childlike objects that can be literally toyed

---

[6] In *Die Gesellschaft der Singularitäten* Andreas Reckwitz examines different components of late capitalist lifestyles; one component is the hegemonial juvenilization of the middle class. Beck was promoted as something akin to a man-child at the beginning of his career. Reckwitz draws out that ever since the 1990s, there was hardly any need for another youth movement because the demands for self-fulfillment and anti-conformity have been fulfilled through capitalism (see Reckwitz 2017a, 338). It is interesting to see that Beck's career started at exactly this moment, after the Grunge era came to a close with Kurt Cobain's suicide.

with; this fact problematizes the relationship between Beck and the song reader even further. While *Song Reader* subverts the conventions of the rock star field, what Beck does, ultimately, is to transform his fans into childlike incarnations of himself, into hipster marionettes. The way Beck undermines his own persona and positions his fans as amateurs can be read through Pierre Bourdieu's notion of how

> every gesture, every event, is, as a painter nicely put it, "a sort of nudge or wink between accomplices." In and through the games of distinction, these winks and nudges, silent, hidden references to other artists, past or present, confirm a complicity which excludes the layperson, who is always bound to miss what is essential, namely the interrelations and interactions of which the work is only the silent trace. (Bourdieu 1993, 109)

In this game of distinction, of who *needs* to put effort into the project and who can just make music effortlessly, Beck demarcates himself from his fans and clarifies that his fans might not really be his accomplices. Bourdieu stresses how the layperson will miss the essential components of the work, such as esoteric references within *Song Reader*.

This is, for the fan, a reminder of her subordinate position in relation to the author, the bored rock star. She is never able to attain the mastery and effortless cool of an artist like Beck. The fan can try to emulate Beck's cool, but then again, Beck makes himself available to the public as a *marionette*. Or, to put it even more crudely, how can the song reader ever be Beck's equivalent, if she is basically turned into a child (i.e., watching marionettes on stage like a Punch and Judy show) while her idol is a puppet himself, mouthing along to the songs? These notions stress the significance of audiences, cultural capital, gender, and accessibility in Beck's work.

We might wonder, then, how the dichotomy of creativity and the affective responses of smugness and coolness ties together with the "anti-institutional *desire* for creativity and the institutionalized *demand* for creativity" (Reckwitz 2017b, viii) visible in Beck's work. To elaborate, it is "important to take seriously the affective dimension of the creativity dispositif, the importance of aesthetic practices in contemporary society, the existence of what I have termed *aesthetic sociality*, and the way the dispositif directs audiences' sensuous, affective attention" (Reckwitz 2017b, viii, emphasis mine). Reckwitz's comment detects a slightly different affective response that *Song Reader* would make available in comparison to Ware's work, which explores feminine affective labor of caring for material (such as the aesthetic category of the "cute" that Sianne Ngai defines in *Our Aesthetic Categories*).

Song Reader examines the coolness of male rock stars[7] and how the song reader must emulate this position. This intersection involves the object of *Song Reader* and Beck's role of the auteur, whose seemingly effortless songwriting (i.e., his nonsensical, aloof lyrics) stands in stark contrast with the song reader's position in the project, who adopts this detached stance toward stardom and labors to emulate Beck's (fluctuating) positioning.

Following this line of thought, Andreas Reckwitz places large emphasis on the historical importance of the emergence of the star system in the twentieth century. He explains how the star's

> apparent uniqueness and cultural productivity can be realized and expressed both in works and in the presentation of a public image. Modern stars turn out to be the successors of the figure of the artist. . . . They are not people with whom the public communicates or has dealings in any way except as objects of an aesthetic—i.e., a sensuous, affective regard which is enjoyed for its own sake. (Reckwitz 2017b, 154)

Celebrities, according to Reckwitz, are mobile objects that allow for aesthetic and affective responses of the rather passive audience. Further, the star (be this a rock star or a film star) assumes the popular appeal of the creative subject as an *ideal* and indexes how an individual performs (and commercializes) her creativity. Stars are "made exceptional by the fascinating idiosyncrasies of the works they produce, by their performance or their personality, which escape conformity to any familiar type and thus come to be invested with an aura" (Reckwitz 2017b, 156). The emergence of mass media is indicative, for mass media is to place "masses of people over long periods in the position of receivers, of members of an audience who, instead of actively engaging with or generating events, are merely involved in their cognitive, aesthetics, sensuous observation" (Reckwitz 2017b, 157). Andreas Reckwitz underlines how the star is "embedded within mass-media representation and is thus a result of the revolution of media technology" (Reckwitz 2017b, 157). And if mass media can produce these positions, the rarified object of mass culture like the sheet music song of an indie rock star might bring about effects that pertain to cultural practices of the digital era,

---

[7] In relation to female rock stars, Kim Gordon's *A Girl in a Band: A Memoir*, Patti Smith's *Just Kids* and *M Train*, and Carrie Brownstein's *Hunger Makes Me a Modern Girl* mark a surge of female musicians' memories that shed light on the role of women in the male-dominated music business and on stage.

whose aura is distorted by copy and paste.[8] To generate answers to these questions, we must turn toward the object itself, *Song Reader*. We need to investigate in the materiality and ephemerality of music in the twenty-first century to further think about the song reader subject position. Because it is not only the premise that stands out in Beck's efforts to redefine the borders of what an artist or rock star can do but also how music and its shapes are manipulable in the twenty-first century.

Song Reader's negotiations of music's materialities and ephemeralities

Beck's latest album comes in an almost-forgotten form—twenty songs existing only as individual pieces of sheet music, never before released or recorded. Complete with full-color, heyday-of-home-play-inspired art for each song and a lavishly produced hardcover carrying case, *Song Reader* is an experiment in what an album can be at the end of 2012—an alternative that enlists the listener in the tone of every track, and that's as visually absorbing as a dozen gatefold LPs put together.
— Description on the songreader.net website

Song Reader allows us to think about the connection between the star, the fan, and changes in media and technology—by way of an obsolete medium. Martin Heidegger's notion of the broken tool, wherein an object only reveals itself as a thing at the moment it fails to work, offers a useful segue for thinking about Beck's *Song Reader* project, once the idea of the rock star is "broken up" and made porous by Beck's subversive gestures. In Heidegger's sense, then, *Song Reader* is a broken record: a curious, outdated guise for a music album at the beginning of the twenty-first century. As a self-proclaimed "album," it comes in a large blue folder and with colorful pieces of sheet music tucked

---

[8] In relation to the copy in the digital spheres, David Banash explains that from "the perspective of the copy and its digital worlds, the anxieties and transformations of the twentieth century become suddenly clearer; collage is the art of the assembly line, the newspaper, the film, the fragment. As these forms have been exceeded and enmeshed in the digital, collage has been liquidated or mutated into a process of copying" (Banash 2013, 29). I take Banash's idea of the flexibility of the (digital) copy as a cue to examine how conceptual art, consumerism, and media archaeology congeal to online practices of storing and documenting—or the failure thereof. After all, it seems as if *Song Reader* is destined to proliferate online, on platforms such as YouTube and songreader.net (the website created especially for collecting cover versions). But these spheres elude the control of an editor or curator; they seem to grow wildly, without oversight or interference.

inside of it neatly. Kate Maxwell underlines that the folder looks like a gatefold LP, and that "every track has individual artwork on its front cover, and an advertisement on its back cover. Within these is the musical notation: appealing to the eye, the ear, and the touch" (Maxwell 2016, n.p.).

While contemporary music persists in ever-shrinking media, *Song Reader* deliberately takes up space as an object and time as a hobby. Arguably, music has never existed and been mediated in more formats (i.e., MP3s, CDs, vinyls, cassettes, MiniDiscs, YouTube, soundcloud streams) than at the beginning of the twenty-first century: changing formats accommodate the music listener and offer a wide spectrum for consumption. CDs, Sony Walkmans, vinyl records, and cassettes become obsolete in just a matter of years but are then rediscovered as nostalgic retro treasures in the next heartbeat. "The form and matter of music remain closely bound today, especially if we consider the ways in which recordings move across formats and milieus," Jonathan Sterne writes in *MP3—The Meaning of a Format* (Sterne 2012, 186). In this sense, music seems to be many things at once: technology, commodity, property, idealized work, bundle of affordances, and digital things (see Sterne 2012, 189–98). The resurgence of the vinyl record, for example, indexes this trend how music now takes up space again and becomes a collectible, refusing to vanish into the clouds of online data. Sterne refers here to Bill Brown: "If the topic of things has attained new urgency . . ., this may have been a response to the digitization of our world," and, I would add, to the digitization of pastimes and past times (Brown 2001, 18).

While music seems to be and afford many different "things" at once (i.e., commodity, technology, idealized work), an album compiled as sheet music inserts itself as something like a sneering side glance at the long list of obsolete media, pirated video footage from concerts, and pre-release album leaks. It facetiously suggests yet another way of music production and consumption that comes back from the nineteenth century in the style of twenty-first-century digital culture. Yet, a sheet music album caters to a weird notion of nostalgia present in the digital age—for things that are touchable. Something that might be coined "digital nostalgia" traces the recalcitrance of some objects toward digitization processes and emphasizes the individual's interaction with said objects. Svetlana Boym helps approach this idea, who argues how technology and the internet do not necessarily *cure* nostalgia, rather, the digital sphere *anticipates* nostalgia: "Technology and nostalgia have become co-dependent: new technology and advanced marketing stimulate *ersatz* nostalgia—for the things you never thought you had lost— and *anticipatory* nostalgia—for the present that flees with the speed of a click" (Boym 2007, 10). This implies changing conceptions of space and time—and our relation to fleeting moments and transient spaces, of clicking the moment away or archiving it instantly (i.e., tweeting, instagramming). Archiving becomes the pastime.

Suddenly, the place or the moment we long for but cannot restore oddly lies in the future—we already anticipate being nostalgic *for* and the impending loss *of* the moment that we currently live in. Yet, as Beck maintains, music does not necessarily rely on technological innovations, but "there's something human in sheet music, something that doesn't depend on technology to facilitate it—it's a way of opening music up to what someone else is able to bring to it. That instability is what ultimately drew me to this project" (Hansen 2012c, n.p.). To Beck, the album is about the participation of his fans to make it viable; as Jody Rosen points out in his introduction to *Song Reader*,

> The kind of participation called for by *Song Reader* will seem far-fetched. Pop music fandom today is a mostly passive endeavor; we are used to cuing up records, sitting back, and letting the sound wash over us. In the age of MP3s, music has become even less hands-on. Once we had a tactile thing to go with the sound—a shellac 78, an LP inside a gatefold cover, a CD in a jewelbox. (Rosen 2012, n.p.)

It does so, interestingly, by anticipating nostalgia for a long-lost consumer market. *Song Reader* imagines the nostalgia for consumer life and consumption habits of the early twentieth century (i.e., ordering something off the back of a sheet music song) to create the subject position of the song reader. The advertisement on the back of the sheet music for "Why Did You Make Me Care?" speaks to this—what unfolds is a fictional universe nestled into a time long lost and irretrievable—but with trite everyday objects. *Gift Time Is All the Time* invites the song reader to buy personal music accessories: playing cards, a keychain, or a Jiffy can opener will unleash the song reader's creativity (and all presuppose dexterity: holding cards in your hands, turning the key in the lock, opening a can with your fingers). The items for sale underline the "shuffling" nature of the imagined world created by the ads in *Song Reader*. The playing cards promise to produce "a new composition, to be interpreted as you wish."[9] They are waterproof

---

[9] Shuffling cards is a metaphor promising a reading experience focused on contingency. This is reminiscent also of aleatory postmodernist writing, which refers to a ludic experience of fiction. Things are left to chance and accident: *The Unfortunates* by B. S. Johnson is a book in a box, which relies on the shuffling of twenty-seven unbound sections; "Heart Suit," a story by Robert Coover on a deck of cards, was published in the McSweeney's Issue #16; similarly, *Building Stories* offers the reader to rearrange the story with every reading.

and the basis for every tonal system known to man, as the advertisement claims. The Jiffy can opener will "uncan" the song reader's creativity as she would open a container of tuna: "The music is locked within you—this is the tool you need to extract it. Also can be used for actual cans; no more cutting fingers" (Hansen 2012e, n.p.). The analogy between opening a can and unleashing creativity plays on cliché. To unleash your creativity, you need a tool to open yourself up. Everyday objects are repurposed and sold as merchandise to stimulate creativity; they are cheap objects made for marketing and quick consumption. These commodities promise a practical sense of the objects at hand (pun intended)—they allude to the materiality of everyday life and their own transferable, figurative version of creativity. But they also promise the song reader a way to remain in the *Song Reader* market: unless her creativity is unleashed, she cannot function as a valuable musician. Her creativity, after all, is the asset in which she (and other consumers) must invest.

Gift Time Is All the Time spoofs (useless) expensive merchandise sold at rock concerts or in online stores (i.e., a friend of mine recently wore merchandized flip flops by one of his favorite bands). But it simultaneously evokes a nostalgic feeling similar to when we buy old magazines (or sheet music!) on a fleamarket and flip through the pages. Companies that are now long out of business or objects tied to their time create a feeling of a world lost and forgotten—inaccessible to us. *Song Reader* merges digital nostalgia with analog nostalgia. *Song Reader* looks exactly as the song reader would expect it to look like: arabesque and antiquated fonts, in a certain "mode retro" pastiche style.[10] This ambiguity asks in which spheres

---

[10] Fredric Jameson famously turns to pastiche in *Postmodernism, or, the Cultural Logic of Late Capitalism* and urges to distinguish these strategies from that of parody—a statue with blind eyeballs. He writes, "The disappearance of the individual subject, along with its formal consequence, the increasing unavailability of the personal style, engender the well-nigh universal practice today of what may be called pastiche" (Jameson 1991, 16). He continues to underline that pastiche is, indeed, the imitation of a peculiar or unique, idiosyncratic style" but devoid of any of parody's ambitions—instead, it is "the wearing of a linguistic mask, speech in a dead language. But it is a neutral practice of such mimicry . . . amputated of the satiric impulse, devoid of laughter and of any conviction that alongside the abnormal tongue you have momentarily borrowed, some healthy linguistic normality still exists." (Jameson 1991, 17).
  Similarly, Linda Hutcheon and Richard Dyer work on parody and the pastiche mode. Dyer interrogates genre, history, and media, and turns to neo-noir and Spaghetti western, for example; Hutcheon sees a political momentum within pastiche, for "parody signal show present representations come from past ones and what ideological consequences derive from both continuity and difference" (Hutcheon 1989, 93). Acknowledging this blindness and "neutral practice" gives an idea of pastiche modes in nostalgia movies, for instance, and project it onto cultural and social debates. Linda Hutcheon's idea of the

Song Reader belongs: on the fleamarket or in the digital ether? Why not both? Its beautiful covers cater to our idea about how sheet music might have looked in the nineteenth century, and now the medium comes back in a crisp, new façet, printed in China, distributed by McSweeney's, sold online, never used before. In this sense, Beck resuscitates the feeling for sheet music—but only through the lens of a twenty-first-century consumer who looks for an "authentic experience" among other consumer options. Jeffrey Nealon posits that in the "past twenty or thirty years . . . the work of commodity consumption has been rebranded as part and parcel of the work of individuation and subversion, and thereby a certain style of consumption has become a royal road to authenticity (rather than an assured off-ramp)" (Nealon 2012, 56). This is an important insight into the nostalgic mechanisms of *Song Reader*, for it posits that consumption[11] (be this buying something off *Gift Time Is All the Time* or the *Song Reader* per se) leads toward and creates authenticity.

Beck has repeatedly explored and expanded the sensory and consumer boundaries of what goes "with the sound." In this sense, both Beck and Chris Ware seek out media that presuppose (authenticate?) collecting and a dedicated fan community who is not reluctant to protect (expensive) objects from dust or cigarette smoke. To be a Beck fan is to collect Japanese-only editions of his albums with rare b-sides or highly priced releases of early albums such as *A Western Harvest Field by Moonlight* (early editions came with a customized finger painting). Sought-after vinyl records like the Bong Load Records releases of *Mellow Gold*, *One Foot in the Grave*, *Odelay*, *Mutations*, and *Midnite Vultures* sell for astronomic prices. A first edition of *Mellow Gold* is sold for over $50 on websites such as eBay and discogs,

---

politization of pastiche helps untangle the larger implications of *what* pastiche in a given era can express about the past, the future, and the present. It begs the question what kind of "lost reality" is evoked and unearthed in the contemporary moment. (I believe that 2018's "lost reality" is the early 1990s, before the implementation of commercial internet.) Richard Dyer sees, among other things, historical circumstances that make the production of pastiche possible and intriguing. He argues that periods "in which new media suddenly make available a huge range of hitherto inaccessible work, such as the printing press (enabling the work of Cervantes and Rabelais) and audiovisual innovations since the nineteenth century . . ., the suddenness and multiplicity heightening a sense of variability of ways of doing things" (Dyer 2007, 131). Dyer outlines the intermingling of media innovations and their reworking of the past(s), projecting them, through media, into the future.

[11] Nealon's argument extends the idea that consumption in the "present cultural market for music has largely become unmoored from newness as the ultimate test of authenticity and value; and in the offing this cultural shift gives us an inkling of the passing of the high postmodern phase of US cultural production into something not exactly new, hardly 'better' or 'worse,' but something that's certainly different: cultural and economic post-postmodernism" (Nealon 2012, 64–65).

and miniscule differences in covers, pressings, barcodes, and colored vinyl records drive the market price of the albums even higher. Yet, Beck's *Song Reader* seems even more recalcitrant or inaccessible than an obdurate object like *Building Stories* or a rare pressing of *Midnite Vultures*. As an early means to record and sell music, reaching well back into the nineteenth century, sheet music puts music back onto the page and back into a musician's hands.

Beck's continuous attempts to redefine the boundaries of what a music album should look like and what space it should take up in the fan's imagination begin prior to *Song Reader*. With *The Information* (2006), Beck took the first steps toward receding into the background as an authorial voice, while he simultaneously bolstered discussions of records and their market value as collectables. The limited-edition vinyl release of *The Information* is a $300 behemoth (which is a lot of pocket money for his child-fans) that comes with stickers, a coloring book, and felt-tip pens. The limited-edition album also includes rare remixes and b-sides. Unlike *Song Reader*, *The Information* offers artistic design choices, as the fan can decide how to design the cover of the album. Nonetheless, these gestures remain merely playful: releasing a rock album with stickers and a coloring book subverts conventions of the field. Coloring pens are hardly rock and roll: "Beck" becomes a brand that can be colored in with "Beckpens," and he blends in almost like a ghost, leaving the blueprint to his fans to implement their own artistic vision of how the cover should look like. Yet, *The Information* is a very expensive object, and its resell value would decrease if the fan made poor design choices. *The Information*, ultimately, is a poor investment for a fan who might be eager to explore her creativity, as the cover must remain pristine for the album to retain its value and prestige. It is a collector's conundrum, similar to Ware's *Multi-Story Building Model*—should the guidelines of the collectables be executed or should the objects remain pristine? Do creativity and interpretation come at the expense of market value?

We must thus consider *Song Reader* within the context of contemporary music's (im)materiality: at first sight, *The Information* and *Song Reader* are comic, almost facetious comments on market value and creativity. *The Information* interpellates its listeners as children who should color in and put stickers onto the cover to individualize the record while simultaneously depriving it of its market value. In relation to this, Beck explains how *Song Reader* is a "book that's able to stand alone as an object, aside from the music. Traditional album releases can have a self-contained value in their physicality; the photos and art and titles can draw you in before you ever hear the songs. This is a book that takes inspiration from that feeling. The art, the ads, and the other text hopefully convey something all by themselves" (Hansen 2012c, n.p.). David Fricke of *Rolling Stone* underlines how *Song Reader* is a "book-form *anthology* of new compositions for others to interpret" (Fricke 2013, n.p., emphasis mine). Yet, as much as it is a book or an anthology to be flipped through, *Song Reader* is a fickle and fragile object: the pages are not bound together and can be subject to tearing, easily lost or destroyed. This music album can tear and break, it can be misread and mis-sung, or not sung or read at all. This is the distinction that *Song Reader* makes: it can both occur in immaterial and material formats, in the guise of YouTube clips or as a gimmicky coffee table book. This fact reconfigures both the idea of the album, *Song Reader*, and song reader herself as a mobile, "shape-shifting," and flexible consumer and fan.

It is, when approached from this angle, that *Song Reader* can work as a purely aesthetic or gimmicky object that does not depend on an audible interpretation to *function* or have value. *Song Reader* speaks to the fault line between the subject position of the creative-industrious reader and its retro-chic materialities. How music stands out among the noise of the twenty-first century is one of the guiding principles of *Song Reader*. According to Beck, songs compete with so much "other noise now that they can become more exaggerated in an attempt to capture attention. The question of what a song is supposed to do, and how its purpose has altered, has begun to seem worth asking" (Hansen 2012c, n.p.). He continues that learning to "play a song is its own category of experience; recorded music made much of that participation unnecessary. More recently, digital developments have made songs even less substantial-seeming than they were when they came on vinyl or CD" (Hansen 2012c, n.p.). Music, then, in Beck's words, has lost part of its substance, and it is the song reader's task not only to bring the music on the page to life but also to regain a first-hand, affective experience with music. This *experience* is meant to reveal the ways that music has been diluted or diminished by technological changes. Must the music lover now also collect pulpy sheet music along with records only released in Japan? It is here where *Song Reader* draws on the impossibility of its own collecting. *Song Reader* depends on the tension of materiality and ephemerality; it cannot be collected like a vinyl record or other fan memorabilia. Instead, the album is a ready-made and, paradoxically, it does *not* exist as a thing in the first place.

Collecting music seems to make this experience available again: "In the 2000s . . . obsessive collecting of music seemed to spread from the fringe to the mainstream, thanks to the new technologies of distribution and storage" (Reynolds 2011, 95). The internet "allowed people to divorce the pleasures of collecting (not just listening but categorising, compiling playlists, and so forth) from the 'downsides,' such as the physical effort to finding stuff, the problems with storage space and organising the collection" (Reynolds 2011, 96). But these collections remain largely digital, revealing a gap between the materiality of music and its digitized incarnations. Therefore, processes of digitization are another point of departure to think about music's materiality in relation to Beck's endeavors. The transformation from haptic objects into material possessions and, ultimately, into raw data serves as an interesting way for approaching what Simon Reynolds calls the dematerialization of music.[12] He underlines how music was first "reified, turned into a thing (vinyl records, analogue tapes) you could buy, store, keep under your own personal control" (Reynolds 2011, 122). Music was liquefied, according to Reynolds, and "turned into data that could be streamed, carried anywhere, transferred between different devices. With the MP3, music became a devalued currency in two senses: there was just too much of it . . ., but also because of the way it flowed into people's lives like a current or a fluid" (Reynolds 2011, 96).

In contrast, Beck urges the song reader to become an expert in a part of music history that seems foreign in the digital moment. The song reader subject position, thus, entails specialized knowledge about the different media of music production and consumption through the prism of nineteenth-century print curio. *Song Reader* urges the reader to acknowledge both the ever-changing materiality of music and its inherent logics of production, consumption, and dissemination. We might wonder, then, how the questions of devaluation, ready-made art, and the song reader as childlike Beck fan resonate within the concept of curatorial labor in the digitized moment. The materiality of music is shape-shifting, from bits and bytes back to sheet music back to CDs and vinyl, Beck's efforts in *Song Reader* subvert the manifold, liquefied materialities that music has assumed. We might think here of Zygmunt Bauman's idea of liquid modernity: as Bauman suggests, the melting of the solids, which he distills as the permanent feature of modernity, focuses now on "the bonds which interlock individual choices in collective projects and actions—the patterns of communication and co-ordination between individually conducted life policies on the one hand and political actions of human collectivities on the other" (Bauman 2012, 6). Bauman's arguments about liquefication prove to be intriguing when thinking about

---

[12] In 2002, David Bowie predicted in an interview with Jon Parales of *The New York Times* that music itself is going "to become like running water or electricity" (Bowie in Parales 2002, n.p.). Bowie continues,

> The absolute transformation of everything that we ever thought about music will take place within 10 years, and nothing is going to be able to stop it. I see absolutely no point in pretending that it's not going to happen. I'm fully confident that copyright, for instance, will no longer exist in 10 years, and authorship and intellectual property is in for such a bashing. (Bowie in Parales 2002, n.p.)

David Bowie's clairvoyance and confidence are resonant within the copyright and distribution logics that *Song Reader* comments on so playfully.

the individual and the possible alliances that *Song Reader* interrogates and initiates.

Song Reader rather contributes to an affective, idiosyncratic interest in "forms of music which are not available to any individual, anytime and everywhere" (Fleischer 2015, 256). In fact, forms and liquefication stand in contrast here. Beck's project resists streaming and downloading by drawing on the experiences of engaging with sheet music and its medium-specific qualities. These experiences can be individualized and intensified, materialized and dematerialized. The song reader is forced to interrogate the haptic or ephemeral guises of a medium and test its incarnations across centuries and across the online-offline divide. Through these efforts, Beck's project reflects upon the ongoing economization of creativity and intervenes in discourses in and around digitization, illegal file sharing, piracy, and online streaming. After all, Beck's music is tightly linked to market fads and commodification (i.e., $300 vinyl records and re-issues with remixes and b-sides) and is something to hunt down and collect. Where should we start looking if and when the object itself relies upon ephemerality and obsolescence? Borrowing from a largely outmoded and forgotten tradition, *Song Reader* interrogates participatory culture's premises and embeds itself in a long, American musical and cultural history of copying and covering. Beck shifts the song reader's attention to the fact that current practices find their predecessors in earlier, related cultural practices. To argue more forcefully even, *Song Reader* (and the same can be claimed for *Building Stories*, too), the reader and the text enter into new haptic relations that feel both antiquated and contemporary.

Sheet music, now and then

Song Reader's sheet music design effortlessly blends today and yesterday—just by flipping through *Song Reader* allows for a mix of visual and textual imagery that spans centuries. Some song cover pages are designed by artists Beck has collaborated with previously (i.e., Marcel Dzama, who also designed Beck's *Guero* album cover), others are covers from old sheet music editions (such as the cover of "Eyes that Say I Love You" and "The Wolf Is On the Hill"). This initial intertwining of old and new connects the spheres of sheet music today and yesterday. The merging of old and new also echoes within the themes that the *Song Reader* songs touch upon. Sheet music songs in the nineteenth and early twentieth centuries were usually playful and tongue-in-cheek; the songs told stories about shipwrecks or wooden legs, love relationships or failed journeys, hence stories meant to be relatable or amusing and easy to croon along to. Beck finds absurd, distorting contemporary imagery. His songs are inhabited by parking valets and apostles who work in malls, floods that turn to droughts, and an enemy's misfortune rains down like rotten eggs. His images echo an ambivalent sense of contemporary life in a post-capitalist wasteland dominated by mixed metaphors. A doubling is brought about, as the songs allude to the past through their mediality, but to the present in regard to their themes and subject matter. But also toward the future: if sheet music has always been universal and open to interpretation, as people over centuries and decades sing the same songs in different voices and with a different range of skills, *Song Reader* might sustain through centuries, too, turning into a song book for future generations. If sheet music can make a comeback in 2012, it might as well come back in another hundred years time, stuck in the process of transitions ad infinitum.

We can approach sheet music as a recalcitrant, obdurate medium in our cultural moment that marks contemporary media being in transition. It can be seen as a celebration of the print medium in digital times, aligning itself with the playful efforts of the McSweeney's publishing universe, which is famous for its idiosyncratic formats and designs. Beck's project echoes a time when music was not available immediately or instantly online, but when making music was a communal activity that brought people together in parlors or around campfires.[13] Its potential to align and bring together people speaks to notion of creative alliances and creative industries, and it draws attention to the overlap of the sheet music medium and its potential in mobilizing its readers both in the 1850s *and* in the 2010s. A medium dormant for years now displays aesthetics of transition vis-à-vis a new moment of participatory culture that is negotiated largely in the online realm. As Henry Jenkins and David Thorburn outline for the aesthetics of transition,[14] a medium such as sheet music, even after

---

[13] This is what Rasmus Fleischer identifies as postdigital strategies, which are key to creating "common notions" and bringing "collective experience into the individualized experience," that could largely also just be predigital to begin with (Fleischer 2015, 266). This puts a strong emphasis on how Beck incorporates old and new to evoke seemingly obsolete practices that are, at second glance, still current in mobilizing the collective and the individual experience.

[14] Kate Maxwell outlines how *Song Reader* works with hypermediacy and immediacy. She points out that on the one hand,

> the book-album is intrinsically hypermedial: it refashions older media (the song sheet, the gatefold LP) into something new; its various media play dual roles (the notation is part of the artwork, which is an intrinsic part of the tracks and the book-album, which is a *mise en abyme* of itself). On the other hand, the very invitation to reader participation brings a form of immediacy to popular music that had been lost with the advent of recording technologies and the music industry: individual, authentic interpretations of pop songs. (Maxwell 2016, n.p.)

140 years, is bound to adhere to the processes of "imitation, self-discovery, remediation and transformation" (Jenkins and Thorburn 2003, 12). This is part of how "cultures define and renew themselves. Old media rarely die; their original functions are adapted and absorbed by newer media, and they themselves may mutate into new cultural niches and new purposes" (Jenkins and Thorburn 2003, 12).

And *Song Reader*, by boldly and explicitly referencing the styles, themes, and contents that were prominent in the United States around the time of the Civil War up until the era of Tin Pan Alley, draws connections to the (media) history of the United States that might reveal itself as one of consumer options and predilection and taste. These specificities of the sheet music medium reflect on the curator's task to tessellate and dissect, to choose and select, to appropriate and to update—working as both a sheet music historian and fan, fluent in nineteenth- and twenty-first-century media practices. It is a medium that reflects upon the consumer and simultaneously draws out technologies that perpetuate the cultural history of the United States forward. Hence, sheet music in the twenty-first century might be able to comment upon its status as a medium in transition, predicated upon, quite literally, interpretation, transformations, imitations, and compromises made by the song reader. And by Beck's efforts to create a fictional universe in which his sheet music collection exists—emulating the style and tone of the commercials, songs, and designs—we are shown a flashback on sheet music's nineteenth-century appeal and popularity based on consumer options.

Questions of universality and access come to the fore. Commenting on the writing process for *Song Reader*, Beck reflects on how sometimes "the lyrics were too clichéd, the sentiments were too shop-worn sometimes. But if the song was too clever or self-conscious it wouldn't have that universality" (Hansen in Barton 2012, n.p.). Beck hence tip-toes around challenges of generalization of styles and voices. For *Song Reader* has to be "relatable" enough to be brought to life by a broader public, yet it still has to be distinctly recognizable as an album containing music by Beck Hansen, and thus, to a select group of fans. But in the self-description, Beck conjures up the practicing of the songs, the performance around campfires and in parlors, and the communal dimension of sheet music that is accessible to anybody. Beck envisions how

> all different types of people would be possibly singing and playing these songs. . . . It made me think of that abstract notion of an American songbook, whether it includes standards, jazz tunes, things from the rock era, singer-songwriter songs—you know, all these songs that people know and love, the kind of songs that you play around a campfire or

at a gathering. Those are the kind of songs that I was thinking about. (Hansen 2012b, n.p.)

It is important to raise awareness toward Beck's rather contested and romanticized term of "universality" here. Beck might see the universality of his songs in the generic layout and cliché lyrics, but his terminology fails to address class, race, ethnic, or regional specificities in the nineteenth *and* the twenty-first centuries.

Given its long intertwined history with the minstrel show and traveling troupes, sheet music is much more politized than Beck's bucolic imagery of campfire. It dips into a history of racial segregation, social privilege, and the question who was entertained by what. In this way, Beck paints over concepts of class, distribution of labor, and social status within the pastoral of bourgeois social gatherings.[15] Sheet music is interwoven with a lost feeling that *Song Reader* now attempts to evoke. Beck's fascination with the colorful history and "universality" and consumer option shines through in his introductory words:

> I came across a story about a song called "Sweet Leilani" that Bing Crosby had released in 1937. Apparently, it was so popular that, by some estimates, the sheet music sold 54 million copies. Home-played music had been so widespread that nearly half the country had bought the sheet music for a single song, and presumably gone through the trouble of learning to play it. (Hansen 2012c, n.p.)

This gives us an idea that 70 percent of all Americans owned and sang "Sweet Leilani" at home. In *Song Reader*'s case today, though, the number of participants might be miniscule. But who knows how often Beck's hit album *Odelay* was downloaded or disseminated on cassettes.

In the nineteenth and early twentieth centuries, sheet music was *the* predominant medium for songs to travel through the United States. After the American Revolution, sheet music was imported from England; publishers in Boston, New York, Philadelphia, and Baltimore would distribute sheet music and make songs available to the American public. At one point in time, sheet music became so popular that it was published as supplements in newspapers and was therefore made available to an even broader reading public. It is here where sheet music closes a gap between professional and

---

[15] Eric Lott's *Love and Theft* has been among the most influential studies in regard to minstrel and race. His book analyzes the most popular form of entertainment in the nineteenth century and uncovers the racial ideologies, divisions between high and low culture, and interrelations of music, literature, performance vis-à-vis race and sexuality.

personal entertainment, since the former was not available or affordable for everyone. It was mostly women, excluded from public spaces such as theaters,[16] who had to make their own theaters: "Singing was a popular pastime and sheet music was in great demand. Hundreds of thousands of Americans in homes all over the country sat down at the piano to hammer out the popular songs propped up over the keyboard, while millions more gathered around for loud and lusty vocal accompaniments" (Levy 1971, vii).

The songs were rather formulaic and the companies releasing the songs "produced sheet music as systematically as factories poured out individual goods. Songs were constructed on the basis of predetermined formulas, and once a particular scheme of words and music transfixed the public imagination, countless replicas of that process appeared virtually overnight" (Sanjek 2001, 11). Sheet music became a commodity and thus a means to sell products—sheet music songs were turned into singable commercials or jingles, as companies "even issued series of sheet music to help advertise their products, notably the Emerson Drug Company's promotion of Bromo-Seltzer. During World War I, publishers promoted the war effort by using the margins of the music for such slogans as 'Food will win the war, don't waste it'" ("About Sheet Music" 2015, n.p.). In this way, sheet music covers are "important to understand the strategies of advertising employed by the publishers as well as the dominant forms of representation" (Silva 2016, 226). But taking representation at face value, we must acknowledge that the author or composer was hardly ever credited; instead the name of the singer who popularized the tune was printed on the sheet music.

Lester Levy points out that it "soon became evident that music of a period was closely tied to the history and mores of the country's development. . . . We sang the virtues of a war or a president. We touched on the American sense of humor. We sang about our mode of dress or advances in technology" (Levy 2013, n.p.). And this happened through the advance of printing technologies: "Newspapers and magazines, postcards, posters and sheet music covers were a clear sign of the spread of the printed page. This highlighted the commodity-in-display, a major tendency of modern consumer culture" (Silva 2016, 226–27). Sheet music and its distribution, consumer, and dissemination practices draw me to Benedict Anderson's idea of imagined communities and its link to the widespread emergence of print systems. Print technologies made it possible for "rapidly growing

---

[16] David Monod in *The Soul of Pleasure* traces the history of theater spaces that catered to a predominantly white, male audience and mostly excluded women. Women either were present in theater spaces for the uplift of morale (hence what could be called "family-friendly entertainment") or as waitresses, actresses, and prostitutes.

numbers of people to think about themselves and to relate themselves to others, in profoundly new ways" (Anderson 2003, 36). The self-conception of the United States and the colorful, funny, humorous sheet music of the early twentieth century are tightly linked to and created by a reading, or rather, singing public that seems to sing itself into existence (i.e., Levy's point regarding the mode of dress or advances in technology). Nonetheless, this also indexes a public manifested by consumers. Nation-ness, according to Anderson, relies on cultural artifacts of a particular kind, and here, the nation is tied together through pulp printings of music sheets and supplements in newspapers (see Anderson 2003, 4). Sheet music was inexpensive to produce, easily disseminated, easy to trade, and even easier to toss out and overhaul. This idea can be adjusted slightly to explain how sheet music might create not imagined communities but, more specifically, a creative *alliance* of individuals united by the commodity-in-display.

Thousands of people who would never meet in person sang the same songs, shared at least some of the same musical taste, the same passion to bring those songs to life, and told the same stories with their different voices and skills. To relate back to what Beck mentions about Bing Crosby's song: "54 million homes singing 'Sweet Leilani' in 1937 would have felt like some weird convergence. That time is long gone, but the idea of it makes one wonder where that impulse went" (Hansen 2012c, n.p.). Recognizing this fact gives us a picture of a diffuse group of like-minded people, primarily created through affinity and zeitgeist. To draw back on Benedict Anderson's study, print-capitalism and print-consumerism brought into being, if perhaps entirely incidentally, an alliance of (song) readers separated by physical distance, but brought in virtual proximity to one another through their shared love for sheet music and the desire for entertainment.

With his romantic vision of an imagined alliance of sheet music song readers, Beck traces the alliances that are created among like-minded people who we can also simply call "fans" today. Sheet music here generates an individualized act by the song reader, be it in 1890 or in 2012, who appropriates and modifies the songs for her own amusement and in line with her own skill set. But the history of sheet music suggests that the form is a deindividualized/deindividualizing medium, accessible to a broad public, one that interpellates the song reader as a fan who pours in time and effort to bring Beck's vision to life. Further, it is blind to questions of race, class, and gender but universalizes the song reader into a consumer position of equal skill and opportunity in the digital age.[17] Sheet music

---

[17] See here gender-neutral practices that Andreas Reckwitz outlines (see Reckwitz 2017a, 339).

augments the emergence of mass culture and the grouping of consumers, of access, of fan involvement and active participation in culture and music, and of notions regarding interactivity in the nineteenth century that is purely based on adapting a "pre-given" creative vision. Most importantly it shows that creative labor is not a solely contemporary phenomenon brought forth by the logics of late and digitized capitalism, but earlier media and technological advances such as sheet music/mass print already generated such forms of labor, publics, consumer options through the covering of a song. Through its democratic and universalizing claims, *Song Reader* is invested in questions regarding copyright,[18] piracy, illegal downloads. To inquire further into this set of questions, let's hold a piece of sheet music in our hands and look at it closely.

Copy of a copy: "Title of This Song"

Cut, copy, and paste have become cultural imperatives and keyboard shorthands in the digital era. A work of ingenuity, like *Song Reader*, is now made consumerist within the framework of such imperatives; it can be purchased and practiced—copied and pasted from its original point of reference (Beck's rock stage) into the fan's living room. Quoting, adaptation, homages extend and reiterate the meaning of the copy and the creative culture of reference within a society immensely.[19] In his book *Mashup*, Dirk

---

[18] For more on copyright and copyright infringement, refer to Jamie Lund's article "Fixing Music Copyright" in which he takes Beck's *Song Reader* as a segue to analyze the Lay Listener Test. Jamie Lund distinguishes between musical composition and sound recording: the "anomaly of Beck's sheet music album demonstrates the often-elided distinction between a musical composition and the sound recording of its performance; each is separately copyrightable. This article contends that the audience for those two kinds of works—compositions and sound recordings—is different. This insight has significant implications for the test for copyright infringement of musical compositions" (Lund 2013, 62).

[19] The full quote reads as follows (no German translation available):

Zum einen das reine Vervielfältigen, ein Bereich, der angesichts der Digitalisierung von grundlegenden Veränderungen steht und in dem Umbrüche notwendig sein werden. Mit den Schwierigkeiten (und auch Kämpfen), die dieser Aspekt des Kopierens mit sich bringt, befasse ich mich unten ab Kapitel IV, beginnen möchte ich jedoch mit dem zweiten Aspekt der Kopie, den ich als kreative Referenzkultur beschreibe. Dabei handelt es sich um eine Technik der Bezugnahme, des Zitats und der Adaption, die schon immer Grundlage unseres Kulturverständnisses war, die jedoch—ebenso wie die Vervielfältigung—durch die Digitalisierung einem Veränderungsprozess unterworfen ist, der ihre Bedeutung noch verstärkt. In beiden Fällen rückt die Kopie in den Mittelpunkt, weil sie einfach von sehr viel mehr Menschen genutzt werden

von Gehlen discusses the musical cover. He points out how the copy has become an important cultural technique that we encounter, again and again, mostly without even knowing that it is a copy we are dealing with. In terms of sheet music, we might also be able to talk about a "cover": a cover version of a song is, according to von Gehlen, better than its reputation, because it is the basis for creativity and a quintessential necessity in and for our culture[20] (see von Gehlen 2011, 12–13). Just by turning the car radio on, von Gehlen's idea blossoms and blooms: the song "Nothing Compares 2 U," for example, was released on The Family's eponymous album (which was one of Prince's side projects in the 1980s), but was an international commercial success for Sinéad O'Connor, who covered the song a couple of years later. Likewise, Leonard Cohen's song "Hallelujah" has been reinterpreted by artists such as Jeff Buckley, John Cale, and Rufus Wainwright. Or when Johnny Cash sings "Hurt," it is not the "same" song that Trent Reznor of the Nine Inch Nails first recorded.

To cover and reappropriate is a means for perpetuating culture and to add nuances and new perspectives to a cultural object—and make a song or artwork accessible to groups of people who might not have come across it otherwise (i.e., there might be merely a small correlation among Johnny Cash and Nine Inch Nails fans). If we take covering as a cultural technique that illuminates hidden contours and facets of an artwork, we see that to copy is to be productive in consumer culture; a question that goes alongside with the copy is why we give labor (both cognitive or physical) away for free. Particularly in digital times, these questions of the blurring of copy and cover remain imperative.[21] We can subsume that the cover does not devalue

---

kann. Einerseits im Sinne der Vervielfältigung durch beispielsweise das Duplizieren einer Datei, andererseits aber auch durch die vereinfachten Formen der Bezugnahme. Wo Inhalte digital vorliegen, können sie leichter adaptiert, parodiert und geremixt werden als zu rein analogen Zeiten. (von Gehlen 2011, 19)

[20] I am paraphrasing Dirk von Gehlen here, for there is no German translation available of his book: "Kopien begegnen uns allerdings häufig an Orten, an denen wir sie zunächst nicht erwarten, sie sind notwendiger und präsenter, als ihr schlechtes Image vermuten lässt, sie sind eine Grundlage der Kreativität, und ja, sie sind überlebensnotwendig für unsere Kultur" (von Gehlen 2011, 12–13).

[21] Again, I am paraphrasing Dirk von Gehlen here. This is the German original:

Die digitale Kopie als Vervielfältigungsform verwischt die Grenze zwischen Vorlage und Nachahmung, Original und Kopie sind nicht mehr zu unterscheiden. Dateien, Songs und auch Filme können ohne Qualitätsverlust dupliziert und verbreitet werden—wenn sie einmal, das ist die zweite entscheidende Innovation, von ihrem analogen Datenträger (Vinyl, Papier, Film) gelöst und digitalisiert worden sind. Die digitale Kopie und die Befreiung der Information vom Datenträger bilden die beiden grundlegenden Herausforderungen des Zeitalters, das als Ära der Digitalisierung beschrieben wird—auch für das Urheberrecht. (von Gehlen 2011, 15)

the original, but much on the contrary: the cover adds important layers to the self-conceptualization of a culture and its economy. Yet, the cover has gone through complicated times in the advent of (global) internet culture. Copying entails illegal file sharing and plagiarism—a new version is just one click on the mouse away. Here, Jonathan Sterne underlines the economic value of pirating:[22]

> The mass piracy of music was actually quite productive as an economic force. Record companies may view mass copying as a threat to capitalism, but copying generates all sorts of value for other industries like consumer electronics, broadband, and even other kinds of intellectual property, like the patents on MP3s. Piracy also reveals and calls into question the social organization of music. (Sterne 2012, 188)

But Beck uses *sheet music* to comment on these processes. Sheet music and the manifold incarnations of the songs must be understood as a creative cultural technique and a creative culture of reference (what Dirk von Gehlen calls "kreative Referenzkultur"). Here, Beck draws attention to the cover as a cultural technique and his role of the "author" in "Title of This Song." It is a song written by _____ for _____, with the suggested tempo being _____ (see Figure 3.3). This song in the sheet music collection seems to be so open to interpretation that it does not even need a name, and the reader must quite literally fill in the blanks on the cover. It poses questions about the role of the song reader within the project, and asks us to think further about plagiarism and copying. On its cover, the blanks are filled in with a generic handwriting font to suggest that Beck beat other song readers to the chase. Beck might have hastily filled those blanks out[23] himself, deciding that he wrote the song for piano. It might as well have been written for guitar or xylophone. This suggests that Beck, too, appropriated the song before releasing it under his name within *Song Reader*. From the get go, then, before the song reader even starts learning the song, "Title of This Song" enacts a game between author and song reader. Blanks occur when

---

[22] Vis-à-vis pirating, Jonathan Sterne explains in what way "more recordings now circulate through channels that do not carry the official sanction of recording industries or states. The iTunes store may be the world's largest music retailer, but an extended web of Gnutella and BitTorrent sites and the users who frequent them make up an even larger, transnational swap meet for recordings" (Sterne 2012, 185).

[23] Wolfgang Iser's notion of gaps is illuminating here. Iser claims that "whenever the reader bridges the gaps, communication begins. The gaps function as a kind of pivot on which the whole text-reader relationship revolves. Hence the structured blanks of the text stimulate the process of ideation to be performed by the reader on terms set by the text" (Iser 1978, 169).

Figure 3.3 "Title of This Song" © used with permission by McSweeney's.

something crucial is missing from the text: What is a song without an author, a tempo, let alone an instrument? What kind of communication can emerge now between Beck and the song reader?

The song's title is a meta-comment on nomenclature and authorship; whoever fills in her name into the blanks first on the cover can claim "Title of This Song" as her creation. This makes the design of the cover entirely generic: unlike the other songs in the collection, the cover only includes the name of the song, but no further images or goofy illustrations that set the "mood" for what follows. Beck has said of "Title of This Song": "It was a puzzle, a logic that was convoluted, a tangle of ideas that I had to put to a metre" (Hansen in Barton 2012, n.p.). The lyrics of the song contribute to this ambiguous mode: the song is about the challenges of naming a song, of writing and performing a song that is not your own, and of love that is lost. It mocks the endeavor of *Song Reader* and the spheres in which it could exist and flourish. The "you," the addressee in the song who might or might not be the song reader, has taken the title of the song from "a life that's beyond something that you could belong to" and from "a book that goes on and on till you can't find the ending," and let alone the beginning of it (Hansen 2012d, n.p.). Funerals and weddings happen in the same line and get mixed up, and a bride, whose affection has died, tells a story only in her head. "Title of This Song" is the most open-ended song in the *Song Reader* collection; it explicitly alludes to the object's qualities, or the lack thereof—thus, if there is meta-media, this is a meta-song, a song about the role of the song reader and her plagiarizing efforts. Dirk von Gehlen's ideas about the creative potentials of the copy are undermined, as it can be inferred that the song breaks when the song reader touches it.

Ironically, she must sing a song that mocks her artistic and emotional investment in the project. While I argued earlier that the fan rehearses *Song Reader* as a song reader, "Title of This Song" complicates this very subject position that it encourages. "Title of This Song" warns the song reader of what might happen if and when she invests too much into the songs, because she runs the risk of destroying the song that she has appropriated: "You've taken the notes from your head and played them out loud on a public announcement instead. / 'Cause all of your thoughts get distorted / The feedback goes on and you've ruined the song / While ev'ryone just plays along" (Hansen 2012d, n.p.). Now the notes from her head (i.e., her thoughts, her feelings, her worries) are channeled into a public announcement, while everyone just plays along in the fakery and forgery. "It's only the notes that you've played / that drowned out the thoughts from a song that was lost / And the song you sang it didn't have a name" (Hansen 2012d, n.p.) "Title of This Song" highlights the challenge of relating to something so generic and adaptable: How, in the end, can an individual appropriate the material to make it her own when such appropriation is already built into the object? The most poignant statement might be the refrain of "Title of This Song": "I'm tired of this old refrain / Is the chorus you sang when you had no one to blame / but yourself for singing it all in vain" (Hansen 2012d, n.p.). Thinking back to what Carrie Brownstein claimed about slackerdom and a detached coolness toward stardom, the song reader is *too* invested. She is not "slacker" or cool enough, not sufficiently detached from the project.

"Title of This Song" criticizes an over-enthused song reader and her eagerness to insert herself into the process of creation and creativity. By taking himself out of the picture, Beck communicates, yet again, a diluted notion of authorship and rock stardom. Nineteenth-century sheet music hardly ever credited a composer, but merely the artist/interpreter of the piece: forgotten authorship, a washed-out notion of who wrote the songs originally is one important feature of both sheet music and *Song Reader*—and ultimately copy and paste culture in and of the twenty-first century. These songs are meant to be adapted by a variety of people, but if Beck asks his readers to adapt his songs, why does he claim "Title of This Song" for himself? This suddenly tells a different tale about *Song Reader*: Is this song maybe a found manuscript, a piece of sheet music in a bargain bin, personalized by the one who stumbled upon it? Could Beck himself be just another song reader, on equal footing with every fan who covers his music? The boundaries between author and interpreter become even more opaque, and the infamous death of the author seems both complete and reversed.[24] Beck annuls himself as the author by positioning himself alongside his fans as just another song reader.

"Title of This Song" can therefore be seen as the most straightforward claim that Beck makes in *Song Reader* about not only how the medium easily overhauls and turns against itself but also how the song reader, as curating instance who implements the artist's vision, has to remain aloof and cool to make her subject position work out. The song's generic qualities (no tempo, no author, no title), and its constant references to open-ended ("a book that goes on"), awkward ("The feedback goes on and you've ruined the song / While ev'ryone just plays along"), and public ("You've taken the notes from your head / and played them out loud on a public announcement instead / Cause all of your thoughts get distorted") mediations of the song gesture toward a (fickle) self-referential mediality of sheet music. "Title of This Song" ends, quite literally, with a feedback loop that dwindles out of control to the point of meaninglessness. It is just the "songs we are singing," depraved of meaning and authorship. If and when there is nothing left but the songs we sing, there is not much creative potential left to the copy as a means for innovative, creative cultural referencing that von Gehlen attributes to the cover song. To argue even more forcefully, "Title of This Song" addresses the difficulties of participatory culture in terms of the self and the other "participators"—the many different renditions create a polyphony that is out of sync with the zeitgeist and its peers. No dialogue

---

[24] As Jeffrey Nealon posits, "Postmodernism, performativity, and the death of the author are no longer 'emergent' phenomena, but they've become 'dominant ones' in post-postmodernism" (Nealon 2012, 64). Beck's game of distinction and his status as a marionette speak to this.

is created, much on the contrary, for the question of conceptual art remains imperative here and underlines the implementations of the intertwining of a borrowed voice and an artistic vision.

What a bleak outlook for the career of the song reader and the career of the song itself. While the nineteenth-century idea of sheet music's popularity and a song's success was to travel and to be sung by many, "Title of This Song" makes it clear that the perpetuation of a song can also be an ambiguous, if not precarious way to propel culture forward. Here, I am taking my cues from Igor Kopytoff's idea of the social biography of things and the way it may relate to *Song Reader* (see Kopytoff 1986, 66–67). If the highest goal of an object is to be introduced into a museum, what should the goal of a song be, if it being sung and copied deprives the song of its message? If a dilettante now plays the rock song by a musician such as Beck, whose *Song Reader* fuses effortless cool of his performance with labor and rehearsing, what will happen to the cultural competencies of both author and fan? The main ideas of "Title of This Song," just like most of the sheet music songs collected in *Song Reader*, illuminate how the songs can easily collapse. *Song Reader*, thus, illustrates the curation of the mass medium, not the singularity, and challenges the reader to think about where and how Beck's project can live on. The song reader acknowledges that the value of the work might not lie in her hands, but rather in the question of how an artistic vision is made consumerist. Late-capitalist individualization creates specific niche needs to authenticate the self—individualization and the self are created by consumption and the desire for ever-new commodities. We can infer that the changing media landscape of the twentieth century and also the twenty-first century, alongside with an altered perception of the self, "do something" with and to the medium of sheet music and the audiences and stars it produces and consumes.

The conceptual slacker

Song Reader stretches a tightrope across the chasm between star and audience, inaudible song and a tune that breaks when the song reader implements it: but is it an interrogation of the nature of artwork or the nature of the commodity? Of the star or of the audience? Of passivity embedded within mass culture or of over-eager participation in the digital age? Both Chris Ware and Beck take rarified objects, like a musician's song or a scattered collection of leaflets, and make them everyday consumer objects. This gestures, again, toward Umberto Eco's open work, for *Song Reader* interrogates the "theoretical, mental collaboration of the consumer, who must freely interpret an artistic datum, a product which has already been organized in its structural entirety" (Eco 1989, 11–12). If Beck makes his creative vision available in a bookstore or in an online store, he transgresses several genre boundaries, such as publishing a "mute" rock album and recontextualizing the songs as printed ephemera through outlets that are detached from the music business.

To unpack this, let us briefly return to the early twentieth century and look at the stratification of media in relation to the aforementioned star system that Andreas Reckwitz sees as one quintessential part of the culturalization and commodification processes of creativity (i.e., from the Romantic genius to the consumerist starlet). Sheet music's demise at the beginning of the twentieth century came rather sudden, but not entirely unexpected. The medium fell victim to changing consumer habits and technological innovations; newer technologies, like the phonograph,[25] the radio, magazines, and film, superseded sheet music as a cultural technique, entertainment, and art form. And, as a weird historical side note, a "printer's strike and a paper shortage caused production costs to triple, and almost overnight the phonograph recording replaced sheet music as the chief means of popular music's circulation" (Crawford 1993, 216). Benedict Anderson's imagined community created by print-capitalism fell victim to fires and worn-out fads. Sheet music hence became too expensive and cumbersome to produce and distribute and was just simply not *en vogue* anymore. Also, sheet music presumably did not produce stars the way other media could or, rather, it did not produce the stars that the budding consumer culture asked for.

American middle-class consumers then were "entering a world of mass culture, in which goods—including cultural goods such as sound recordings, forms, and more—were produced and consumed on a scale previously unknown" (Taylor 2012, 3). The United States wanted to shop: a consumer economy emerged that was "facilitated by the rise of new forms of payment, or deferred payment, such as credit and installment-plan purchasing . . . by new forms of retail, such as department stores and chain stores, and the rise of advertising industry" (Taylor 2012, 3). This changing from primarily produced-oriented to consumption-oriented economic structures in the entertainment industry speaks to passive *consumption* of and in culture, how perpetuating culture forward meant to replace the old with the new. Music hence turned into "a commodity and object of consumption" (Taylor 2012, 3). Catapulting culture forward (i.e., the copy), bluntly speaking, meant consuming and replacing, and not appropriating anymore.

---

[25] For more on the phonograph and media changes in the late nineteenth and early twentieth centuries from a media historical point of view, see my introduction, as well as John Durham Peters, *Speaking into the Air* (1999) and Lisa Gitelman, *Scripts, Grooves, and Writing Machines: Representing Technology in the Edison Era* (1999).

Radio stars, rock stars, movie stars, theater stars: the individual-cum-star is turned into such an object of consumption, performing and embodying creativity in the public. As Andreas Reckwitz points out, the budding star system of the early twentieth century has been brought about by media changes and laid the foundation how the "view of the artist expressing herself, her inner ideas and her imagination, in a concrete work makes her a prototype of the self-creating expressive subject" (Reckwitz 2017b, 156). The constitution of the star has been aided, ever since the end of the nineteenth century, by the emergence and dissemination of the "technical, reproductive media of photography, recording, film, television, and more recently, the internet" (Reckwitz 2017b, 157). The star becomes a mobile, reproducible object for the aesthetic projections of the audience. "Despite their recognizability, stars are not fixed subjects but, rather, 'epistemic objects,' constantly transforming themselves in such a way that their audience can never quite pin them down" (Reckwitz 2017b, 158). In turn, and I am most interested in these notions that Reckwitz outlines in regard to the audience, the star "as an object of admiration presupposes the emergence and expansion of [the] observer of the audience" (Reckwitz 2017b, 157). The star is to be seen as an aesthetic *event* and affords affective stimulation; the audience is pinned into a rather passive role of observers. modern capitalist society, since the 1920s, has been trained to "approach human beings as perceptible bodies with faces and voices. . . . On the level of the affects, the relation between the observer and the star image oscillates between two modes: objectification and identification" (Reckwitz 2017b, 159). And, of course, Horkheimer and Adorno in *Dialectic of Enlightenment* draw an even bleaker image of mass culture and the star system.

Song Reader takes this rather peculiar moment of music media history of the twentieth century (i.e., the demise of sheet music, shift toward consumption rather than production) as reference point to comment on the star system and the value of creativity in mass culture in the twentieth century. Sheet music was pushed to the margins by a budding consumer culture that turned to newer other forms of entertainment. Sheet music's demise happened right on the threshold of this new system, and Beck releases an album as sheet music that alludes to this moment of the history of mass culture and media changes that call for an individual to be associated with a work of art. In this sense, Beck now resuscitates an outdated medium *by way of* digitization processes. If and when music had been turned into a "passive" commodity, and not a piece of art by an ingénue, Beck undermines the album's status once again and makes his creative vision an interactive experience within the digital era.

We may recognize how the passivity of the audience in the star system and the conceptual angle of *Song Reader* congeal. *Song Reader* turns the product (the star, the album, the CD) into a process of objectification and identification—and, in the next instance, this process into a concept to be implemented.

When approached through this lens of the concept album, *Song Reader* becomes an intriguing thought experiment about participation in an artistic vision, which is, then again, embedded in the practices of mass culture. *Song Reader* initiates a dialogue between the conceptual and the consumable and illuminates how these distinctions become contested, but maybe also porous. Yet, it seems as if the snake bites its own tail: Beck's creative vision turns into a malleable, interactive *process* between author and reader, and reader and material. Its material "loosening up" further accentuates this, for it is— similar to *Building Stories*—a jumbled mess of loose leaflets, of pop songs stuck in a silent medium. Nonetheless the song reader also needs to care for the creative vision of the artist, and she must rehearse and appropriate a catalog of ready-made options into a unified vision that is labeled "Song Reader." So what to do? "Title of This Song" will crumble no matter what, and the curator comes to the fore and with a vengeance: the preset components help her adopt a vision that is dependent on her own skill set, yet that gives credit to the star, Beck.

We can further inquire into questions of how and why the project remains merely conceptual or tedious to implement. If and when the artwork becomes conceptual à la Marcel Duchamp or Jeff Koons, the spectator is not invited to participate. She simply cannot, because the everyday object has now been elevated into the field of art, put on display in a museum. This changes the economic context of an everyday, consumer object like a urinal (Marcel Duchamp) or a basketball (Jeff Koons) or a can opener (à la *Gift Time Is All the Time*) and illuminates how boundaries between art and consumerism become contested, not only in the digital moment. This does not, per se, amount to a reflection upon institutional critique or the transgression of the medium. Yet Beck's *Song Reader* (the inaudible song by the avant-garde artist) becomes consumerist for a specific consumer group that is "in the know." The previously distant spectator of celebrity culture (i.e., one that is fascinated with Beck as a rock star) and fan is now invited to participate in high culture; yet Beck's *Song Reader* may not even be meant for performance, but unfolds in the song reader's hands through its inaccessibility. In what way Beck emerges as a conceptual artist in the vein of Marcel Duchamp is up for speculation, but *Song Reader* simultaneously de- and recontextualizes the song into a consumerist mass-produced object that everybody can sing along to.

To return to Dirk von Gehlen, the copy/the cover song is a technique to perpetuate culture forward, and, to argue even more forcefully, it undermines singularities and authentic experiences. What a perplexing parallel development in the twenty-first century: mass products offer up unique experiences while unique experiences become reproducible and consumerist. What emerges is a contorted, möbius-strip-like inversion of the consumer, seeking both an extension of the self through consumption, yet likewise seeking singular, authentic objects to complete the curation of the self. In the dimensions of *Song Reader*, the song reader must see herself in context within a larger fan base of song readers, in which her "unique" experience of rehearsing and sifting through *Song Reader* turns into a (imagined) duplicating of unique experiences. Curating here is therefore based on implementing the conceptual vision of *Song Reader* and the experience of the production and rehearsing of a song—to be "in the know," and to fallaciously cash out of the mass consumer market, by, well, engaging in it.

By drawing parallels to this mass culture moment in the 1920s and interrogating his slacker stardom through an obsolete medium, Beck examines how music is consumed, produced, perpetuated in the 2010s. What we can distill from this discussion is how the singular, rarified object turns into a copy of itself—both consumerist and artistic, a cover song and a unique experience. *Song Reader* illuminates processes that stage dialogic relations between the conceptual and the consumer, in the twentieth and in the twenty-first centuries. Sheet music remains in transition, and of course large parts of participatory culture today are located within online spheres, and the publisher McSweeney's could not imagine Beck's project without an online presence—a new realm into which the distant, passive audience can project affective responses toward the reluctant star, Beck Hansen.

The online archive and its digital ruins

As the discussion of music's materialities has shown, today we think of music as instantly accessible and available. In online streams, we encounter the figurative, digital version of Reynolds's and Bauman's notions of liquidization. Platforms such as YouTube and Spotify have brought forth new ways to consume, share, create, and experience music. YouTube especially creates a community of those who are eager to fill in gaps that previous, older, less flexible media have created. Simon Reynolds writes that "YouTube serves as both major player and potent symbol: the astronomic expansion of humanity's resources of memory. We have available to us, as individuals, but also at the level of civilisation, immensely more 'space' to fill with memorabilia, documentation, recordings, every kind of archival trace of our existence" (Reynolds 2011, 56). The website requires competency at navigating the apparently endless possibilities of digital memory; it is "a field of cultural practice, remediation, post-broadcasting" (Reynolds 2011, 59). Rare live appearances and b-sides are suddenly unearthed and uploaded for the users to sift through; quality and convenience are flattened and the user is often asked to ignore sound and video quality in the upload comments. YouTube has become an expansive cultural space that underlines how we do not archive[26] but much rather document our lives and our commodities (i.e., shopping haul videos, unboxing videos, movie trailers, reviews, and, of course, music).

If the phonograph or the radio contributed to the demise of sheet music in the twentieth century, digitization processes undoubtedly changed the media landscape yet again, causing the demise of the Compact Disc or the cassette. YouTube's economy takes shape around the new and the old: the past seems to be instantly accessible, for it intertwines with the present like never before on the sidebar where rare live footage, b-sides, forgotten video clips are unearthed and mingle with ads or popular new videos. The past seems to be copy-paste-able, or at least upload-able. The website seems like a final resting place for many songs and albums. The messiness of YouTube shows how music occupies virtual spaces differently, sometimes chaotically. The challenges of recreating and storing *Song Reader*'s experience online taps right into these characteristics of YouTube's random, cluttered access to memories and our desire to keepsake oddities and rarities. As much as Beck sees the value of learning a song as a "material" (qua offline) experience for oneself, one that has been largely lost in the moment of digitized music; it is, after all, the experiences we share and upload that have become the main currency of our digital lives. The years 2010 and 1850 no longer seem so far apart. In both times, both forms speak to a disposition to collaborate and to share, to categorize and to consume, to experience and to be communal. Anderson's communities once imagined become virtually visible and connected. Yet, there is something irreconcilable with *Song Reader*'s online and offline possibilities, and their collision produces productive questions vis-à-vis the role of the distant spectator now turned into *Song Reader* archivist.

---

[26] For more on archives, see Derrida (1996), Foster (2010), and Foucault (1972). The question of digital archives is explored in Ernst (2013), Manoff (2004, 2006), and Schwartz and Cook (2002).

Why does *Song Reader* not proliferate and spread online? Bluntly speaking: Why has it been so invisible digitally? This becomes clear when turning to the platform songreader.net, a website that has been created solely to archive *Song Reader* renditions online. While YouTube merely documents and stores data, the platform songreader.net accumulates versions of Beck's songs and makes them accessible and navigable to other song readers; the front page says, "Only you can bring Beck Hansen's *Song Reader* to life. Download select sheet music and share your interpretation here" ("Beck—Song Reader" 2012, n.p.). Another tagline says, "Take It and Make It Your Own" ("Beck—Song Reader" 2012, n.p.) These are tempting imperatives: People interested in the project can download MIDIs of the songs for Apple's app Garageband and watch other people's videos (arranged in categories, i.e., most popular or the individual song titles). It seems as though the marketing team at McSweeney's was under the impression that *Song Reader* could not function as a stand-alone object but needed a digital companion piece to encourage people to engage in the project. The website makes visible a tension inherent to *Song Reader*: while its textual, material form takes the songs offline, it is at the same time primarily envisioned and marketed online. Jody Rosen facetiously suggests that we "have returned to the parlor room, with the laptop camera taking the place of the upright piano" (Rosen 2012, n.p.). The keys of the piano are now the keys of the song reader's computer.

But what exactly happens on songreader.net if we speak of shortcomings? When clicking through the website, something seems peculiar: No "upload" or "share your cover" button entices the song reader to upload her rendition, but it appears as if an algorithm mines YouTube and other video platforms to unearth covers by fans and musicians. But what was once envisioned as a closed-off archive for *Song Reader* songs is permeated by a ceaseless flood of YouTube driftwood. Between the cover versions, there are clips of teenagers who goof around in front of a webcam, of a stop-motion video that tells the story of a sunbathing potato, of a baby who refuses to eat food, of a person falling off a Segway, of a tutorial for the computer game Minecraft, among many other apparently unrelated videos. Relying on algorithms in lieu of curation, songreader.net seems like a jumbled website that hardly speaks to the mission of *Song Reader* and its neighbor *Building Stories*, which both hope for a curating and collecting hand to take care of its legacy. Particularly because *Song Reader* as a material object is such a meticulously designed object, the wild archive of songreader.net seems like an accident. The website actually documents the failures of the archive, the "most recent" videos and soundcloud clips are awkwardly mixed up with those from years ago. Many *Song Reader* renditions on YouTube are not even caught by the algorithm of the website. What is the logic that interweaves the sunbathing potato with "Title of This Song," or teenagers goofing around with "Why Did You Make Me Care"? The carefully curated universe that the advertisements and sheet music aesthetics created now go awry in a blur of Segway accidents.

To return to the case of "Title of This Song," we see a very problematic existence of the song on the online platform. About thirty cover versions of "Title of This Song" are filtered either as YouTube clips (visual) or as soundcloud snippets (audio). The same cover versions appear on different pages again, repeating themselves and just being contingently mixed with other songs (which, to relish in the poetic irony of it, speaks to "Title of This Song"). Most icons bear the generic cover (or other cover pages from other sheet music songs), others show screenshots of the videos (a smoking person wearing an alien mask, instruments, or, again, the sunbathing potato). The site intended for *Song Reader* connoisseurs has been turned into a platform that offers an illogical catalog of files that cannot support any legible form of community. Most importantly, there is no dialogue: even if people can add comments or "heart" for the song (click a little heart symbol to show their appreciation of the song), hardly anybody has done so (the "most popular" videos of "Title of This Song" have generated six hearts; hardly anybody has left a comment on a soundcloud clip. This is systemic: the most popular video on the website generated "only" eighty-three hearts). Unlike YouTube, songreader.net does not lure its audience "away" or draws their attention to a new clip, a new movie trailer, a new "suggested video" outside of the spheres of the enclosed *Song Reader* universe. There is no sidebar that embeds the *Song Reader* videos into a larger scheme of documentation or alludes to a space outside of its confines.

In this way, songreader.net is a chaotic, disorganized archive—closed off, relying on an algorithm that was meant to retrieve every *Song Reader* rendition, but instead allows random videos, audio files, and images to infiltrate Beck's music project. Just like "Title of This Song" already suggested, the archive has collapsed upon itself. It is a diluted scrapbook that has been infiltrated with unrelated contents. To this end, songreader.net exemplifies how contents move across cultural landscapes and contexts, yet not to the extent that the utopian vision of instant sharing and participatory culture in the digital spheres might suggest. What, then, if *Song Reader* remains simply recalcitrant to these practices, not intended to be embedded into larger social networks? Instead, it is targeted toward a coterie who wants to be visible to one another, yet it does not provide "share" buttons. Does this suggest that the imagined community of song readers is too cool to go digital and archive their cover versions? What if songreader.net is merely a graveyard for audiovisual ephemeralities? What shines through, in the end, is that the participating fan and the distant spectator go hand in hand, for internet tumbleweed and rapid media overhaul have won: as of spring 2017, songreader.net seems to be defunct—my browser tries to connect, but there seems no response to the server. *Song Reader* did not leave behind digital ruins but vanished altogether in the ether of the internet.

Slacker competence

In February 2016, a triumvirate consisting of Sir Paul McCartney, Taylor Hawkins (the drummer of the Foo Fighters), and Beck was denied access to a Grammy aftershow party in Los Angeles. Incredulous at the stubbornness of the bouncer (or maybe his ignorance who he was turning away from the door), Sir Paul McCartney half-mockingly asked his fellow rock stars: "How VIP do we gotta get? We need another hit!" A paparazzo filmed the embarrassing incident, and the scene at the nightclub door made headlines the following day because the bouncer did not recognize the famous ex-Beatle. Yet, there was no mention of Taylor Hawkins or Beck Hansen. This speaks toward the way that, despite media saturation, the rock star of the 1990s and early 2000s has become a mysterious stranger. Ultimately, this is what Beck comments upon in *Song Reader*. Not only does he test the fictional and material limits of music, but the fiction of the rock star as well. On the one hand "Beck" is steeped in mystery and obscurity: if bouncers do not recognize him anymore, Beck, too, might "need another hit," because the stardom he evokes with his public persona and *Song Reader* feels like it comes from another era, like a book competing against an LCD screen, to paraphrase Caroline Hamilton. It is here where the marionette meets the star system of the early twentieth century, and we can wonder who, really, the puppet is: the song reader or the rock star?

The medium of sheet music ultimately raises claims toward the fragility of the star system and audiences. The creative designing of the song reader now also reaches her creative investment in envisioning the rock star that Beck is. To idolize a rock star, it seems, also requires creative labor (i.e., collecting records, collaging pictures from magazines, going to concerts). The song reader must acknowledge Beck's role as both puppet and puppeteer, as a distant spectator and creative genius, as artistic persona and foil at the same time. To this end, the Japanese media artist Ham uploaded a tutorial onto her website to create a cut out version of Beck and one of his band members. I believe the cut out encapsulates perfectly what is at stake here. Similar to

Chris Ware's strategies in *Jimmy Corrigan*, "Beck" is something the fan needs to cut out and build in order to bring him into existence (see Figures 3.4 and 3.5). He is both brand and phantom, and to hold him in our hands, we need to first create him.

Song Reader's mission is the creative design of both the song reader *and* of Beck, because the subject position of the song reader and Beck himself comes to life only through the investment of the fan. *Song Reader* is a strange game of distinction and competence: on the one hand, the song reader must acknowledge that she will never be able to obtain Beck's cultural capital (i.e., he goes clubbing with Sir Paul McCartney!) and that she will never stand on stage with a laissez-faire attitude (i.e., the gender divide of male breezy rock star and female affective labor) or sing the songs the way only Beck could (i.e., the shortcomings of the songreader.net platform), plus she cannot slack like Beck does. On the other hand, though, Beck acknowledges that his rock stardom is a fiction and that he serves as nothing but a projection screen for our creativity, that he facilitates and enables our analog engagement with music in digital times. Not only do work and leisure conflate but also dream and reality: we hold in our hands our own little DIY rock star kit, approved by "Beck Hansen."

Figure 3.4 Hambeck's "Paper Beck and with Cameron" (2009) © by Ham, used with permission by the artist.

Figure 3.5 Step-by-step manual to assemble Paper Beck © Ham, used with permission by the artist.

This object of inquiry presses on contemporary modes of competence. The reader must identify *Song Reader* as a part of the McSweeney's universe or as a new Beck album, but she must also display that she "gets it" and that she can navigate the self-referential system and universe that *Song Reader* has become. The doubling of this very specific, highly specialized competence—

of understanding what *Song Reader* is as an album/as an object and *also* being skilled and talented enough to play the songs—lies at *Song Reader*'s core. This model of doubled aptitude helps illuminate texts such as *Building Stories* and *Kentucky Route Zero*: the reader has to understand and categorize what is happening within the confines of *Song Reader* and must demonstrate a certain "*Song Reader* competence" or even "Beck competence," just as much as she must attain a "*Building Stories* competence" or "*Kentucky Route Zero* competence." She must navigate the fictional universe with a cool detachment and smug irony, reveling in her role as the distant audience member. Ultimately, then, *Song Reader* and its song readers tap into how creativity is figured within the cultural moment, how the subject is both encouraged and condemned to be creative, self-sufficient, able to align and disband with others, to practice and appropriate, to create something that both *is* and is *not* of her own making. Fandom has been now refigured as unpaid labor, but what happens when we fail to work *Song Reader* out, fail to understand its ironic play on a previous medium, or simply cannot play an instrument?

Beck would argue that failing or refusing to engage is a legitimate response to his project (i.e., the slacker position). The French film maker Michel Gondry's comment on Beck's *modus operandi* is a nice addendum to what happens to the song reader: Beck "talked about the imperfection, clumsiness, and unassuming qualities that make debut work so special, and often cannot be surpassed when skill walks in" (Gondry in Wilde 2011, n.p.). *Not* being competent in working out *Song Reader* is, paradoxically, another legitimate competence to *Song Reader*. To be aesthetically amused by *Song Reader*'s gestures toward times past or to the empty gestures of rock stardom seem to be as important as playing the songs and uploading them onto YouTube or rehearsing them with friends. *Not* being able to decipher the notes on the page or to laugh at *Song Reader*'s jokes, even if this runs contrary to what Pierre Bourdieu would see as art competence, is another way of engaging with the music, another response to the project, another encounter with the object. This resistant form of engagement is something we might call *slacker competence*. Thus, with *Song Reader*, creativity can be purchased, and the song reader reaches its apogee when she refuses to engage, when she becomes a slacker herself. The song reader can be the marionette, but she can also be the ventriloquist. How can we trace and characterize the highly skilled yet bored slacker laborer that Beck envisions his fans to be? The song reader is encouraged to bring the project to life, but, really, she can also just let it be. Whatever.

4
Kentucky Route Zero's Netherworld of Slowness

In his unfinished *Arcades Projects* Walter Benjamin watches flâneurs closely, those cosmopolitan figures who take slow walks through the arcades with turtles on a leash: "In 1839, a rage for tortoises overcame Paris. One can well imagine the elegant set mimicking the pace of this creature more easily in the arcades than on the boulevards" (Benjamin 1999, 106). To Benjamin, it is a way of showing that one has the luxury to let a turtle set the pace for one's day (see Benjamin 1999, 834). And about 180 years later, in 2018, the arcades of the internet are populated by flâneurs who luxuriously lounge in the digital ether of twitter time lines and sub-reddits and who walk a different animal on an imaginary leash: the chaperone of the digital flâneur[1] is the sloth. Sloths are all the rage, and in an endless stream of YouTube clips and animated .GIFs popping up in newsfeeds, sloths hang from trees or eat hibiscus leaves, with a knowing smile on their face. With calm indolence, the sloth has all the time on the World Wide Web.

The sloth denies immediacy: it subverts quick loading times but toys with slow buffering on fast devices. A sloth .GIF on a high-end cellphone defers closure and sets the rhythm on timelines: slow, repetitive movements

---

[1] For Walter Benjamin, the street

> conducts the flâneur into a vanished time. For him, every street is precipitous. It leads downward—if not to the mythical Mothers, then into a past that can be all the more spellbinding because it is not his own, not private. Nevertheless, it always remains the time of a childhood. But why that of the life he has lived? In the asphalt over which he passes, his steps awaken a surprising resonance. The gaslight that streams down on the paving stones throws an equivocal light on this double ground. (Benjamin 1999, 416)

This modern urban figure of the nineteenth century gains new traction as a postmodern social figure; Zygmunt Bauman is interested in the flâneur, the vagabond, and the tourist:

> Like his hope, the *flâneur* wants to be wide open and unprejudiced: he hopes to re-open the options that have been closed, to tear off the labels of class, status, or trade, to be once more innocent and innocently receptive. . . . The *flâneur* lives his life as a succession of absolute beginnings From the past, there is an easy exit; the present is just a gateway; the future is not yet, and what is not yet cannot bind. (Bauman 1994, 139)

mirror the internet user's repetitive clicking, swiping, typing. While we flip through the web with a quick flick of the thumb, sloth content defers and delays; a sloth can stretch and distort time.[2] The flipside of this fascination with the slow sloth indexes that the internet user always already anticipates a kernel of slowness within the device she holds in her hands to browse the web. While a fast internet connection helps watch a YouTube clip of a sloth more fluently, it does not make it move any faster. The internet user's smittenness with the sloth can be read as one symptom of Lutz Koepnick's diagnosis that Western society suffers from too much speed. Slowness marks a counterbalancing to a perceived acceleration of cultural and social dynamics[3] and the evanescence of information and substance in the digital era. Koepnick explains how "we no longer take the time to contemplate an image, develop a profound thought, traverse a gorgeous landscape, play a game, or follow the intensity of some emotion. Life is faster today than it has ever been before, it is concluded, but in accumulating ever more impressions, events, and stimulations we end up with ever less" (Koepnick 2014, 1).

Neither passivity nor boredom,[4] but slowness can offer a key to understanding curatorial reading practices in the twenty-first century, be this the entanglement of domestic activities (the slow learning of a song) or digital routines (the buffering of a YouTube clip, mindless browsing at 2 am in the morning). Similarly to Ngai's aesthetic categories that have guided my readings of *Building Stories* and *Song Reader*, inquiries into the aesthetic category of slowness untangle the confluence of rapid capitalism,

---

[2] The sloth as the digital animal of the twenty-first century broadly relates to other cultural phenomena, ranging from decluttering to "simplify your life," from slow food to mindfulness. These phenomena cater to such fascination with slowness in everyday routines.

[3] Sociologist Hartmut Rosa has been invested in theorizing (social) acceleration and its influence on the changing structures of time in (late) modernity; see Rosa and Scheuerman (2009) and Rosa (2013). Paul Virilio in the 1970s saw the logic of speed not only as one of the foundational aspects of a technological society but also as an engine for destruction and militarization, see here Virilio (2006). Further reading includes Armen Avanessian's edited volume *#Akzeleration* (2013). For speed, late modernity, and its influence on changing sleep patterns, see Crary (2014).

[4] A word about boredom: The word itself has only been lexicalized in the nineteenth century, and this testifies to the modern nature of the phenomenon and mood. Yet, there is nothing like "boredom studies," but a plethora of philosophical reflections on boredom and acadia do exist. For more, see Busch (2012); Martin Heidegger's lecture on different kinds of boredom in relation to Dasein (das Gelangweiltwerden von etwas, das Sichlangweilen bei etwas, and die tiefe Langeweile als das 'es ist einem langweilig') in Heidegger (1983); a more literary approach offers Patricia Meyer Spacks (1995); a beautiful collection of quotes by many different philosophers offers the weekly newsletter *Brain Pickings Weekly*, see Popova (2015).

neoliberalism, globalization, as well as consumption habits and media interaction: slow denotes a *Kippbild*, similarly to cuteness or zaniness, of capitalist activity in the twenty-first century that marks the luxury of deceleration entwined with the deferral of the luxury of immediacy (something we might describe as aggressive impatience).

I argue in my introduction that the internet seduces us into thinking that it might be boundless or infinite (but never slow!). These dichotomies between finitude and openness, between haptic and digital, meaningful experience and banal routines are among the most significant characteristics of media interaction made open and strange by Chris Ware and Beck Hansen. *Song Reader* and *Building Stories* rely on haptic interaction and remain decidedly offline and recalcitrant toward digital translations. Further, *Building Stories* and *Song Reader* presuppose a readership that contemplates the *slow* progression of the panels in Chris Ware or likewise indulges in the tedious intensity of learning one of Beck Hansen's sheet music songs. Both objects are deeply invested in the subversion of quick market overhauls and obsolescence by staging themselves as collector's items (i.e., their media-specific affordances, the tossed-out newspaper or the sheet music leaflet picked up at a flea market). Unlike sheet music or comic ephemera reminiscent of early twentieth-century mass media, the medium of the computer is already steeped in late-capitalist logics. Particularly the rise of the personal computer in the late 1980s and 1990s speaks to a confluence of hyper-capitalism and self-expression and curation. For this last chapter, then, I am invested in the subversion and "strange-making" of the medium of the computer—by way of the computer.

The computer game *Kentucky Route Zero*, a retro point-and-click computer game by the game developing company Cardboard Computer Inc., illuminates the tension between the finitude of the internet and the seemingly unlimited, interactive possibilities with the computer, indexing the meaningful interaction between reader[5] and game and the *banality* of the experience per se. *Kentucky Route Zero* replicates online interaction on twenty-first-century devices through broken computers and slow machines, and I read *Kentucky Route Zero* as a subversion of both the genre of the point-and-click game and the medium it is embedded in. By both prolonging time and (fictionally!) breaking the computer it runs on, *Kentucky Route Zero* does something weird and strange to the device that must not fail us. I argue

---

[5] I decide to call the player of *Kentucky Route Zero* a reader, for the game privileges reading over "using" the computer game. I acknowledge that the choice of words bears consequences, but "reader" is a better-suited term for the curatorial positioning toward the object than user.

that the game gestures toward how its reading- and/or gaming experience interrogates art in the digital age—one that the curator has to download, install, load, save, and perhaps even cheat through—all with the click of a finger on the trackpad or the computer mouse.

The game incorporates games-within-games and a meandering plot that, weirdly, does not lead anywhere. It reads like a Southern Gothic novel while employing a gaming tradition that borrows from LucasArts games like *Day of the Tentacle* or text-based early interactive computer games such as *Zork* or *Adventure*. At one point, the computer game even crashes entirely, and the reader, by way of the characters she controls on the screen, has to fix her own computer to continue the story. In this sense, *Kentucky Route Zero* distorts and subverts the medium of the computer and its temporalities, creating a mise-en-abyme that is frustrating and slow. It layers a slow computer game into a fast device and filters media interaction by way of a retro-fitted computer game that is then shifted back onto a state-of-the-art device.[6] This medial and temporal mise-en-abyme is part and parcel of the medial and cultural work *Kentucky Route Zero* performs: it privileges the individualized experience of the reader over the end product, and yet the gaming experience relies on detours and errors. The computer game journalist Dan Whitehead points out that the game is released from "the expected right/wrong structure of traditional gameplay, you're freed to approach the game like a shot of sipping bourbon—slowly savouring [sic] the taste, taking it at your own pace, relaxing into the experience without expectation" (Whitehead 2013, n.p.). Whitehead's comment (particularly the "bourbon" part) carries gendered, elitist assumptions about who will play the game, yet this "experience without expectation" unshackles the reader from the burden to make the "right" choice.

The computer game's genesis is marked similarly by delays and detours. *Kentucky Route Zero* is set to be released in five installments over the span of several years. Acts I–IV have already been released on online platforms such as Steam, and the final act is expected to see the day of light at the end of 2018. In early 2011, *Kentucky Route Zero* was crowdfunded through the website kickstarter.com. Within a month, the developing team consisting of Jake Elliott, Tamas Kemenczy, and Ben Babbitt received $8,583 for the implementation of the game, though they asked for only $6,000 from supporters and potential customers. By doing so, the

---

[6] Nintendo recently announced the adaptation of *Kentucky Route Zero* for one of its latest consoles, *Switch*, which gives indication that *Kentucky Route Zero* will be available for another medium/console, and, ultimately, for a broader audience. I will gesture toward *Switch* and Nintendo *Labo* in the coda.

game developers embedded the game in common twenty-first-century infrastructure for the production and consumption of (digital) games, like Kickstarter projects and online downloading platforms. But things do not always go so smoothly: Cardboard Computer long struggled with the implementation of Act IV and every once in a while posted apologetic tweets on their twitter account, much to the chagrin of impatient fans. Maybe this delay (and the *sprezzatura* of the developers) speaks to how the pastime gaming can be made unusual and weird, unmoored from the traditional infrastructures and connotations gaming takes up in today's culture (i.e., "blockbuster" video games, add-on game patches, browser in-games).

The game puts emphasis on the way media-bending facilitates the cross-pollination between theater, art, literature, and computer game. Interactivity here is evoked through intertextual references, making the computer (and gaming on it) peculiar and idiosyncratic. In addition to the five acts, for instance, the programming company released shorter, free games on the website to bridge the waiting period between the main acts. *The Entertainment* is an interactive theater production that the reader has to put on; *Limits & Demonstrations* is a retrospective/interactive installation for one of the characters' artwork; *Here and There Along the Echo—A Guide to the Echo River for Drifters and Pilgrims* is a pink telephone on which the reader has to make phone calls.[7] This already gives indication what gaming in the Cardboard Computer universe entails.[8]

Reconfiguring the act of reading as a *game* in itself "weirds" and "makes strange" the medium it harnesses as a narrative device. The game diagnoses shifting parameters in regard to reading *as* interaction with art in the digital age. The aesthetic experiences that the game makes available—disorientation and disarray—and the medial questions it evokes draw a picture of how the reader meanders, like a flâneur, through stories, through media, through art. Reading, here, is culturally coded as slow, and makes us "say to ourselves 'Oh, this feels drawn out'—even at the risk of boring us. Herein lies the deep divide: on one hand aesthetic forms in which time is neutral or invisible; on the other

---

[7] In order to make the boundaries between game and reality even blurrier, the production company auctioned off an actual pink telephone on eBay. The computer-generated telephone, rendered digitally, suddenly occupied a virtual market place as an actual object.

[8] Particularly questions of narrative structures in computer games have arisen in the advent of games such as *Life Is Strange*, *The Stanley Parable*, or *Braid* and challenge seriality and temporalities. *Kentucky Route Zero* and its niche status generates budding academic interest in light of its disarraying gaming experience (see Mitchell 2014) and the challenges of character development throughout the game (see Joyce 2016).

those in which tempo, whether fast or slow, makes itself integral to the work" (Reed 2017, 19). Through the connotation of slow and detailed reading[9] on a decelerated machine, the game extends questions of obsolescence and nostalgia in a Kentuckian (post-)capitalist cultural moment.

Nostalgic deferral, deferring nostalgia

Kentucky Route Zero draws a dystopian vision of a post-industrial United States of America. Internet-less, dark, and slow, it is a desolate, interactive version of long-gone American prosperity. The game introduces Conway as its protagonist, a deliveryman working for *Lysette's Antiques*. Conway comes across as a solemn *Death of a Salesman* figure, and his last job before being laid off is to deliver a mysterious package (which is never seen, but remains in the back of the truck[10]) to a peculiar address he has never heard of: "5 Dogwood Drive." This address is nowhere to be found in Kentucky. In the course of the first act, Conway learns that there is a parallel underground network running underneath Kentucky, called "The Zero." And 5 Dogwood Drive is located on this netherworld highway. Conway sets out to find Dogwood Drive, and in the course of the game, more and more characters join Conway's quest: drifters, ghosts, and, naturally, academics, who all seem lost and lonely in dark and solemn Kentucky. The "elegant set" of people in the Parisian arcades are now working-class Kentuckians: slow, unbound, and aimless, desperately trying to make ends meet. The flâneur is not the emblem of modernity in the way that Walter Benjamin or Charles Baudelaire understood it. In the twenty-first century, flânerie is a cultural practice of figures of the "Make American Great Again" era who walk aimlessly through a post-industrial landscape. They embody the flipside of the luxury that nineteenth-century

---

[9] This attention toward miniscule details and everyday life already comes into focus in the very first scene of the game: Conway arrives at a gas station to ask for the way to Dogwood Drive. In this scene, attention is placed upon the naming of the dog, of reading emails, of fixing the power generator rather than to solving riddles or other components of point-and-click games the reader might anticipate—thus, it attends to everyday life (even though Conway meets *ghosts* who play a board game in the basement). Yet it should not be mistaken for a "slow-motion version of postmodern life," but it acknowledges "patterns and practices, like others in contemporary culture, are non-synchronous, albeit deliberately and consciously" (Parkins and Craig 2006, 3).

[10] The mysterious suitcase, box, trunk, or package that might bring misery and death is a reoccurring trope in film noir and its neo-noir incarnations. Movies such as *Kiss Me Deadly* (the box carries an atom bomb and detonates at the end of the movie) and *Pulp Fiction* (what the suitcase's yellow shimmer is . . . nobody knows), as well as in movies like *Raiders of the Lost Ark* (the opening of the Ark) and *Repo Man* (the opening of the trunk of the car results in death) employ this motif.

flânerie afforded; they have too much time and nowhere to go—*Muße haben* turns into *müßig gehen*.

The game carefully sets up a social diorama of the lives of members of the American working class.[11] The characters of *Kentucky Route Zero* have financial problems and live in broken-down buildings, drive shabby trucks, and have been out of their job for a long time. As Jake Elliott, who is one member of the programming team, points out in an interview with Nathan Grayson, one question that *Kentucky Route Zero* tackles is how people go into debt and how they cope with their financial and personal hardships: "It's about different ways that people deal with hard times, and the different ways that economic downturns affect people who live at the margins, who are disempowered, and how they make use of those situations or how they deal with those situations. And also this idea of debt is a really central theme of it" (Elliott 2013a, n.p.). *Kentucky Route Zero*'s characters are burdened with "contemporary tragedies: debt, predatory lending, people being displaced from their homes" (Elliott in Rougeau 2013, n.p.). To underline the despair of the characters, the game is set exclusively at dusk and nighttime (and underground: in caves, in underground factories / distilleries). Unlike *Building Stories*' characters, who are round and soft and have no sharp edges, *Kentucky Route Zero*'s characters seem to have been put together by geometrical shapes—squares, circles, oblongs; they do not have faces and look rather rudimentary—recognizable, but without distinct features.

As much as the game formally aligns itself with earlier incarnations of text-based and point-and-click computer games, there are no puzzles to be solved like in a traditional point-and-click adventure game. *Kentucky Route Zero*'s strategy relies on disorientation and getting lost in small talk. As much as Conway's quest to find Dogwood Drive rings up quest tales such as Homer's epic poem *The Odyssey* and even Thomas Pynchon's postmodern novel *The Crying of Lot 49*, it similarly underlines the burden of choice (i.e., experience without expectation). In Pynchon's novel, the protagonist Oedipa Maas faces a similar conundrum. She is obsessed with the underground mail delivery system Trystero. But as she accumulates more and more clues and piles up more evidence for the existence of said

---

[11] Elliott expresses the necessity to embed marginalized, financially disadvantaged characters into a medium that has gained traction within the last decades. He explains to Michael Rougeau that he and his programming partner Tamas Kemenczy

> spend a lot of time down in that part of the country visiting family, so it's pretty close personally for us. There's a lot of stereotypes about the south and Kentucky . . . it's a lot more real for us than some of these stereotypes. The portrayal of southern characters in video games has been pretty bad so far, generally speaking. (Elliott in Rougeau 2013, n.p.)

secret network, her search is turned into absurdity, mirroring the reader's futile efforts to make sense of Pynchon's complex novel.[12] Oedipa might be closer to understanding who she is at the end of the novel, yet the last scene cuts off the very crying of lot 49. Similarly, *Kentucky Route Zero* sends off its protagonist (and its readership) on a never-ending journey through the American netherworld.[13]

Kentucky Route Zero's strategy of deferral is crucial on medial and narrative levels. The infinite deferral of Conway's mission makes the moment of nostalgic "homecoming" seem impossible. It is in line with what Svetlana Boym defines as a marker of restorative nostalgia,[14] for it "is more oriented towards an individual narrative that savors details and memorial signs, yet perpetually defers homecoming itself" (Boym 2007, 15). The game feels deeply nostalgic for a time and place that cannot be restored. Interestingly it also codifies nostalgia for outdated *technology*. The game, designed to look retro, is set in a time that is distinctly "pre-internet," devoid of twenty-first-century cultural markers. Nostalgia

---

[12] Aside from the similarities to Thomas Pynchon's novel, the developers have drawn on American Gothic fiction writers like Tennessee Williams, William Faulkner, Carson McCullers, Arthur Miller, and Flannery O'Connor for literary inspiration (see Elliott 2013a, n.p.). For its circular structure (some scenes are repeated from a different angle), *Kentucky Route Zero* draws on James Joyce's *A Portrait of the Artist as a Young Man* (i.e., Stephen Dedalus's circular epiphanies), Thomas Pynchon's *Gravity's Rainbow* (whose novel ends with the detonation of the 000001 that Roger and Jessica witness at the near-beginning of the novel, I think) or David Foster Wallace's *Infinite Jest* (whose novel ends with the beginning and begins with Hal Incandenza's end). Similarly, these novels in themselves are overwhelming as aesthetic experiences.

[13] The game dreams up a mythological past of the American South in which gigantic eagles fly around and people cross fated rivers, similar to Styx or Lethe, or, like Huckleberry Finn, the Mississippi. This is the self-description of the game, as published on the Nintendo website:

> An antique furniture delivery man trying to make his small shop's last delivery gets lost along the way and meets a haunted TV repairwoman, a young boy and his giant eagle brother, a pair of robot musicians, and dozens of other characters. Together, they explore the nocturnal highways and country roads of Kentucky, the storied Echo River by ferry, and the mysterious Route Zero, the secret highway that runs through Mammoth Cave. ("Kentucky Route Zero: TV Edition" 2018, n.p.)

[14] In "Nostalgia and Its Discontents," Svetlana Boym distinguishes between restorative and reflective nostalgia. There is a difference between dwelling in *algia* (loss and longing) and *nostos*, the idea of returning home after a long journey; reflective nostalgia "is concerned with historical and individual time, with the irrevocability of the past and human finitude. Re-flection means new flexibility, not the reestablishment of stasis" (Boym 2007, 15). She draws a distinction between restorative and reflective nostalgia, even for they "might overlap in their frames of reference but do not coincide in their narratives and plots of identity. In other words, they can use the same triggers of memory and symbols, the same Proustian madeleine cookie, but tell different stories about it" (Boym 2007, 15). For *Kentucky Route Zero* emplots a journey, Boym's ideas of homecoming as a nostalgic affect are prevalent in the game.

is a "symptom of our age, an [sic] historical emotion. . . . In a broader sense, nostalgia is a rebellion against the modern idea of time, the time of history and progress. The nostalgic desires to turn history into private or collective mythology, to revisit time like space, refusing to surrender to the irreversibility of time that plagues the human condition" (Boym 2007, 8). The irreversibility of time and likewise the rebellion against the modern(ist) idea of the progress of time stands in line with the game's idea of deferral. Why/how retreat into a past if the game does not even seem to warrant motion or progress? Similarly, Angela McRobbie points out that nostalgia is capable of bringing "history into an otherwise ahistorical present" (McRobbie 1994, 130). McRobbie's assertion explains the way how *Kentucky Route Zero*'s layering of temporalities (and the layering of historical moments! Pre-internet versus twenty-first-century digital capitalism) brings about a sense of nostalgia for when computer gaming was more rudimentary.

Boym and McRobbie offer a bridge between nostalgia, deferral, and slowness—but also to "restoring": This layering of temporalities and the nostalgic gesture toward a time and place that cannot be restored is compellingly intertwined with the refusal for one single integrated, coherent narrative, let alone one fixed point of observation. The game contorts timelines and makes available an atemporal space of perception and experience (and hence subverts the notion of nostalgia—to long to go back to *one specific* time or space). Notice in Figure 4.1 how the options relate to the hopelessness the characters feel about their life's work being in shambles. These emotions are now made interactive; the options do not necessarily drive the narrative forward, but they carve out the backstories and emotions of the characters—to whose past is nostalgia directed? Whose past is the one safe to restore?

The reader can here select responses from several different characters, indicating a shift in perspective and focalization. It mirrors a social reality of despair and hopelessness—made out of mosaics of different voices and fates (i.e., disappearance of family, no lease, no job). By choosing dialogue options on the screen, the reader carves out the emotional matrix of the characters, but not necessarily a "fixed" or stable past. Jake Elliott emphasizes how "we're less interested in giving the reader ethical or strategic choices, and more interested in giving them poetic or performative choices" (Elliott 2013b, n.p.). Choice[15] is one of the fundamental properties of *Kentucky*

---

[15] To explore this focus of the game on its poetic and performative choices, Astrid Ensslin's concept of "verbal art" helps identify how verbal language is a constructive force in the gameplay. It privileges *reading* over *puzzle-solving*, and Ensslin underlines how such

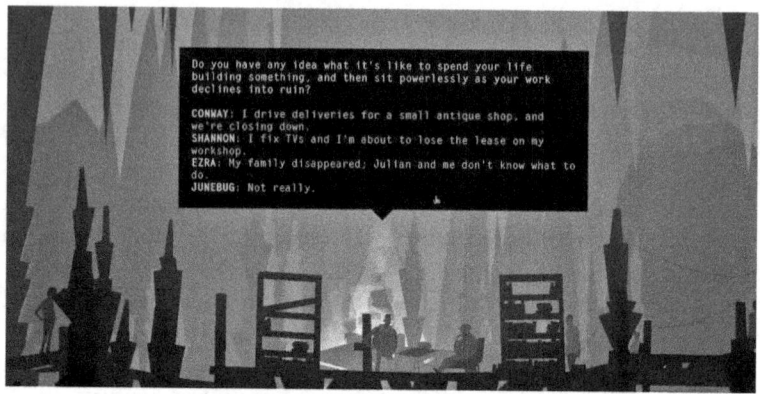

Figure 4.1 A screenshot taken from the third act in *Kentucky Route Zero*. © used with permission from Cardboard Computer.

Route Zero, and choosing here means curating emotions and ambience. This, of course, rubs against the desolation and hopelessness of the characters within the game. Living in the present means to no longer know "one integrated dynamic, grand narrative, or stable point of observation.... Slowness ... sharpens our sense for the coexistence of different and often incompatible vectors of time and, in doing so, it invites us to reflect on the impact of contemporary speed on our notions of place, subjectivity, and sociability" (Koepnick 2014, 4). And we can elevate this onto the poetics of the game (and its investment in nostalgia and hardware, too—different machines co-existing in one computer) and the nostalgic gestures it makes available.

Kentucky Route Zero employs narrative strategies that are coined *branching narratives* in gaming. These are often employed in point-and-click computer games, and the reader can create different versions of the same reality, with some options that she chooses freely, but there are also some mandatory events that need to happen in the game. Employing

> games like *Kentucky Route Zero* "include texts that employ and foreground spoken and written language in unconventional ways and embed them, kinetically and multimodally, in what are essentially digital *Gesamtkunstwerke*, rather than following a rigid page-under-glass trajectory. The term 'literary,' thus, has to be dissociated from print and its implications for reception ... and production" (Ensslin 2013, 77–78). *Kentucky Route Zero* unfolds within this tension, and it reveals "literary and poetic techniques [that] are employed in order to explore the affordances of rules, feedback, challenges, performance monitoring, and other ludic mechanics" (Ensslin 2013, 77–78).

branching narratives, or, rather, parallel paths (which is a subdivision of branching narratives) allows for semi-autonomous decision-making in the gameplay. The game programmers harness the formal poetics of a point-and-click computer game to explore societal and medial instability and precariousness. The narrative branching of the game illustrates the multiplicity of meaningful plots, and this technique acknowledges and facilitates such co-temporalities to exist. Again, this goes for the mood and ambience. For nostalgia, too, can create "mood." Linda Hutcheon outlines that "nostalgia is not something you 'perceive' as an object . . . it is what you 'feel' when two different temporal moments, past and present, come together for you and, often, carry considerable emotional weight. In both cases, it is the element of response—of active participation, both intellectual and affective—that makes for the power" (Hutcheon 2000, 199). And we cannot perceive *Kentucky Route Zero* as such an object either: we cannot hold it in our hands; it is code on the computer.

Jake Elliott insists: "We're thinking of the way the player interacts with *Kentucky Route Zero* like how an actor interacts with a play. . . . They make decisions about how and when to move, what tones or emotions to inflect spoken dialogue, and what fictional back-story to construct for the character they're playing" (Elliott in Whitehead 2013, n.p.). The game developers formally align the game with theater (i.e., stage directions, acts and scenes, the structure of the Greek tragedy, references to Henrik Ibsen's play *Peer Gynt*) or movies,[16] and not with computer games per se. We can subsume that these strategies of reader engagement, such as carving out the mood, interaction with the preset options and choice that unravel nonsynchronous patterns, speak to remediation processes and the fluidity of media boundaries. Here pointing and clicking is more about curating a beautiful story, finding the right words, making small talk than to solve riddles. Filtered through the lens of slow and outdated devices, which encapsulates considerations of deferral, the game unravels a spectrum of (nostalgic) narrative and material expressions in and through digital media.

---

[16] The game's ambience, shadows, and darkness clearly draw inspiration from the American film noir cycle of the 1940s and 1950s or even David Lynch's dystopian movies about American small town life (i.e., *Blue Velvet* or his television series *Twin Peaks*). The game's existentialist themes, such as disorientation and the helplessness/powerlessness of the characters, interlace the game with the film genre and recalibrate the game as a bizarre interactive effort to carve out doom and premonition.

Dazzlingly small steps

I began thinking about slowness as an aesthetic parameter after having noticed a peculiar overlap between *Kentucky Route Zero* and *Building Stories*: the respective protagonists have either an injured leg or wear a prosthesis. In Ware's graphic narrative, the unnamed protagonist lost her leg in a boating accident when she was young. She wears several prosthetic limbs throughout the graphic narrative; parts of *Building Stories* depict her slowly walking to work, making small talk about the prosthesis and the social stigma it brings along, or her sitting in the bathtub shaving her leg. Her disability is never explicitly at the core of the narrative,[17] but it alludes to the motif of slowness and incompleteness in *and* of *Building Stories*. The missing leg stands in relation to the material[18] of *Building Stories*, for the reader might not notice if the collection is complete, if this is a complete "body" of work.

Building Stories and *Kentucky Route Zero* rely on a dichotomy of able-bodiedness and disability to explore bodies of and at work in the twenty-first century. I do not intend to equate disability with cumbersomeness—much on the contrary, for *Building Stories* and *Kentucky Route Zero* both demonstrate the importance of narrating alternate rhythms and parallel paths. *Kentucky Route Zero*'s retro point-and-click technology prolongs the progress through the upper world and the underground of Kentucky through specific narrative strategies (i.e., branching and parallel paths through the narrative, deferral through small talk, the idiosyncratic gameplay vis-à-vis twenty-first-century technology) as well as through the nonnormate body of

---

[17] Chris Ware's description of the protagonist "strangely elides disability as a characterization . . ., relegating it to a de-privileged position in his account of the narrative" (Fink Berman 2010, 191). Margaret Fink Berman remarks that it is Ware's *style* that "directs the reader's eyes to a frank confrontation with her legs by depicting her in close-up shots from the knee down" (Fink Berman 2010, 192). In *Kentucky Route Zero*, it, too, is style: the rudimentary stick figures, the solemn tone, and so on.

[18] My forthcoming article "'Her Leg': Chris Ware's Body of Work" (in *PathoGraphics: Narrative, Aesthetics, Contention, Community*, edited by Susan Squier and Irmela Marei Krüger-Fürhoff. University Park: Penn State University Press, 2019) explores the interlacing of material and disability in *Building Stories*. I discuss Ware's comic spread titled "Her Leg," in which the protagonist of *Building Stories* shaves her shorter leg in the shower. She had a humiliating experience on public transportation, and a woman whispered "Her leg" to her boyfriend. She ponders, "Besides, my real leg is buried in a decomposing biohazard bag somewhere, or incinerated, or whatever it is they do with stuff like that. . . 'part of the earth,' 'feeding the flowers.'" In the article, I suggest a careful recalibration of *Building Stories* vis-à-vis themes of incompleteness and present/absentness. The metaphor of the disabled body helps unlock the remarkable book that *Building Stories* is (and vice versa!), both reliant on nonnormate materialities and readers.

its protagonist, Conway. Pretty much at the beginning of the game, Conway injures his leg in a mining accident and needs immediate medical attention. But he delays his visit to the doctor to continue his quest on the Zero and limps through the scenes of the first and second act (which can be seen as a comment on the American health care system—his job at *Lysette's Antiques* probably does not include health insurance). Through the missing leg, the game creates "awkward, labor-intensive rhythms" and delays and retracks "narrative development, waylaying readers with constant interruptions and slowing their progression" (Banita 2010, 178). Georgiana Banita's comment refers to Chris Ware's earlier graphic narrative *Jimmy Corrigan*, but it rings true for *Kentucky Route Zero* as well as *Building Stories* and the reading experience these texts make available to the reader.

When we distill Banita's keywords—awkward, labor-intensive rhythms, delaying and retracking of the narrative development, waylaying readers, interruptions—we get a picture of poetic and aesthetic components of slowness. Banita coins the miscroscopic gestures[19] in Ware's graphic narrative *Jimmy Corrigan* "dazzlingly small steps" (Banita 2010, 177). These gestures underline the slow progression through the narrative *and* material; slowness helps the reader engage with the present, one panel or text option at a time. (Think here also of the co-temporalities of the "Rubik's Cube" in *Jimmy Corrigan*'s cut out of the barn.) Banita points out that this stands in relation to Victor Shklovsky's concept of "narrative retardation," which foregrounds "such deceleration techniques as digression, defamiliarization, repetition, and narrative embedding" (Banita 2010, 179–80). The conceptualization of dazzlingly small steps as a narrative (and material) strategy foregrounds lateness and detours. Due to his broken leg, Conway and his troupe cannot help but saunter, walk slow, and rest. But also the crafting the story is a slow endeavor in itself: the dialogue options the reader can choose from appear just very slowly on the screen—row after row after row. And even in the menu, the reader has the option to select the pacing of the "text speed"—the options are "sudden," "steady," and "drowsy."

In Act II, Conway finally does see a certain Dr Truman to cure his leg. He prescribes Conway an experimental drug called Neruypnol™. Conway's leg heals miraculously, though Conway does not get his human leg back. The leg

---

[19] Chris Ware's notorious, almost painfully slow-paced progressions of panels depict one slice of a second, like the old landlady shooing away a fly. This detailed depiction of one microscopic moment renders both the reading experience and the "performance" of the reader within the gutters infinitesimal and minute. If Ware's comics are so slow and tightly controlled, where can the reader insinuate herself? How can she creatively and autonomously connect the panels in her imagination in the gutters? This can be understood as Chris Ware taking full control of the narrative progression.

turns into a ghost leg, or rather into a glowing skeleton leg. This glowing limb makes him swift and agile again, and in the scene following his miraculous healing, Conway runs around like a child. But the shady doctor warns him of side effects: the drug will give him a sense of *lateness*, as well as "daydreaming, déjà vu, passiveness, fugue states, irregular perception of time." When we look at these side effects, we get an idea of the governmentability of bodies,[20] as postulated by Lauren Berlant. What she coins "slow death" of obese bodies in her eponymous article lies within a zone of temporality "we can gesture toward as that of ongoingness, getting by, and living on . . . a condition of being worn out by the activity of reproducing life, agency can be an activity of maintenance, not making; fantasy, without grandiosity; sentience, without full intentionality; inconsistency, without shattering; embodying, alongside embodiment" (Berlant 2007, 758–59). This turns the nineteenth-century flâneur bonvivant into a twenty-first-century figure burdened by debt and desolation, whose life is that of maintenance, not making, of going on and not of sauntering. The body (of the medium, of the characters, of the reader) is bound to grow old, wear out, and fail. Berlant's considerations therefore unfold on the narrative (i.e., the characters merely "get by"), material (the data lives on, more on this later), and bodily level (i.e., double layering of protagonist's and reader's body).

It is equally indicative that *Kentucky Route Zero*, *Song Reader*, and *Building Stories* delay the reader's labor through fragmented media, mirrored on the level of bodily interactions. One question that lingers is, If the protagonist's slow body is affected by these side effects, what happens to the *device* that narrates his slow journey? This makes me wonder in what way "slow reading" could be a condition of "wearing out" and "ongoingness" in the twenty-first century of both bodies and machines. The game might be able to comment on slowness as a curatorial, narrative strategy that retards and delays mass-produced commodities and devices and, inherent within this, the reader's entanglement with (and addiction to) devices. The computer, now, equally "goes on" and "goes slow" (i.e., the speed of the text—drowsy,

---

[20] The work of the body is significant from a media-philosophical vantage point, and Mark Hansen diagnoses in *New Philosophy for New Media* a shift toward "affectivity": "the capacity of the body to experience itself as 'more than itself' and thus to deploy its sensorimotor power to create the unpredictable, the experimental, the new" (Hansen 2004, 6). In these terms, slowness inverts and makes the reader experience the unpredictable, drawing its effects on both affective responses and the body (i.e., routinized motoric gestures of clicking on the mouse, or sitting in the computer chair for too long, or hunching over the laptop). Hansen's ideas stand in contrast to Berlant's question of ongoingness, for he urges for the unpredictable, while Berlant detects the ongoing routine. The body as "more than itself" in Berlant is not marked by affectivity, but affected by political and economic circumstances that render bodies nonnormate.

sudden, steady—comes back in a different guise). What could be at stake here is a commentary on routinized, ongoing interaction with material, text, and media—and likewise the material slowly wearing out by these routines (think of the way a keyboard key turns loose, or the slowing down of the hard drive, or the breaking down of the iPhone's home button) and then breaking altogether, going black. But to conceptually arrive at the breaking of the machine, we first must do a little detour through museums.

Limits of demonstrations: The interaction with art *through* art

After so many pages of thinking about curation, *Kentucky Route Zero* opens reclaimed and repurposes spaces, which now function as museums, factories, mines, caves, dive bars, and abodes. But what, really, *is* a museum here? A closer look at the game *Limits & Demonstrations*, one of the free add-on games expanding the fictional universe of *Kentucky Route Zero*, allows for dissecting the precarious interactivity and malleability of aesthetic experiences within the game—through an art exhibition. The reader has to *organize* and curate aesthetic and affective responses within the museum context, and I argue that these museum spaces negotiate a distorted, contorted sense of choice. We need to pay close attention to what these museums display and *how* they are rendered within the game. *Limits & Demonstrations* is an interactive retrospective of Lula Chamberlain's art installations. Set in a large warehouse that has been remodeled into an art space, the reader encounters the characters Ben, Bob, and Emily—ghosts she met before in the basement of the gas station in the first scene of *Kentucky Route Zero*. They saunter through the exhibition to look at Lula's art, and the reader tags along.

Time is not an issue here: The reader and the characters linger in front of individual artworks for as long as they want and let the eerie, alienating installations sink in. There are five pieces in the exhibition, which Lula created over the course of thirty-five years. Due to their fragility and, well, weirdness, they were almost impossible to install in other museums, as the accompanying museum catalog explains. Lula Chamberlain's installations are made out of found materials, wire, and "unknown media," among other materials. The works are called "Basement Puzzle #2 (artist, sunset and horse)" (1976, poster and wire), "Spinning coin, suspended, correcting for angular motion" (1976, found materials), "Overdubbed Nam June Paik Installation in the style of Edward Packer? (1965, 1973, 1980, Magnetic tape, hand-help tape playback head, speaker system, voice of the artist, computer-synthesized speech), "Visage" (1985, unknown media), "Vertex Texture Fetch (Three, Television, and Suspended Cathode Ray Tube)" (1968, found materials). Her art is exhilarating: horses in fragile steel cages, a teletype computer tipped to the side, a face formed out of long strings of paper, a tentative map of Kentucky and "interactive" tape recordings.

Inscription media such as tapes, machines like TVs and teletype terminals, or PDP tape cabinets are all obsolete curio in the twenty-first century, sidenotes of technological progress; Lula turns them into artworks that evoke suspense and loneliness. Fragile, yet obdurate, the artworks dwarf Emily, Bob, and Ben to tiny stick figures. The exhibition catalog explains that galleries and museums

> balked at the scale, power requirements, and highly-skilled labor involved in maintaining these works for display. Some of their debuts collapsed under the weight of logistics, only to be successfully executed much later.... [The] works on display here also trace the extremes of our capabilities and the frontiers of our patience as both viewers and exhibitors. Are we capable of viewing these works as they were meant to be viewed?

Lula's art pushes the frontiers of patience: she is an artist who makes art with obsolete media and office supplies—that are repurposed, reshaped into a new contour. Teletype scripts form a tornado that resembles a face; the coin in the computer is merely an *image* of a coin. But her art does not reinscribe, but changes its purpose altogether. John Durham Peters facetiously suggests that obsolescence is "good for art, since it invites the materiality of objects once submerged in the Lethe of Use to shine forth. Most people toss their old media, but a few made art from them" (Peters 2015, 92). He continues that obsolescence can be a form of "foregrounding or strange-making" (Peters 2015, 92). But Peters's comment also tackles the significance of art in today's economic sphere: Lula sees the cultural value of obsolete media—not necessarily the market value. She puts old machines into a museum and gives them a new purpose—storing cultural history.

She might even be one of those people whom Jared Gardner has earlier identified as compulsive combers through archives, warehouses, and dumpsters, who seek out rare comic book issues, the broken Macintosh, or other prized ephemera. *Building Stories* and *Song Reader* similarly incorporate obsolete media—elevating the comic book and the sheet music page into a rarified, sheltered existence in collections and music folders. These comments mediate the self-referential construction (and deconstruction and repurposing) of the works of art. In *Limits & Demonstrations* it takes a connoisseur like Lula to recognize outdated technology. She has long ago understood to elevate and recontextualize the tossed-out wish coin, the unreadable tape, or the teletype into the museum. She repurposes and recycles technological history into artistic practice—she obscures the original purpose of these machines and creates something new out of the old. Can these fragile objects ever break or is their conservation in the museum their final resting place, à la Igor Kopytoff?

What is there even to say about Lula's art? What kind of mood does it create? Bob, Emily, and Ben slowly walk from one piece to the next, as art gallery visitors would do in a "real" museum. The camera pans along with them. The interlude game of course mocks presumptuous artsy museum small talk, but it creates a complicated aesthetic experience of guessing and interpretation. As Dan Solberg opines in his online article: "These conversations are less about informing you about the art on display as they are about fleshing out the characters via their points of interpretation" (Solberg 2014, n.p.). There is no story in this add-on game, though. It merely consists of the reader of *Limits & Demonstrations* curating the visitors' conversations about the meaning of Lula's art. This is a bold move—privileging experience and affect over coherence and plot. Tamas Kemenczy continues in conversation with Dan Solberg that "meaning, themes, or narratives encoded into visual forms can often be pretty diffused, non-linear, and hard to articulate back into words . . . [They] carry the potential for equally compelling and estranging experiences" (Kemenczy in Solberg 2014, n.p.). And this is also true for the descriptions of the artwork, which sometimes do not even match what is on display. One piece, described as "Spinning coin, suspended, correcting for angular motion" (Figure 4.2), really is a computer that *simulates* a coin on its screen. It hence displays "merely" a digital reproduction of the object that it presumably is.

Notice the responses in the point-and-click dialogue box for "Spinning coin": the characters interpret "Spinning coin" as "lonely," yet "strangely alive" (see Figure 4.2). This affective response toward Lula's art is rearticulated within the curatorial efforts of the *reader* curating the experiences in the museum. While interacting with the options on the screen, the reader is reminded that her task is to *select* text fragments and sift through the stylized list of data options inside the dialogue box (which looks like DOS code from the 1980s). She carves out the mood in the eerie exhibition space. As much as there is no story in this add-on game, the reader clicks through the game that already has a predetermined path. (The reader cannot select freely which artwork she wants to look at next, but she trots along slowly with Bob, Emily, and Ben who walk from right to left until they reach the exit.) She therefore *implements* the options made available—a role that is staged as an integral part in making the add-on game progress, but that does not necessarily has effect on the game

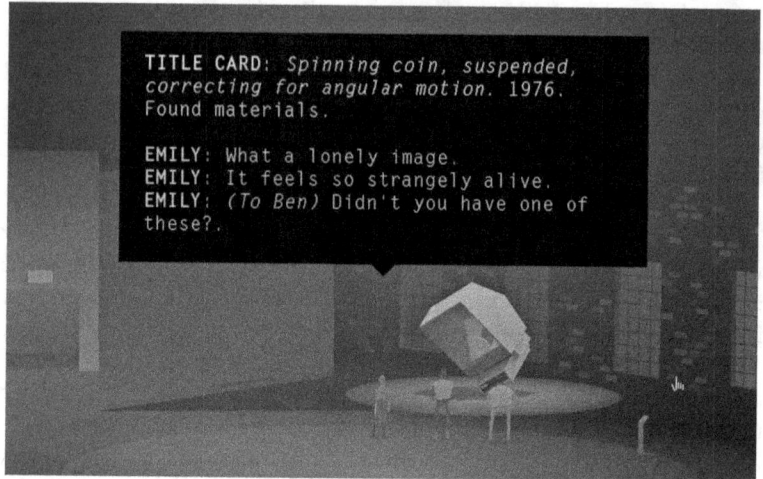

Figure 4.2 Screenshot from *Limits & Demonstrations*: "Spinning coin, suspended, correcting for angular motion." © used with permission from Cardboard Computer.

or its outcome in the larger scheme of things.[21] *Kentucky Route Zero* signals this shift as a recalibration of curatorial labor toward curatorial *reading* and assumes the laborious dimension of play within late capitalism[22]—on the art market, on Kickstarter, or in the reader's gaming den.

To explain this complicated aesthetic experience Lula's experimental art makes available—and the viewer's concern if she is "capable" of viewing works as they were meant to be viewed—I'd like to linger a bit longer on Lula's sculpture "Spinning coin" and draw out the artwork's intertextual references.

---

[21] Labor itself is now figured as play, as Alexander Galloway underlines, "just as play becomes more and more laborious" (Galloway 2012, 23). To paraphrase Alexander Galloway, art, too becomes more and more laborious for the reader and the characters alike to experience. And here, this curating of affective responses is reconfigured into emotional labor in the most literal sense of the word.

[22] Alexander Galloway continues to enunciate the intertwining of play and labor in late capitalism:

> Consider the model of the market, in which the invisible hand of play intervenes to assess and resolve all contradiction, and is thought to model all phenomena, from energy futures markets, to the "market" of representational democracy, to haggling over pollution credits, to auctions of the electromagnet spectrum, to all manners of supercharged speculation in the art world. Play is the thing that overcomes systemic contradiction but always via recourse to that special, ineffable thing that makes us most human. It is, as it were, a melodrama of the rhizome. (Galloway 2012, 23)

It is made of "found materials," and who knows where Lula found them. The joke is not lost, for the artwork is of course reminiscent of the Rubik's Cube, the retro cult toy from the 1980s that comes back into style every other decade. We can find gestures toward the Rubik's Cube[23] logic within the larger gaming structure: we engage with a fixed, yet flexible "toy" with multiple possibilities (but only one solution), or we abandon it altogether. Similarly, *Kentucky Route Zero* and the road, the Zero, twist and turn around their own axis. Also, Lula's art virtually renders a coin on a screen. This coin maybe feed a coin-op television or a snack machine. "Spinning coin" therefore underlines how the game can only work once we put our money into a machine, through Kickstarter, for example—and how art becomes valuable if there is money "in it"—as an investment on the art market. Does that mean that we can shuffle stories and art like Rubik's Cubes? Twisting and turning them until we are out of patience or until our hands grow tired? Feeding them coins to make them work?

There is no story in this game, but there is a story tucked away in one of the art installations: Lula exhibits an immersive artwork in her exhibition, which is called "Overdubbed Nam June Paik Installation in the style of Edward Packer." This piece examines the relationship between Lula, Donald, and Joseph like a Choose Your Own Adventure book, rendered on tapes. In a meta-gesture, this artwork, too, relies on branching narratives and trial-and-error: the characters engage with Lula's artwork like the reader of *Kentucky Route Zero* engages with the game. While interacting with the installation, Emily stalls and is unsure about how to proceed—she deliberates with Bob and Ben about the options to choose and whether or not they would like to go on and venture "deeper" into the artwork. In "Overdubbed Nam June Paik," it is both the character *and* the reader who learn more about a doomed cave mission that Donald, Joseph, and Lula undertook together. At one point, they only have one option: to go into the cave (Emily asks in a surprised manner if that is the only option available). And so, Bob, Emily, and Ben

---

[23] The installation also makes bold visual references to Tony Rosenthal's public sculpture Alamo, a popular hangout spot in the East Village in New York City. In a *New York Times* article, Colin Moynihan explains that Alamo is "made of six eight-by-eight-foot panels of Cor-Ten steel and weighs about 1,800 pounds. Its surface features geometric indentations and grooves, and it turns on a pedestal" (Moynihan 2005, n.p.). The site-specific art installation is interactive—for the cube rotates on its axis when pushed, and over the years, "the cube has become a cherished neighborhood symbol. It has been listed in travel guides and has been a sort of giant rabbit's foot that people rotated for good luck. Skateboarders and afternoon tipplers have congregated there. . . . 'It was a meeting place for tourists and for drug dealers,' Ms. Rosenthal said. 'People came and talked to it'" (Moynihan 2005, n.p.).

"read" art as much as they interact with the given components within the exhibition—at arm's length, behind the museum's barrier.

This is a crucial (and depressing) meta-moment, hidden away in the *Limits & Demonstrations* add-on game. Notice the non-sequentiality here: the reader has not even encountered this doomed cave expedition (it plays a major part in Act III). Emily's engagement mirrors the reader's engagement in a similar vein as when Jimmy and the reader build the zoetrope together—it bridges temporal and medial planes, and it deepens character identification—which is ironic, because Emily is a ghost and does not return for the remainder of the game. *Limits & Demonstrations* hence illustrates the flexibility of the term of the curator and the role of art within the framework of the game. The reader curates art, dialogue, and affects, and "Overdubbed Nam June Paik Installation" instantiates this very play of co-temporalities and of co-medialities: temporalities and materialities collide and the game, in its messy non-sequentiality, moves through time and space like a razor.

Can we label this as "slow art"? As Arden Reed points out, slow art names "an encounter between object and observer; it refers to a class of experiences, not a group of things. Slow art is what transpires in the space and time between beholders and beheld. . . . The viewer needs the artwork in order to receive pleasure, understanding, consolation—all three, or something else" (Reed 2017, 10–11). This certainly rings true for the avatars on screen. Yet the add-on game appears to be playing a deliberate in-joke on the expense of the reader, for the characters talk about events the reader has not yet encountered. It is because Lula's retrospective is a glimpse forward, a slice through time, space, and form: the allusions the art exhibition makes and the interconnections it conjures up are (still) beyond the reader's scope, merely priming her for what is to come. And it does so, ironically, through media that has been discarded and rendered obsolete by technological progress. The art exhibition *Limits & Demonstrations* thus gives first indications toward the question of how the computer game is able to negotiate notions of obsolete media and storage devices—their brokenness notwithstanding.

The black screen: Glitches in and of narrative

Kentucky Route Zero showcases during a scene in the so-called "Museum of Dwellings" in what way narrative and poetic strategies intertwine to delay the gameplay and break the reader's machine altogether. For it is suddenly the reader's computer screen that goes completely black—the reader's machine fails. In Act II, Conway and his troupe enter the forsaken "Museum of Dwellings," where houses are on display that have been relocated because of economic and environmental changes. Middle-class family homes are now re-embedded into a museum, showcased as art (and not as homes!), preserved from demolition. Conway and his group look at every house on display in the museum. Conway walks into one of the houses and vanishes for quite some time. It remains unclear what exactly happens in the house— whether this might possibly have been Conway's childhood house—because the reader cannot enter the house along with him. She remains aloof. (Here, it is also the camera work that is indicative, for the scene is shot from a high-angle vantage point, thus she is kept at a distance as an observer. The reader is literally not "on the ground" with the characters in the game.) The scene is narrated by a ghostly "voiceover" of an unknown group of people, called "Museum Staff." The scene is set up as an interview between the museum staff and people living in the houses on display.

This shift in perspective completely alienates the reader from the character she has been invested in and whose affects she has curated thus far. From the get go, the reader is stymied in her options about how to look at the dwellings on display. To make the scene progress, she has to look at each and every house and read every corresponding descriptive plate. She cannot saunter around freely, nor can she fast-forward or go back. One can make the point that the Museum of Dwellings is an aesthetic experience *about* an aesthetic experience, something like a meta-effort where the reader curates the experience of the characters. Similarly to the options in *Limits & Demonstrations* the reader selects emotional responses to what is put on display. But to add insult to injury, the characters suddenly in charge of narrating the game are people whom the reader has never even encountered before. The reader takes up an even more distanced role and conducts the interviews as "Museum Staff." Characters called Fred, Thomas, Sadie, and Flora watch the troupe roam around. Here is an exemplary dialogue from the Museum of Dwellings (the "man" is Conway, the "lady" is Shannon, Flora is one of the inhabitants of the houses, presumably a child). The reader decides vicariously by way of Flora what Conway experiences/experienced and feels/felt in the house.

> FLORA: I heard the man and the lady talking when they first came in, but they did not see me.
> MUSEUM STAFF: What were you doing up that late?
> MUSEUM STAFF: What were they talking about?

Notice how the options are suddenly in past tense: It elucidates how Conway lives in "multiple times and spatial orders at once, in competing temporal frameworks where time often seems to push and pull in various directions simultaneously. Time today is sensed as going forward, backward, and sidewise all in one" (Koepnick 2014, 3). The game makes visible this effect of slicing through time (i.e., past tense and present tense combined) and it *visually* abandons the reader and turns the screen black slowly.

When Conway vanishes into one of the houses, a most compelling effect unfolds on the reader's screen: the *visual* and the *narrative* planes diverge from one another: the screen gradually turns to black. The screen solely displays a list of options to click on. The game suspends the narrative visually and leaves it to the reader to fill out the darkness by making choices on the screen. Now the interview/"voice over" is merely a silent progression of text options on the screen. The following dialogue describes the very moment when the screen turns black (bold print indicates the choice I made to proceed):

FLORA:	He went upstairs and he also looked around the other rooms. I played with the dog.
MUSEUM STAFF:	**What did he do upstairs?**
MUSEUM STAFF:	What did he do in the kitchen?
MUSEUM STAFF:	What was the dog like?
FLORA:	He looked in some boxes. He looked out the window. He could see the museum better than when he was downstairs—he could tell how it was all put together. And the cabin, too, he could see the shape of it better from up there. Now that part is weird. He said he went into the basement.
MUSEUM STAFF:	That cabin doesn't have a basement.

By the end of this dialogue, the screen has turned completely dark (see Figures 4.3 through 4.5). Conway's magical story in the house continues as following (these are my choices; I am leaving the other options out): "He said he found a secret door in the floor. . . . He was surrounded by giant aphids. . . . He ran away from the aphids, into a river to hide. . . . He was a good swimmer, so he found his way back to the cabin." Conway will, no matter which path the reader chooses, always find his way back to the cabin (see here the idea of parallel paths), and the screen will always return to the reader. But the computer game seemingly abducts its own protagonist—and Conway's adventure will remain in the dark, merely imagined by the reader

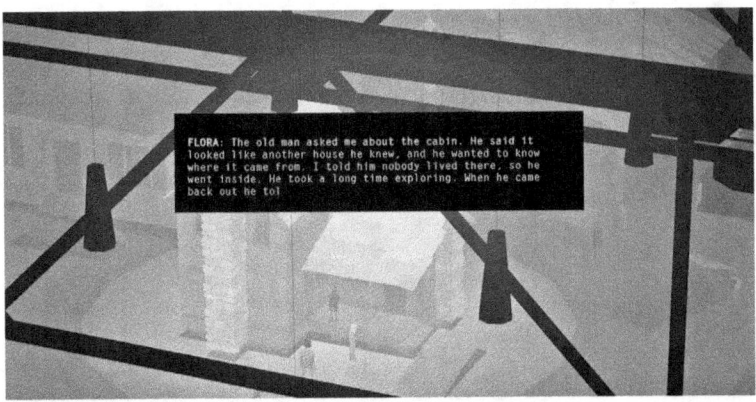

Figure 4.3 The slow fading of the computer screen to black, to be understood as a glitch that reveals the code behind *Kentucky Route Zero*. © used with permission from Cardboard Computer.

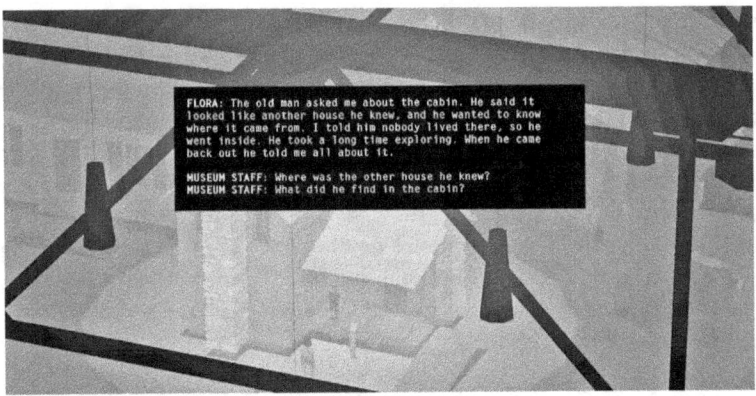

Figure 4.4 The slow fading of the computer screen to black. © used with permission from Cardboard Computer.

staring at the black screen.[24] The reader is placed on the outside, as a tourist, alienated from her surroundings, and her efforts to curate the museum experience draw a literal blank.

The *reader*'s experience is now one of lateness and passiveness (in line with Dr Truman's drug!): why is this temporal lapse intertwined

---

[24] Since the game toys with nostalgia and the deferral of homecoming, I find it remarkable that the computer breaks the moment when Conway reaches his home.

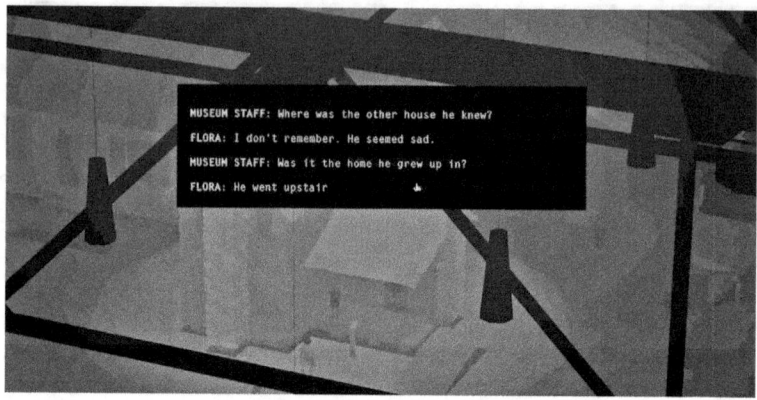

Figure 4.5 The slow fading of the computer screen to black. © used with permission from Cardboard Computer.

with the lapse of technology? We could say that by breaking down, the skeleton of the game becomes visible. The reader sees a DOS-esque list of options from which to choose narrative options from. In this way, the reader now curates *code* and turns it into narrative. The gaming journalist Dan Whitehead comments: "Oh, those wonderful blanks. There are lots of them in *Kentucky Route Zero*, and a large part of the game's pleasure comes from the realisation [*sic*] that this is not a game where the answers will be laid out in a neat sequence or suddenly made clear by choosing the right dialogue options" (Whitehead 2013, n.p.). Further, the reader needs to draw on her previous gaming experience within *Kentucky Route Zero*'s universe to imagine Conway's tumultuous adventure in the house. And Jake Elliott explains to Michael Rougeau in their interview: "It was kind of jarring for some people to see those text-only parts of the game. We've definitely had people asking us a lot if we did that to save time or something. But it wasn't really about saving time; it's a form that we are interested in" (Elliott in Rougeau 2013, n.p.). The DOS-esque screen lays bare what crowdfunders have paid Cardboard Computer for: coding, which then becomes story.

Computers tempt us to think that when they are not showing something, they are not working. In case of *Kentucky Route Zero*, I posit that the glitch leads the reader away from the game toward its code to show underlying mechanisms. As Wendy Hui Kyong Chun argues, code becomes source "through its simultaneous non-presence and presence"—self-effacing as game, but visible when gaming (Chun 2011, 25). Building on Chun's work, Zara Dinnen explains that source code remains an "unresolved present—what it is and what it will have been" (Dinnen 2018, 12). To extrapolate, the game reveals the machinations of both the device we are operating and the (individualized) story we are immersed in— but it does not efface the source code, but rather the game, contorting the source code into an aesthetic, retro, DOS-esque experience. Dinnen continues that "the task of representing code in its material and symbolic state and as an effacing gesture that is also a political reality of everyday life" (Dinnen 2018, 22). In this sense, it acknowledges that there are parallel temporalities lingering within the story *and* computer. In line with this, Alexander Galloway wonders, "A computer might remediate text and image. But what about a computer crash? What is being remediated at that moment? It can't be text or image anymore, for they are not subject to crashed of this variety. So is a computer crash an example of non-media?" (Galloway 2012, 21). Code and narrative, these glitch moments seem to suggest, are copresent, following their own temporal logics, by diverging from each other.

More generally, as Olga Goiunova and Alexei Shulgin observe, a glitch is a "singular dysfunctional event that allows insight beyond the customary, omnipresent, and alien computer aesthetics. A glitch is a mess that is a moment, a possibility to glance at software's inner structure" (Goiunova and Shulgin 2008, 114). Notice here how "immediacy" stands in direct contrast to Dinnen's "ever-present." We must simultaneously visualize information *and* evaluate data to "read" and curate *Kentucky Route Zero*. This dark screen as glitch, as Thomas Apperley argues, "makes it explicit that complex processes are underway beneath the assumed user-friendliness of the contemporary interface, disrupting the illusion of smooth, invisible mediation by revealing the artifice of the digital software and platform" (Apperley 2013, 147). I am intrigued by Apperley's argument, as it helps explain how these processes "underneath" the user-friendliness disrupt the gameplay immensely. This effect toys with the idea of our machine breaking down, of the fading to black, left with white text on a black screen to click on. On the other hand, we as readers are well acquainted with a *white* page and *black* letters—that is reading a book.

So the black screen does not surprise us, but it tantalizes us and reveals the backbone of the game that is ever-present. And by being situated within the museum context, it also draws on, ironically, Pierre Bourdieu's art competence: the reader does not only have presumptuous conversations about art (i.e., *Limits & Demonstrations*), but she needs to render the invisible experience "legible" for a "fluent" gaming experience. How ironic, though, that this fallacious and complicated "competence" in data curation is tested within a museum setting. It conjures up a doubling of art competence and what we might see as a *loss* of gaming competence or agency. For the dark screen might fascinate the reader, it nevertheless shows malfunctions in the game that are beyond her scope. To withhold and delay become key imperatives to showcase the disruptions of material and narrative interaction.

Kentucky Route Zero turns its readership into data analysts whose job is to rewrite and overwrite the same story, over and over again—and this might end up being tiresome and soporific and strange, resulting in frustration and another black screen: turning the machine off. The kind of curatorial labor that the computer game enables cannot solely be examined as an artistic/aesthetic involvement with the text, but it must be challenged in regard to the machines it operates on. Reading and curating, here, are literally "mending" activities to make the broken computer work again—and alluding to its own "data-ness" or "code-ness"—both effacing and ever-present. But to turn it around and to be a bit more facetious: Why would dragging on small talk in the game be a more "legitimate" readerly experience than to, say, scroll through a list of options in a database? What the game challenges is what might be understood to be magical about its poetics.[25] Is it the *story* and its stunning visuals that entice the reader or is it the coding of the program itself that is "magical"?

"Strange-making" media

Robots, zoetropes, floppy disks: machines do not feel or tire, they simply work or do not work, they break and can be repaired. Susan Stewart reminds us that they stand in the service of the dead awakened, of the

---

[25] This evokes Lev Manovich's notions of data and narrative. Manovich's arguments on the logics of the database identify a complicated aesthetic experience as characteristic of a database or archive. Database and narrative have a complicated relationship; he writes how databases can "*support* narrative, but . . . nothing in the logic of the database itself fosters the generation of narrative" (Manovich 2001, 225). Manovich explains, "As a cultural form, database represents the world as a list of items and it refuses to order this list. In contrast, a narrative creates a cause-and-effect trajectory of seemingly unordered items (events). Therefore, database and narrative are natural enemies. Competing for the same territory of human culture, each claims an exclusive right to make meaning out of the world" (Manovich 2001, 225). As much as Lev Manovich postulates that narrative and database are natural enemies, maybe code and database are, in *Kentucky Route Zero's* case, legitimate tools to tell a story and to turn a list of information into a narrative (and vice versa).

inanimate brought to life, of vanished and lost ones recovered and simulated. While the objects in their ongoingness and "ever-presentness" arguably do not degrade or *feel*, they do call for affective responses from reader and characters alike. The two scenes discussed so far showcase experiences *about* experiences, art *about* art, computers *about* computers, all embedded within museum that display and repurpose technology as curio and curiously outdated. Lula Chamberlain's art speaks to these concerns, for her art utilizes forgotten inscription media to foreground their obsolescence.

I outlined earlier how the dark screen/the glitch in the Museum of Dwellings hijacks the reader's machine and enables the curation of *data* to negotiate a strange ever-present. This scene is not the only "hijacking" of the screen that *Kentucky Route Zero* employs: in Act III, reader and character interact with a supercomputer called XANADU[26] that hijacks the reader's computer screen. The interaction with a computer is mirrored through a computer that the reader *and* the crew have to fix together to make the story proceed. It is the most curious mise-en-abyme that takes interaction with art *through* art and data *through* data into different terrain. XANADU stores information on a cave expedition, but its operating system has grown on its own, unguided by any external influence, but solely based on entropy and mold. XANADU unfolds as a broken machine that has started to write itself and exemplifies an auto-poetic system that tells itself, *without* any curating hand. While the reader has been made to believe that the narrative cannot proceed without curation, XANADU undermines this notion: this is a new nuance in the "strange-making" in and of *Kentucky Route Zero*. The computer simulation establishes its own network of nodes and feedback loops to connect dreams and academic endeavors of its programmer, Donald.

---

[26] The term "Xanadu" carries larger implications in the history of cybernetics. As Janet Murray explains, Ted Nelson coined the term "hypertext" in the 1960s

and called for the transformation of computers into "literary machines" to link together all of human writing, [and he] has been more in love with the unsolvable labyrinth. He sees associational organization as a model of his own creative and distractible consciousness. . . . Nelson has spent most of his professional life in the effort to create the perfect hypertext system, which he has appropriately named Xanadu. (Murray 1997, 91)

Initiated in the 1960s, Project Xanadu was among the first attempts to create a hypertext to instigate a magic place for literary memory, but the project has repeatedly been stalled, redeveloped, and is considered as the first "vaporware." For more on Project Xanadu, see Nelson (1981), Dechow and Struppa (2015), and Gary Wolf's article in *Wired*, "The Curse of Xanadu."

What happens is this: on their quest, Conway and his troupe reach the Hall of the Mountain King, an underground cave system in the depths of the Zero. At the center of the Mountain King hall sits Donald, the writer and programmer of XANADU, who escaped the realities of the world and now stares at a large fire burning at the center of the hall.[27] Describing XANADU to the group of travelers, he relates that "before its ruin, [it] was faultless as an oracle: a shrine to perfect simulation." It was once an "ornate labyrinth of memory, exhaustively-simulated parallel cave ecosystems. Real artificial intelligence built on sophisticated neural network algorithms! The birds in the forest could flock in three dimensions. The bats could learn to sing." Donald's supercomputer documents and simulates a cave exploration that was undertaken by Donald, Joseph, and Lula (and that Lula turned into art in one of her installments in *Limits & Demonstrations* that the reader could interact with). XANADU is Donald's *Magnum opus*, but it now rots in damp caves, hidden from the public, haunting the old man. Unsupervised and broken, the program has continued to accumulate data about the cave expedition, and XANADU has grown out of proportion during the years of its dysfunctionality. Lula (the artist) and Joseph (the gas station attendant), people Conway and his troupe have met on their way to the cave, suddenly appear in the simulation. They exist not only on the Zero but *also* in that computer.

[27] Is the Hall of the Mountain King a Platonic "virtual cave"? The hall's fire throws shadows on the walls: but not only of the characters' but also that of the reader. Tom Boellstorff argues that Plato's allegory of the cave can be regarded as an early elaboration of the idea of the virtual. In this light, Tom Boellstorff offers an intriguing overview on philosophical and technological ideas of virtuality. He makes an important observation that in "Plato's story it is the physical world that is 'virtual.' Between Plato's time and our own, a reversal has taken place with regard to dominant Western understandings of what is real; we now presume that nonphysical worlds are ontologically subsequent to physical ones" (Boellstorff 2008, 34). He relates how the act of writing "allows ideas, stories, and beliefs to persist over time and move to places distant from their point of utterance, and computer programs are forms of writing. Like virtual worlds today, in earlier times writing, as a form of techne or human craft, was seen as threatening" (Boellstorff 2008, 33). Boellstorff refers to Walter Ong, who posits that most

> people are surprised, and many distressed, to learn that essentially the same objections commonly urged today against computers were urged by Plato . . . against writing. Writing, Plato has Socrates say . . . is inhuman, pretending to establish outside the mind what in reality can only be in the mind. It is a thing, a manufactured product. It is a thing, a manufactured product. The same of course is said of computers. (Ong 1997, 79)

Kentucky Route Zero exceeds and twists Plato's allegory into a new shape. While there is a huge fire burning in the middle of the Hall of the Mountain King, the computer simulation XANADU bears its own simulation within the simulation. The characters of *Kentucky Route Zero* repair the computer and play the simulation to make sure the *other* simulation can perpetuate and continue to burn.

The troupe (and the reader) must click through XANADU to make the game proceed. Acknowledging this helps understand the conflation of "personal time" with what one can coin "machine time." XANADU asks questions pertaining to gaming sessions and reading sessions and it showcases the way human temporalities and technological temporalities collide and interweave. *Kentucky Route Zero* emphasizes varying temporalities meshing and twisting around one another: the temporal (and even spatial) structures of the medium, the experience of time for the reader (media-consumption, "working out"), and temporalities within the narratives (story time and plot time[28]) interlace. Shane Denson and Andreas Jahn-Sudmann point out the "negotiation and aesthetic mediation of the difference between human temporal experience and the nonhuman temporalities of digital media (e.g. the microtemporalities of computer technics and the apparent synchronization processes effected in networks and databases under conditions of digital media convergence)" (Denson and Jahn-Sudmann 2013, 11). Even more to the point, XANADU is doing something akin to slowing the reader's machine: the viewer can experience the "copresence of various temporalities and learn how to resist collapsing different trajectories into one unified and fully controllable vector of motions" (Koepnick 2014, 8). This meta-medial, self-reflexive, auto-poetic turn in *Kentucky Route Zero* explores narrative relying on restoration *and* anticipation (or, to speak in Peter Brooks's words: the anticipation of retrospection), of breaking and mending.

This idea of restoration and anticipation also extends to the strong cultural connotations the term "XANADU" evokes—the cave borrows from *Peer Gynt*, Henrik Ibsen's poem/play, whose eponymous protagonist enters the Hall of the Mountain King only to steal a bride at her wedding and is then hunted by gnomes through the caves. Samuel Taylor Coleridge's poem "Kubla Kahn; or, A Vision in a Dream: A Fragment" describes the splendor of a utopia, Xanadu, a place that cannot be attained or restored. And, of course, it evokes Charles Foster Kane's estate in Orson Welles's masterpiece *Citizen Kane*. Kane's Xanadu is a castle in which the bygone splendor of the mogul's life is preserved until his belongings are tossed nonchalantly into the chimney fire (among them, of course, his sled, Rosebud). By evoking these multifarious intertextual references, the game draws a picture of its own

---

[28] Shane Denson and Andreas Jahn-Sudmann put this distinction very elegantly: "'Story time' (the time of *histoire*, or of the diegetic world and events being narrated), discourse or 'plot time' (the time of *discours*, or of the narration itself, which can dilate, compress, and rearrange diegetic events for various effects), and the time of actual media consumption (the empirical time of reception)" (Denson and Jahn-Sudmann 2013, 6).

XANADU. But it also allocates the utopia into the machine to encapsulate a bygone splendor of a time and place that cannot be restored.

In contrast to its literary predecessors, and either by design or by accident, *Kentucky Route Zero*'s XANADU turns out to be a long and tedious[29] simulation about the exploration mission, and hardly one that begs to be integrated into the canon (with the canon being another idea of a text being "ever-present"). The reader must take care of logistics (fun!): she hires people, evaluates data, coordinates the cave expedition. The computer game within the computer game evokes organization and order, archives and databases: as dreary as it sounds, the layering of fiction(s) here is fascinating. To turn to a comment by one reader calling themselves Merve on the website *avclub.com*:

> For Donald, it's the ultimate act of preservation—it's a catalogue of better times spent with his former colleagues. It's almost a literal memory bank. And yet, it's presented as some sort of weird, ridiculous fool's errand. For Conway and his gang, Xanadu [sic] is just a means to an end; they're not interested in the substance of the memory, just the information contained therein. (Merve 2014, n.p.)

Donald sees the cultural, historical value of XANADU, whereas Conway and his gang merely see it as a storage device for information, not necessarily the personal attachments its programmer has to the object.[30] Game-reality and

---

[29] *Kentucky Route Zero* is uneventful, and XANADU is a tedious gaming experience that negates tempo/speed and temporality as cultural and textual markers in the twenty-first century. Niklas Luhmann posits that temporality has to be eventful to perpetuate the system forward—well, XANADU is very boring. Luhmann's idea assumes an interdependence of disintegration/decay and reproduction: the end of one action presupposes new action, and the system reproduces itself through this very condition of the possibility of interdependence. Thus, time as *tempo* turns into a critical variable (emphasis mine, translation mine, see Luhmann 1982, 376. In the original, "So muß man zum Beispiel von einer Interdependenz von Zerfall und Reproduktion ausgehen; das Aufhören des Handelns ist Bedingung weiteren Handelns, und das System reproduziert sich über die Bedingungen der Möglichkeit dieser Interdependenz. Damit wird, ganz anders als bei der Suche nach allgemeingültigen Gründen, Zeit, als Tempo, zur kritischen Variable; und schon aus Tempogründen müssen System im wesentlichen selbst für ihre Reproduktion sorgen."). Luhmann's ideas translate to how XANADU just goes on and on—it obscures our engagement with the medium of the computer, hijacks our screens, and reproduces a computer within the screen of our computer.

[30] This line of inquiry begs the question what will happen to our memories and past experiences: Will they become storable streams of data? Where will our dreams unfold—on a computer, in clouds, or academic folders? Will our lives become meaningless options for others to click on? These are bleak questions, and the idiosyncrasy of the computer medium can produce this unique, yet troubling aesthetic effect of the storing of dreams and feelings as well as data and information.

simulation-reality blur, and character and reader are, again, immersed in the same activity, like Jimmy and the reader in *Jimmy Corrigan*.

But who, really, knows how to fix a computer?[31] And does fixing the computer here equate to "fixing" Donald's nostalgic longings? As much as XANADU becomes a tedious and exhausting experience,[32] it functions as an important conceit to blur the boundaries between fiction and metafiction. XANADU asks to reassess materialities of machine and software (virtual computers, virtual caves, the reader's hardware seemingly "hijacked" by the in-game simulation). XANADU is installed on a historical record, and John Durham Peters notes that our contemporary moment is "marked by the odd combination of astronomically large data storage and obsolescence of storage media. . . . The amount of data gathered by social media, city surveillance cameras, web searches, and intrusive state apparatuses is quite unprecedented in history" (Peters 2015, 83). XANADU is more than an ironic in-game reference to text-based adventure games. It acknowledges the cultural work that data performs—the means of how (big) data is being accumulated and processed in the twenty-first century. Donald relates how mold seeped through to leave sticky residues, "forming new connections and creating new circuits. The computer is no longer the pure domain of language or mathematics, but entropy, but we are mere tourists in the ruins. Our keystrokes echo into the tunnels . . . boundless and bare, the caves stretch far away. We are too late." He goes on how XANADU's operating system "Literary Multitudes: Hypertextual Narrative as Poststructural Witness" evolved on its own and then deteriorated by mold: "I'm afraid you are too late, fellow hypertext enthusiast. As the mold accumulated on the circuitry, XANADU blossomed for a moment into something holy and enchanted; then all the charm was broken. . . . Do you have any idea what it's like to spend your life building something, and then sit powerlessly as your work declines into ruin?" And life on the internet weirdly feels the same way, sometimes—and so does academic work.

---

[31] I evoke Friedrich Kittler's question from the preface to his lectures on optical media.
> I don't know how many of you would be able to operate a television studio or even repair a television set. This technology is so extremely complicated in comparison to film that we are also required to pursue television history in order to learn anything about the *modus operandi* of electronic image-processing from its first tentative steps to today's image standard. (Kittler 2010, 24).

[32] XANADU takes about thirty minutes to play. Speaking from personal experience, I honestly was hardly invested in XANADU, for I wanted to exit the tedious simulation as quickly as possible. Basically, I wanted my agency back. If the reader wishes, she can play XANADU for as long as she wants.

To approach *Kentucky Route Zero*'s self-referentiality is to say that the text bears characteristics of auto-poetic mechanisms that operate as self-generating feedback systems that cannot be separated from those who manipulate and use them. Niklas Luhmann's arguments of autopoiesis and the self-perpetuation and self-generation of systems come into play. An auto-poetic system produces its own actions recursively and "realizes the network of productions as a unity in the space in which the components exist" (Varela in Luhmann 1982, 368). Luhmann posits how an auto-poetic system cannot be shown as "autonomous" based on a closed organization of self-referential reproduction. In the realm of auto-poetic systems a circular, inner closed-off-ness is a prerequisite for the self-reproductivity of the system[33] (see Luhmann 1982, 368). The simulation thus functions as a reflexive and recursive open system that relies on internal feedback loops, chaos, destabilization, and nonlinearity to accumulate data and information[34]—in Donald's words: entropy. In Chris Ware's words: collection. In Beck Hansen's words: album.

Luhmann's assertion reflects upon production for sheer production's sake. XANADU does not select or curate, it merely accumulates and makes visible the processes of archiving and data-ization of feelings and dreams in the era of digital memory. Jussi Parikka writes in relation to Wolfgang Ernst's concept of digital memory how it "provides an alternative to the literary-based narrativization that historians provide in their epistemological and ontological premises. Ernst's position is aware of the materialist media grounding of contemporary archives that engage not only with images and sounds but nowadays increasingly with software-based cultural memory" (Parikka 2013, 9). In *Kentucky Route Zero*'s case, a database's cultural memory is "less a matter of representation than of how to think through the algorithmic calculation—based ontology of a memory" (Parikka 2013, 9). The cultural memory of Kentucky is consequently uploaded as data, perpetuated by mold, and the RAM-storage of our computer is turned into

---

[33] Luhmann's article "Autopoiesis, Handlung und kommunikative Verständigung" has not been translated into English (yet). The original quote reads as follows: "Ein autopoeietisches System kann dann dargestellt werden als ‚autonom' auf Grund einer geschlossenen ‚Organisation' selbstreferentieller Reproduktion.... Sie betonen aber, daß im Bereich autopoietischer Systeme zirkuläre innere Geschlossenheit Voraussetzung ist für die Unaufhörlichkeit der Selbstreproduktion des Systems; und daß ihr Aufhören eben Tod bedeutet" (Luhmann 1982, 368).

[34] This can be seen as inverted key concepts of what Frank Kelleter coins "serial agents." Frank Kelleter suggests that we should "describe them as self-observing systems, in the sense that they are never just the 'product' of intentional choices and decisions, even as they involve intentional agents (most notably, people) for whom the generate real possibilities of choosing, interpreting, appropriating, extrapolating, objecting, and so on" (Kelleter 2016, 222).

such calculation-based memory space. And John Durham Peters's idea of the historical record comes back in a new guise, for the historical record now is a record that stores history and memories.

XANADU as historical record is nonetheless a *utopia*, a place that cannot be attained. The game comments on *our* investment to store daily life routines and habits in online databases as well as our efforts to digitize and archive documents, pictures, memories, and the most miniscule data logs. Most importantly, XANADU does not employ images or store pictures (and if so, merely stick figures that are even more rudimentary than the characters appear on the screen). Rather, it evokes the era before even computers rendered information *visually*—a counterintuitive comment on online habits and practices. XANADU taps into nostalgia linked to media changes and asks about the storing, transmitting, and processing of cultural/personal memory, history, and information. In our day-to-day life data also becomes crucial in the ways we interact with information stored on *our* (handheld) devices.[35] By holding up a mirror to our screen in the form of XANADU, it asks us what we would do if information became unattainable and lost once our computers break down. Would our data live on, without us, in moldy circuits? And where would that be?

Routes not traveled: Untold stories and parallel possibilities

The recursive acts of writing and rewriting that the computer game enables ("rewriting" the story whenever we start anew; writing it as we click on the options, XANADU writing itself through mold and entropy) reflect, according to Sianne Ngai, "the structural incompleteness of modern knowing itself" (Ngai 2012a, 370). I am intrigued by Ngai's idea, and I see *Kentucky Route Zero* as one cultural expression that productively comments on this incompleteness (and incompletion!) of knowing, doing, and making, curating, and laboring (after all, one of its main premises is slow ongoingness). *Kentucky Route Zero* is as much *about* the experience of being played and choosing as it is about the options that are *not* chosen, the routes *not* traveled, the feelings *not* carved

---

[35] John Durham Peters weighs in regard to the incompatibilities between devices: "The current strategy is to 'migrate' data across formats. VHS tapes and vinyl records may be functionally dead except among communities of collectors and connoisseurs, but the movies and music they once held are not gone—they have been reformatted into the latest storage medium with, of course, slight but significant changes in their affordances" (Peters 2015, 85).

out, the things *not* said. This "unknowing" is part and parcel of the aesthetic experience the game unfolds toward the reader—previously described with terms such as withholding, delaying, retracking, and deferring.

One strategy in exploring the incompleteness of knowing is the game's investment in a historical moment before the implementation of commercialized internet in the United States, which stands in contrast to the immediacy/ever-presentness of code outlined above. Tying into this, another one is that of giving the reader choices that flicker on the screen that she then will never be seen again—or might not remember the next time she plays the game. Yet another, more prevalent one might be the *material* level, for the game is written and rewritten over and over again by the reader on a device subjected to planned obsolescence. Matthew Kirschenbaum in *Mechanisms: New Media and the Forensic Imagination* looks "backward to electronic objects whose distance from us is measurable not only in years, but also by palpable shifts in hardware, software, data standards, file formats, and other manifestations of materiality" (Kirschenbaum 2008, 9). This can be, for instance, transferred onto Lula's "ever-present" art that eschews any specific marker for historization (when, exactly, are any of *Kentucky Route Zero*'s games set?), but merely by acknowledging the media's outdatedness (i.e., teletype). Kirschenbaum's comment also pinpoints XANADU as a foil to compatibility and data rot. In all these instances, the game "gamifies" a cultural anxiety of the twenty-first century—the fear of missing the ever-present moment. I would like to end my discussion of *Kentucky Route Zero* of what I suggest calling "parallel possibilities" and the fear of missing out.

Parallel possibilities evoke what *could* have been—the potentials of the glitch, the unclicked text option, the delay, the missed connection. This idea is tightly linked to the aesthetics of slowness. As Lutz Koepnick argues, it is slowness that makes "untold stories" available, for slowness "enables us to explore spatial relationships through physical engagement and mobile interaction. It makes us pause and hesitate, not to put things to rest and to obstruct the future, but to experience the changing landscapes of the present in all their temporal multiplicity" (Koepnick 2014, 9). Further, he underlines the "hesitation, delay, and deceleration, in an effort to make us pause and experience a passing present in all its heterogeneity and difference" (Koepnick 2014, 3). Slowness presses us "to account for the unlived and the not-yet-and-perhaps-never-lived. It brings into play the durational qualities of memory and anticipation while drawing our attention to what is irreversible and dissipative about our course through time" (Koepnick 2014, 6). What else but a feeling of "not-yet-and-perhaps-never-lived" does *Kentucky Route Zero* enable?

When thinking back at the various strategies of deferral and withholding in the game, we see that the game works with alternate realities and conclusions that are beyond the reader's scope.[36] Curating practices here are linked to unknowing and contingency (in *Building Stories* and *Song Reader*, the reader can at least see the rest of the options laid out to her). Pointing and clicking are now means to create different versions of the same reality. This is among the most significant characteristics of the game: *not* depending on a satisfying reading experience, but on the idea of how an aesthetic experience might remain incomplete and frustrating at times. In correlation with this, Janet Murray asks similar questions toward the narrative possibilities of the medium of the computer[37] in her seminal monograph *Hamlet on the Holodeck*. Murray is invested in what she coins multiform narratives, which afford "pullulation"—the splitting of reality, the choice between multiple alternatives, and creating various futures simultaneously[38] (see Murray 1997, 37). Murray writes, and it is worth quoting at length here,

> As this wide variety of multiform stories makes clear, print and motion picture stories are pushing past linear formats not out of mere playfulness but in an effort to give expression to the characteristically

---

[36] Umberto Eco in *The Open Work* follows a similar line of inquiry, for he writes,

> The two-value truth logic which follows the classical *aut-aut*, the disjunctive dilemma between *true* and *false*, a fact and its contradictory, is no longer the only instrument of philosophical experiment. Multivalue logics are now gaining currency, and these are quite capable of incorporating *indeterminacy* as a valid stepping-stone in the cognitive process. In this general intellectual atmosphere, the poetics of the open work is peculiarly relevant: it posits the work of art stripped of necessary and foreseeable conclusions, works in which the performer's freedom functions as part of the *discontinuity* which contemporary physics recognizes, not as an element of disorientation, but as an essential stage in all scientific verification procedures and also as the verifiable pattern of events in the subatomic world.... Perhaps we are in a position to state that for these works of art an incomplete knowledge of the system is in fact an essential feature in its formulation. (Eco 1989, 15)

[37] This also allows for a different strand of inquiry undertaken, for example, by Alexander Galloway who begins *The Interface Effect* with a critical inquiry in Lev Manovich's *The Language of New Media*. Galloway argues that Manovich postulates in *New Media* that the computer, essentially, borrows from the cineastic tradition—the question, yet again, lingers what is "new" about new media, questions that Lisa Gitelman and Mark Hansen also pose from different positions.

[38] Janet Murray lists Jorge Luis Borges's short story "The Garden of Forking Paths" and Delmore Schwartz's short story "In Dreams Begin Responsibilities" as proto-examples for such pullulating stories. These are, among films like the cult classics *Groundhog Day*, *Lola Rennt*, and *Rashomon*, what she calls multiform stories—they unearth the roads not taken, the decisions not made. Of course movies such as *Rashomon* and *Groundhog Day* toy with unreliable narration. Certainly, the rise of branching narrative computer games both borrow from and encourage this form of narration.

twentieth-century perception of life as composed of parallel possibilities. Multiform narrative attempts to give a simultaneous form to these possibilities, to allow us to hold in our minds at the same time multiple contradictory alternatives. Whether multiform narrative is a reflection of post-Einsteinian physics or of a secular society haunted by the chanciness of life or of a new sophistication in narrative thinking, its alternate versions of reality are now part of the way we think, part of the way we experience the world. To be alive in the twentieth century is to be aware of our alternative possible selves, of alternative possible worlds, and of the limitless intersecting stories of the actual world. To capture such a constantly bifurcating plotline, however, one would need more than a thick labyrinthine novel or a sequence of films. To truly capture such cascading permutations, one would need a computer. (Murray 1997, 43–44)

According to a *New Yorker* article published to commemorate the twentieth anniversary of Murray's publication in 2017, Murray indeed briefly contemplated on prefacing the reissue of her book with three words: "I was right!" (Murray in Margini 2017, n.p.). (Instead, she decided to give each chapter a "2016 Update.") Matt Margini underlines that her argument made in *Holodeck* might feel "dated at times, superseded by a future that is, broadly speaking, darker and stranger than the one Murray anticipated" (Margini 2017, n.p.). Nonetheless, what Murray establishes in *Holodeck* are multiform stories that work similar to labyrinths and mazes, but that can only unfold through the medium of the *computer*.[39] I find this indicative for the cultural work that *Kentucky Route Zero* performs in comparison to *Building Stories* or *Song Reader*. To Murray, an unsolvable maze holds promise as

> an expressive structure. Walking through a rhizome one enacts a story of wandering, of being enticed in conflicting directions, of remaining always open to surprise, of feeling helpless to orient oneself or to find an exit, but the story is also oddly reassuring. In the rhizome, one is constantly threatened but also continuously enclosed. The fact that the plot will not resolve means that no irreparable loss will be suffered. (Murray 1997, 133)

---

[39] Alison Gazzard's book *Mazes in Videogames: Meaning, Metaphor and Design* explores how "our cultural experiences of real-world maze landscapes may have changed and how, in light of this, contemporary worldly maze designs also may have been influenced through the walker's experience of living in a technologically mediated world" (Gazzard 2013, 2).

Murray's choice of words[40] evokes not only surprise and helplessness but also how everything will be "okay" at the end—the screen will return, Conway's leg will be healed, Dogwood Drive will be found, and if not, then the reader can reboot and start over.

The premises of the "multiform narrative" or slowness unveil multiple realities co-existing: slowness as an aesthetic category can draw attention to simultaneity, the expansion of the present, copresence of "various memories and anticipations, narratives and untold stories, beats and rhythms in our temporally and spatially expanded moment. It not only stresses the open-ended and unpredictable but also the need to unfetter notions of mobility and movement" (Koepnick 2014, 6). Has the flâneur ever taken the wrong turn? Isn't this what flânerie is all about—to aimlessly saunter through Paris and Kentucky, with either a sloth or a turtle on your leash? Unearthing these dead ends, the reader clicks her way through history, technology, landscape: what else does this imagery evoke but one of the mapping of the American continent? And what is the history of the United States but of media expanding, of media excluding, of media mapping the country? *Kentucky Route Zero*'s local history of Kentucky, the question of walking through history, data, and narrative, reflect on larger implications of how media shape personal, local, and global histories.[41] The game focuses on

---

[40] Notice how she uses "walking through a rhizome"—and we do so, tagging along with Conway, slowly, on a skeleton ghost leg. But getting into the maze is the hard part. Writing about dictionaries and encyclopedias, Umberto Eco distinguishes between three kinds of labyrinths: the linear one, the "Irrweg" (the maze), and the net (he also uses the metaphor of the rhizome) (see Eco 1986, 80–81). For my interest, Eco's idea of the net is the most productive one, for he sees it as

> an unlimited territory. A net is not a tree. The territory of the United States does not oblige anybody to reach Dallas from New York by passing through St Louis, Missouri; one can also pass through New Orleans. A net . . . is a tree *plus* corridors connecting its nodes so as to transform the tree into a polygon, or into a system of embedded polygons. . . . [The] abstract model of a net has neither a center nor an outside. (Eco 1986, 81)

Eco urges us not only to understand the geography of the United States as such a net but also to understand the *encyclopedia* as a myopic algorithm: "At every node of it no one can have the global vision of all its possibilities but only the local vision of the closest ones: every local description of the net is a *hypothesis*, subject to falsification, about tis further course; in a rhizome blindness is the only way of seeing (locally), and thinking means to *grope one's way*" (Eco 1986, 82). Engaging with the computer game means to be aware of the alternative possible selves and worlds, as Murray would say.

[41] James Carey harnesses the interlacing of experience, understanding, and communication to read the United States as a "media experiment"—James Carey argues that we should see the United States as a country that is the "product of literacy, cheap paper, rapid and inexpensive transportation, and the mechanical reproduction of words" and thus banking on the capacity, in short, "to transport not only people but a complex culture and civilization from one place to another, indeed between places that were radically dissimilar

how stories and objects are recorded (in museums) on what kind of devices (moldy supercomputers), through which kinds of processes (pointing-and-clicking), for what kind of bodies.[42] In reading *Kentucky Route Zero* through this lens, we come to understand how this computer game of the twenty-first century is determinedly commenting on life mediated on the internet—but the WiFi is down and the home button is broken.

---

in geography, social conditions, economy, and very often climate" (Carey 1988, 3). *Kentucky Route Zero* turns into a *Sinnbild* for media archaeology itself: it acknowledges what has not happened, the media not "used," what detours media and life can take.

[42] But what is the body of work here, exactly? I wager that it is the computer and its narrative possibilities (i.e., branching narratives) and material components (i.e., embedding a slow game into a fast machine). In line with Banita's and Fink Berman's arguments, slowness obscures the interaction with the *computer* and simultaneously makes new means of (digital) storytelling visible and possible. The narrative and the machine are decelerated and delayed, operating on different time layers and points of observation. For my reading of *Kentucky Route Zero*, I would slightly recalibrate this point for a stronger articulation of the idea of slowness through the computer: approaching the game through this lens allows for a shift in focus toward the wearing out of machines and obsolescence.

Coda: What's the Matter, Media?

Questions pertaining to the unruliness, flexibility, adaptability, and nonlinearity of media in the twenty-first century lead me toward cardboard[1] and allow me to take the question of materiality into different terrain. The lament of paper in the age of the lowercase internet fails to acknowledge that cardboard has never been more present in our daily lives. Our consumption habits have rendered paper nearly invisible from our keen analytical eyes, but I urge not to let paper disappear from view and touch. Forget the infamous paperless office for a second, or the cultural objects solely based in the digital ether—think for a second: How did your last order from the online retailer of your choice make its way to you? I'd wager that it probably came in a cardboard box (though plastic bags are popular, too, particularly with sartorial orders) or a brown sturdy envelope. In this coda, I seek a refined approach toward the cardboard box: books might be the mysterious things disappearing from our hands and competing with LCD screens, yet we neglect to realize that the touch we take to the *cardboard* is more than the ripping away of the fishbone from its prefabricated path. Rather, cardboard offers an approach toward contemporary reading practices and media interaction that lay bare different, unrulier, recalibrated media histories. Because paper, cardboard, papier-mâché aren't dead—far from it, our cultural moment brings them back from the recycle can into our hands.

I am intrigued by a peculiar surge of fusing cardboard with state-of-the-art technology at the beginning of the twenty-first century. Companies capitalize on our tactile familiarity with cardboard, and tinkering with cardboard initiates discussions regarding reading techniques and readerly technology: Nintendo *Labo* and Google *Cardboard* are marketed as mass-produced, yet one-of-a-kind toys that combine expensive electronic devices with rudimentary cardboard contraptions. *Labo* and *Cardboard* breathe life back into the cardboard box—literally branding nondescript cardboard with their corporate name, simultaneously rendering gadgets cheap and cardboard expensive. Cardboard stores and protects, is inexpensive and lightweight, and makes visible the transience and obsolescence of objects. In combination with a cellphone, cardboard, in fact, lays bare dichotomies

---

[1] The cardboard I am referring to is corrugated fiberboard. "Cardboard" in and of itself is an unspecific term that indexes several different types of thicker paper.

pertaining to use-value and commodity fetishism as well as rarified object and commonplace material. This play with and on these tensions is hardly a coincidence: *Labo* and *Cardboard* fictitiously turn the expensive cellphone or gaming console into a makeshift object that each and every reader must build for herself. Cardboard as a matter for media here is thus able to simultaneously efface and underline the medium/device it comes to replicate (and not only replicate, but quite literally embrace and incorporate in its contraptions).

This approach through matter and material affordances, and not necessarily through narrative affordances, elucidates on how cardboard negotiates between two contested spheres—in this case, paper toys and electronic gadgets (or, to put it more crudely: the contested boundaries between paper and digitality in the twenty-first century). They are not diametrically opposed, on the contrary: the turning of cardboard digital and the gadget into an "analog" cardboard toy opens up new avenues to infuse terms that I have used throughout this book with extended meaning—interactivity, open source, as well as nostalgia and obsolescence. Google *Cardboard* is a contraption into which a mobile device can be strapped; cardboard here works as an extension to the two-dimensional screen. With the accompanying *Cardboard* app from the Google Play store, three-dimensional worlds await its users behind flat cellphone screens. Newspapers such as *The New York Times* upload immersive journalistic videos to be watched with *Cardboard*. Similarly, Nintendo *Labo* is a DIY cardboard kit that "cardboard-ifies" the Nintendo *Switch*. With *Labo*, the gaming console can be extended—the user can build a piano or even a fishing rod out of the DIY kit. One striking difference to the three case studies that I engaged with in my book is that neither *Labo* nor *Cardboard* asks for the implementation of an *artistic* vision. Rather, they take the mass-produced electronic device—the gaming console or the cellphone—and obscure it via an everyday cardboard object (such as a fishing rod) that first needs to be assembled by the consumer. More precisely, cardboard does not build narrative worlds, much rather, it renders virtual worlds plastic. But the device's main purpose (communication) seems to be effaced in the meantime.

Why am I thinking of cardboard in the first place? I built an IKEA kitchen in the summer when I was writing this book, and the piles and piles of paper trash that accumulated in my apartment got me thinking about the ubiquity yet the strange invisibility of cardboard in our daily lives. It occurred to me that *Kentucky Route Zero*, *Song Reader*, and *Building Stories* all toy with their affinity to cardboard. Of course, at first glance, they toy with their affinity to *paper*: Take how the booklets included in Chris Ware's graphic narrative negotiate the way paper changes over the course of the years. His oversized newspaper can never be folded back into the same shape (much to my dismay), it will grow too big for it and fray around the edges. Likewise, *Song Reader* plays on the nostalgic feeling of music disappearing from our touch in the twenty-first century by way of sheet music (cheap paper). It plays with pretending that the song reader stumbles upon sheet music in an oddities store or in a flea market, showing that music is far from liquefied. *Kentucky Route Zero* performs different work here. *Kentucky Route Zero*'s production company is called, quite tellingly, Cardboard Computer. A cardboard computer, no less, connotes makeshift aesthetics, something a child would build because they do not have a "real" computer. But remember also how XANADU was infected by mold, letting the computer continue to grow on its own, without any human intervention. What would happen if and when a cardboard computer got infected by mold?

In the discussion of my three case studies, I repeatedly returned to their proximity to digital culture, and their replication of online activity via paper speaks to what N. Katherine Hayles postulates: without the opportunity "to build the kinds of traditions associated with print literature, electronic literature risks being doomed to the realm of ephemera, severely hampered in its development and influence it can yield" (Hayles 2008, 40). Hayles's question of *tradition* and *ephemera* can be transferred onto the materialities of print and digital cultures in the twenty-first century. My case studies, as well as *Cardboard* and *Labo*, refer back to cardboard to establish both tradition *and* ephemerality, underlining the simultaneous sturdiness and the transience of its matter. All three case studies evoke passé modes of entertainment and refer to earlier incarnations of media they riff off via paper and print culture. And the cardboard used in my case studies comes in different shapes and sizes and colors and qualities, yet presupposes readerly interaction with the material. *Building Stories* uses the oversized cardboard box to hold together the dispersed collection of comic booklets (as well as a board game included in the collection). *Song Reader* is sold in a blue cardboard box, making reference to artful vinyl gatefold record packagings. Cardboard as a box and a board game, as a music portfolio, as a computer: These are media that have been under immense pressure in the twenty-first century—always in flux, oscillating between the poles of analog and digital spheres.

Cardboard draws attention to the durability and (market) value of the objects and media—the rarified object inside a keepsake box or a cardboard computer, individualized by the reader, taken out of circulation and offering a unique, singular reading experience. Cardboard here is suddenly obdurate, valuable, pricy material that can, potentially, immediately tilt toward questions of ephemerality (i.e., the recycle bin awaits). All such instances index, to borrow from Sianne Ngai, "an uncertain status of performing between labor and play, the increasing routing of art and aesthetic experience through the exchange of information, and the paradoxical complexity of our desire for a simpler relation to our commodities that they are "about" production, circulation, and consumption" (Ngai 2012b, 13). Ngai's argument can be transferred onto cardboard and in what way it indexes ideas *about* circulation, (mass) production, and consumption in the digital age. With its "ordinariness," cardboard simultaneously reveals and conceals such processes—for it is itself sturdy *and* trash at the same time, for it produces and circulates simultaneously. Cardboard speaks to the mass-produced yet rarified, ephemeral object—mass-produced in terms of its material, yet rarified by way of its user who individualizes her gadget according to a manual. Tradition, here, is evoked by activities known to the consumer from her childhood. I would like to shift Ngai's assertions toward the cultural and technological work that *Cardboard* and *Labo* perform. We can see in these two objects how paper and electronic devices are being made, quite literally, compatible, with a cardboard device commenting on the production, circulation, and consumption of both electronic devices *and* paper. This, in turn, circulates ideas about the media *user* of the twenty-first century by staging her as media-savvy but decidedly "offline," attuned to the beauty of spending an afternoon building a computer out of cardboard.

Google introduced its virtual reality (VR) glasses *Cardboard* in June 2014. Its slogan on the website says, "Experience virtual reality in a simple, fun, and affordable way." Naturally, I ordered a set of two glasses for EUR 30, promptly delivered from Ireland to Berlin in a handsome cardboard box. In the online store, there are several different models on sale, with prices ranging from EUR 10 to EUR 39.99. Also, a DIY manual lists the materials the tinkerer needs to build her own contraption at home: cardboard, Velcro tape, lenses, and elastic rubber bands, as well as the blue print. *Cardboard* is primarily marketed to encourage the interest and development of VR applications. And from a media-historical vantage point, Google's cardboard VR goggles refer back[2] to an entertainment device from the nineteenth century, one that is obscure, forgotten, obsolete:

---

[2] Google *Daydream* superseded *Cardboard* in 2016. The *Daydream* headset was introduced in November 2016 and the software is built-in to the Android operating system. *Daydream* is to further encourage the development of VR applications (note that *Daydream* is not available for Apple devices!). Google introduced new headsets for *Daydream*, which are sturdier and, obviously, more durable. In this sense, Google already anticipated *Cardboard*'s obsolescence and quick overhaul and introduced a new gadget to the market that stands more in line with Oculus Rift. Think here, also, the fad of the smart glasses developed by Google, called *Glass*.

the stereoscope, an early contraption that similarly created the illusion of depth. Google *Cardboard* instantiates how the combining of two unrelated devices—cardboard goggles and a smartphone—is able to create a three-dimensional immersive experience. Certainly, *Cardboard* evokes Friedrich Kittler's assertion that I refer to in the chapter on *Kentucky Route Zero*: we probably do not know how to build or repair a cellphone as much as we do not know how to repair a television set. But with the "correct" manual, we build a device that can augment the machinations inside the mysterious, impenetrable cellphone. *Cardboard* replicates the act of building of one device in order to "extend" another one, serving as proxy to the cellphone's mysterious interior wirings.

Cardboard leads us to believe that we, at least, can manipulate this mysterious object and "open it up" to some degree—*Cardboard* creates depth and renders the flat screen three-dimensional while simultaneously engaging us in a ludic, childlike activity. In this way, it offers an immersive experience *about* an immersive device (just think the hours you waste away playing app games or browsing Instagram) to diverge the feeling of the object's impenetrability. What Google *Cardboard* suggests is that we can go deeper into our device than our flat screens suggest at first touch, with our fingers dancing on the screen, swiping left and right and up and down. We encountered a similar strategy in Chris Ware's zoetrope,[3] that, as I have argued in the chapter on *Building Stories*, makes something visible that would have remained hidden otherwise. For Jimmy and the reader, the zoetrope is paper-based entertainment that functions as distraction from everyday troubles and anxieties. To be a bit polemic, *Cardboard* reminds me of something akin to this, namely, that there is a three-dimensional world waiting outside—but we need our cellphone to see these parts of the world (i.e., the website advertises immersive experiences for glacial explorations or skaters doing tricks in a half-pipe). This cardboard object enables interactive, immersive, and participatory modes of building and forgetting. It suggests that we can animate the world and see the beauty of nature with our own eyes—yet we need our screens and our *Cardboards* for that.

[3] Google *Cardboard* stands in close proximity to Chris Ware's artistic visions, particularly explored in his zoetrope included in *Jimmy Corrigan*. My personal fascination with the zoetrope might stem from its obsolescence. Who would be entertained by this odd device, nothing more than a thing long lost and forgotten, a mere foot note on our way toward three-dimensional blockbusters, movies streamed instantly online, and hilarious reaction GIFs we send our friends in emails. The zoetrope, also known as the "wheel of life," with its Greek root words meaning "life" and "turning," creates the illusion of motion by means of a spinning drum. The still images on the strip inside the drum seem to move; the faster the drum is spun, the smoother the illusion of movement and life is.

With Nintendo *Labo*, the everyday object is turned into an entertainment device. *Labo* are tool kit cardboard extension packages for *Switch* that borrow aesthetics from LEGO or that of IKEA manuals. Nintendo *Labo* of course presupposes that there is already a Nintendo *Switch* gaming console in the user's home (which costs about EUR 300). The commercial ad video on the Nintendo website promises the consumer fun hours of tinkering, for she is to build so-called "Toy-Cons" (I assume that means toy constructions) that can be then hooked up to Nintendo *Switch*. The kit includes perforated cardboard sheets that, once assembled, turn into pianos, fishing rods, robots, houses, and even motorbikes. The slogan is "Make"—"Play"—"Discover" but no straying off the predetermined path. I am intrigued by the "Variety Kit" (around EUR 70): it says to "pop up the pieces" and then "fold and combine them to build your Toy-Con creation"—add Nintendo *Switch* and play! Two things strike me here: one selling point is that the *Labo* user can go at her own pace, making the aesthetics of alternate rhythms (borrowing from Lutz Koepnick's ideas of the aesthetics of slowness) a viable component to the gaming experience (i.e., in comparison to more traditional gaming experiences that rely on countdowns, unlocking new levels, or the avatar depleted of "lives"). Gaming and tinkering conflate here to underline the user's unique experience with the "ordinary" material at hand—again, the term "digital" is being taken at face value. But it is also the case that the user cannot diverge from the manual, but she must implement the kit correctly to make it compatible with the gaming console. This speaks, in part, to *The Open Work* and how Umberto Eco stresses that this "openness" does not mean "infinite possibility" or complete freedom of reception (Eco 1989, 6). Rather for Eco these types of contemporary works are "works in movement" that depend on an author's intention[4] and a performer who chooses among options—but *Labo* puts the performer *into* movement by way of the electronic device (i.e., pretending to ride on a motorbike or playing the guitar).

Further, I'd suggest that Nintendo *Labo* and Google *Cardboard* examine notions regarding obsolescence, retro aesthetics, and data rot in the digital age. With *Labo*, cardboard and gaming console *have* to be combined for the full gaming experience. Similar to *Cardboard*, where the user has to download the *Cardboard* app and has to strap her cellphone into the contraption to experience VR worlds (i.e., walking along Paris or looking at an art exhibition), the tension between intangible digital space and the

---

[4] Ha, speak of author's intention: I think it is important to underline that there is the vision of a company implemented here.

re-appearance of the haptic object (like the music album in the guise of a vinyl record or sheet music or the fishing rod) are integral components to the experience. The emphasis, though, is on the distinct and deliberate shabbiness of the objects (i.e., the sleek *Switch* contrasted with the bulky cardboard contraptions; the expensive cellphone vs. EUR 20 glasses). Media archaeologist Jussi Parikka observes that retro-cultures "seem to be as natural a part of the digital-culture landscape as high-definition screen technology and super-fast broadband" (Parikka 2012, 3). But note that *Cardboard* and *Labo* do not necessarily reproduce retro chic or nostalgia or codify the object as mysterious or unique: there is hardly anything mysterious about a fishing rod. Rather, *Labo* cross-pollinates ordinary objects with the "mysterious technology" of a gaming console.

We could say that the combination of materials and objects that at first seem unrelated are integral to digital-culture landscapes. *Cardboard* and *Labo* infuse ordinary material and ordinary objects with super-fast broadband. Further, *Cardboard* and *Labo* turn the everyday object into a one-of-a-kind curio, almost of Duchamp-ian proportions (relocating the ready-made everyday object into the museum context). Here, a fishing rod is repurposed as an extension to the virtual world. Pastimes are being rendered virtual and are being integrated into the logics of the digital spheres. In this sense, *Labo* and *Cardboard* elevate the everyday object into the realm of mass-market technology and gaming culture, ironically replicated through the everyday material of cardboard. This initiates a curious feedback loop: a mutation and metamorphosis in economic and technological terms, signaling the intensification of something familiar, and not something new. We can see Bill Brown's "unmodern world" in full bloom here: the internet of things is man-made and makeshift—and now even a fishing rod can be hooked up onto the internet. And as Mark Miodownik argues, "The material world is not just a display of our technology and culture, it is part of us. We invented it, we made it, and in turn it makes us who we are" (Miodownik 2015, xii). In this sense, the (digital) world we invented through online retailers and online shopping is brought back to us by way of shipping material reconfigured as technology. The device we use to order something on amazon—our cellphone—is now incorporated into the material amazon uses to deliver its goods, and hence *Labo* and *Cardboard* integrate such consumer aesthetics of the twenty-first century into ludic, virtual pastimes.

But the cultural work that *Labo* and *Cardboard* perform does not stop by merely acknowledging their flirting with an outdated entertainment device that renders an image three-dimensional or the fishing rod that now is a DIY cardboard contraption. With *Cardboard* or *Labo*, we are faced with labor performed by a tinkerer who turns goggles, pianos, fishing rods into paper gadgets. Throughout my book the tension between author and fan has been one of my guiding questions in my inquiries toward curatorial labor. Remember how the artistic vision à la Beck Hansen or Chris Ware can be purchased online on amazon or other retailers (i.e., an inverted Duchampian gesture), rendering the curator as a consuming amateur. Much rather, we see a shift from labor to *Labo*: the above questions of repairing and tinkering and "digitizing" pastimes that do not necessarily belong into the digital spheres open up the inquiry toward amateur labor. And, in relation to this, I think that there is a history of cardboard in conjecture with *amateurism* to be told here.

Already in the nineteenth century, cardboard afforded flexibility and was marketed toward the amateur as material to be tinkered with at home. In 1817, the first commercial paperboard was credited to M. Treverton & Son in England (even though cardboard was invented in the 1600s in China); in 1856, corrugated cardboard was patented and mainly used as a liner for tall hats. Beginning in the 1870s, it was used as shipping material, which I find significant, for it alludes to a shift of consumption and a change in trade and exchange networks beginning at the end of the nineteenth century. During my research for this coda, I stumbled upon two handicraft magazines published around this time: *Amateur Work, Illustrated* (I looked at the third volume, suitably titled "The Workshop at Home," from 1883) and *The Young Englishwoman—A Volume of Pure Literature, New Fashions, and Pretty Needlework Patterns* (published in 1869). (Both are available, of course, on Google books. The scans are watermarked with the Google logo.) The latter is a fascinating magazine, for it bookends fiction (there are "nursery stories told to grown-ups" in this publication) with embroidering materials and handicraft tutorials. These tutorials oftentimes list cardboard: cardboard in *The Young Englishwoman* is used for creating needle patterns or a "knitting needle case in shape of a bonbon," and my first response here is to ask: How, when, why, where was cardboard available to the young Englishwoman? At what point in time was cardboard mass-produced to be then turned into an amateur material for the young Englishwoman to use in her embroidery practice at home? Was it a luxury good? Almost contemporaneously, the magazine *Amateur Work, Illustrated* devotes its third volume to "The Workshop at Home." On about 600 (!) pages, tutorials for how to build the most outlandish objects, among them microscopes,[5]

---

[5] The artist Kelli Anderson recently published pop-up books called *This Book Is a Camera* and *This Book Is a Planetarium*. Her works showcase how books turn into something different; the *Planetarium* book also includes a speaker and an instrument akin to a guitar. All of these things included in her book are made out of cardboard.

are included in this magazine, transplanting the scientific object into the home of the amateur.

Notice how cardboard was available for both genders, but that there was still a clear division of gender in place (microscope vs. needle bonbon). To me, this acknowledging of the (female and male) tinkering amateur of the nineteenth century illustrates a strange feedback loop[6] to the strategies laid bare in the three case studies (all of which replicated nineteenth-century pastimes, no less). Cardboard nowadays seduces us to think that there might be endless supply of it (i.e., IKEA or amazon packaging)—but what kind of media history can cardboard reveal? In the twenty-first century, Ware's, Hansen's, and Cardboard Computers' work of genius that, as I have argued in my introduction, is reified by the amateur fan who brings their artistic vision to life. Notice here the shift from genius to amateur, from rarified to mass object in both the nineteenth- and twenty-first century. We could even go as far as to argue that the genius of the twenty-first century appropriates the material of the amateur of the nineteenth century to underline their "failing" artistic vision. But also remember that with *Cardboard* or *Labo*, there is no artistic vision to be implemented here or made consumerist, but a technological and corporate one (which brings us back to the microscope tutorial included in *Amateur Work, Illustrated*).

My case studies interrogated the "singularity"—the Ware collectable taken out of circulation, for instance, or the Beck Hansen song audible only for a small niche group. My three case studies thus toyed with this notion of taking the mass-produced object and re-planting it into a new environment—rarifying the artistic vision and turning it into a mass-produced object. Looking at the objects through the lens of cardboard, "taking out of circulation" connotes to more than preservation and collection (as it is the case with *Building Stories* or *Song Reader*). In the case of cardboard, we might say that cardboard is taken out of the *recycle* circulations, and it is embedded within a new, digitized context to create one-of-a-kind objects. A cardboard object might not be beautiful or artistic, for it is makeshift, but

---

[6] Google *Cardboard* combines two materials of the nineteenth century: glass and cardboard. Granted the glass used in *Cardboard* is made of plastic. Glass, here is of course optics, they are lenses, but they also ironically simulate the idea of *looking through* the glass interface of the cellphone. Glass here facilitates the literal looking through of the medium into a three-dimensional land that lies behind. In *iMedia* Sarah Kember discusses glass as gendered interface of the twenty-first century: "In the twenty-first century, glass is being redesigned as a more haptic, gestural and intuitive interface, neither more nor less visible than the screen or lens but more natural, closer in property first of all to plastic (which bends) and ultimately to skin (which stretches and breathes and has the semi-autonomous status of an organ)" (Kember 2016, 33).

it turns into a foil to the mass-produced device. We might even be able to press Zara Dinnen's question of the "digital banal" and test it on the plane of *material* banality that equally effaces and makes visible again. What else but utterly banal is cardboard? Secondly, what else does *Cardboard* or *Labo* do than to equally draw their attention to the utter banality of their materiality and efface it altogether?

This tension between the singularity and the banal maps the cultural work of cardboard in the twenty-first century. Cardboard in this way is able to index keywords of my book, like labor and flexibility, differently: questions of digitality, of tinkering, of compatibility spring forth, and one way of reading this conflation is to say that cardboard maps out an unrulier media history that is here dominated by amateurs (i.e., think, for example, of pirate radio stations or even amateur scientists with cardboard microscopes), and not by geniuses or pop-culture darlings. Through this lens, cardboard aligns the cellphone with the tinkerer and the amateur—but it leaves no real flexibility or room for the amateur to integrate her own artistic vision. Yet it might ultimately be the affinity to childhood activities that is replicated here. In 2005, the cardboard box was inducted into the *National Toy Hall of Fame* in Albany, NY. The blurb on the museum website reads as follows: "Children sensed the possibilities inherent in cardboard boxes, recycling them into innumerable playthings. The strength, light weight, and easy availability that make cardboard boxes successful with industry have made them endlessly adaptable by children for creative play" ("Cardboard Box" 2018, n.p.). Of course, these cardboard boxes are long gone and thrown away. We may wonder if *Cardboard* or *Labo* replicate this feeling for these long afternoons, or do they rather perform a meta-gesture and replicate the feeling as a marketing strategy with branded cardboard?

In this book, I examined the contemporary and its inherent provisionality to elaborate on curation and creativity in the twenty-first century. Seemingly unrelated skills now become part of the pastime in reading and gaming. The objects I interrogated from this vantage point speak to a contemporary cultural and creative aesthetization and "process-ization" of the new and the novel that, ultimately, evokes old modes, media, and matters. DIY kits for creativity come in boxes, in blue folders, as bits and bytes, in cardboard—and reading is staged as the interaction with and the tinkering, the caring for, the "figuring out" of the material at hand. The objects that I discussed are prefabricated, ready-made, consumerist, targeted to niche audiences to explore and exploit their cultural competences—as sheet music, as comic strips, as files to be downloaded onto the computer, or, ultimately, as cardboard boxes to fill our vacant afternoons. This, indeed, is highly specialized labor: reading now enables a manifold of curatorial and creative practices, which gives us an image of an ostensible naturalizing of the leisure/work dichotomy (or, to refer back to Adorno, unfree and free time). Cardboard, ultimately, leads us back to a time of our lives where we had more free time than unfree time—childhood afternoons.

The methodological approach of media archaeology has proven to be a productive lens for the excavating of the old within the new: the layers of meaning that the contemporary texts encode evoke earlier modes of their respective media, but underline, repeatedly, the process, not the end product that is rendered visible. By presenting themselves as hobbies that enable creativity, my case studies simultaneously evoke discussions on quality and competence.[7] An outlook onto cardboard as a material for media can strengthen this argument and elevate it onto different terrain: it can enunciate the proximity of pastimes to juvenilization and likewise reflect on consumption and production habits. My discussion of cardboard as a material of twenty-first-century digital cultures is not to discredit the achievements of artists such as Thomas Demand[8] and Bodys Isek Kingelez, who both in their own artistic practice recreate worlds with and through cardboard. Rather, by turning to cardboard, I urge to reflect on mass entertainment in the twenty-first century via the positioning of the tinkerer toward it—rooted, again, in the nineteenth century, as a cardboard aficionada and reader of magazines such as *The Young Englishwoman* and *Amateur Work, Illustrated*.

All of this makes me wonder about the quiddity of all these expensive gadgets and devices that we buy and throw away just to buy them again—cellphones, computers, smart watches, what have you. Cardboard parodies its expensive state-of-the-art counterparts. Similarly to Lula's artistic practice in *Kentucky Route Zero* and *Limits & Demonstrations*, who unearths the teletype and gives it new life, our moment takes cardboard out of the recycle bin and reintegrates it at the crossroads of the disappearance of paper and the internet of things. Cardboard hallmarks not only consumer excess but

---

[7] Yet, the characters with whom to identify hold up a mirror to the participating reader. The builder, recollector, and daydreamer (*Building Stories*) builds the life of a "failed" artist living in the suburbs of Chicago; the song reader and sheet music connoisseur (*Song Reader*) meets a ventriloquist rock star, a cut out of his former self; the data analyst (*Kentucky Route Zero*) meets a Willy Loman-esque delivery truck driver and a programmer gone mad.

[8] The German photographer Thomas Demand takes pictures of press photography that he reassembled with cardboard. These are mediated worlds made out of cardboard sculptures. Demand's work speaks toward the augmentation of reality through cardboard in different registers, and as Lauren Graycar explains, Thomas Demand's "paper and cardboard constructions of interiors and environments often depict historically or politically significant locations" (Graycar 2011, n.p.). This creates a tension between the fabricated and the real and makes their already shifting boundaries even more porous. His images, so to say, are truly fabricated.

also the malleable subject position of the consumer: a shift toward cardboard might reveal not a history of print culture, but rather a history of circulation, production, and consumption in the digital age (but also what is consuming and what eats away our free time!) and the ways the consumer is embedded within it. Selling that consumer an object made out of material she would have had thrown away otherwise—cardboard—is kind of brilliant. *Labo* and *Cardboard* ultimately gesture toward something that we cannot predict but must assume: not only the obsolescence of our expensive devices in the future but also with how little we can *actually* make do—a box made out of paper to entertain us and our cats for the duration of a rainy afternoon. Here's hoping that these cardboard boxes will never go up in flames in Chris Ware's post-apocalyptic campfire.

Bibliography

"About Sheet Music." 2015. *Historic American Sheet Music – Rare Book, Manuscript, and Special Collections Library at Duke University*, n.d. Accessed January 24, 2015. https://library.duke.edu/rubenstein/scriptorium/sheetmusic/about.html.

Adorno, Theodor W. 1998. "Free Time." In *Critical Models: Interventions and Catchwords*. Translated by Henry W. Pickford. New York: Columbia University Press.

Agamben, Giorgio. 2009. *What Is an Apparatus? And Other Essays*. Translated by David Kishik and Stefan Pedatella. Stanford, CA: Stanford University Press.

Anderson, Benedict. 2003. *Imagined Communities: Reflections on the Origin and Spread of Nationalism*. New York and London: Verso.

Apperley, Thomas H. 2013. "The Body of the Gamer: Game Art and Gestural Excess." *Digital Creativity* (24.2): 145–56.

Appleford, Steve. 2013. "Beck Remakes Bowie's 'Sound and Vision' with 'No Limitations.'" *Rolling Stone Online Magazine*, February 6. Accessed January 22, 2016. http://www.rollingstone.com/music/news/beck-remakes-bowies-sound-and-vision-with-no-limitations-20130206.

Arendt, Hannah. 1998. *The Human Condition*. Chicago and London: The University of Chicago Press.

Avanessian, Armen, ed. 2013. *#Akzeleration*. Berlin: Merve Verlag.

Bachelard, Gaston. 1994. *The Poetics of Space: The Classic Look at How We Experience Intimate Places*. Boston: Beacon Press.

Bal, Mieke. 1994. "Telling Objects: A Narrative Perspective on Collecting." In *The Cultures of Collecting*, edited by John Elsner and Roger Cardinal, 97–115. London: Reaktion Books Ltd.

Banash, David. 2013. *Collage Culture: Readymades, Meaning, and the Age of Consumption*. Amsterdam and New York: Rodopi.

Banita, Georgiana. 2010. "Chris Ware and the Pursuit of Slowness." In *The Comics of Chris Ware: Drawing Is a Way of Thinking*, edited by David M. Ball and Martha B. Kuhlman, 177–90. Jackson: University Press of Mississippi.

Ball, David M. 2010. "Chris Ware's Failures." In *The Comics of Chris Ware: Drawing Is a Way of Thinking*, edited by David M. Ball and Martha B. Kuhlman, 45–61. Jackson: University Press of Mississippi.

Barton, Laura. 2012. "Beck on His Song Reader: 'It Was a Struggle for Me.'" *The Guardian*, November 26. Accessed May 4, 2015. http://www.theguardian.com/music/2012/nov/26/beck-song-reader-it-was-a-struggle-for-me.

Baudrillard, Jean. 1994. "The System of Collecting." In *The Cultures of Collecting*, edited by John Elsner and Roger Cardinal, 7–24. London: Reaktion Books Ltd.

Bauman, Zygmunt. 1994. "Desert Spectacular." In *The Flâneur*, edited by Keith Tesler, 138–57. London and New York: Routledge.

Bauman, Zygmunt. 2012. *Liquid Modernity*. Cambridge and Malden, MA: Polity Press.

"Beck – Song Reader." 2012. *Beck Song Reader Website*. Accessed July 22, 2015. http://www.songreader.net/.

Beck, Ulrich. 1992. *Risk Society: Towards a New Modernity*. London, Newbury Park, and New Delhi: SAGE Publications Ltd.

Beck, Ulrich. 2000. *Brave New World of Work*. Translated by Patrick Camiller. Cambridge, and Malden, MA: Polity Press.

Beck, Ulrich, and Elisabeth Beck-Gernsheim. 2002. *Individualization: Institutionalized Individualism and Its Social and Political Consequences*. London: Sage Publications.

Bellezza, Silvia. 2017. "'Ugh, I'm So Busy': A Status Symbol for Our Time." Interview with Joe Pinsker. *The Atlantic*, March 1. Accessed January 4, 2018. https://www.theatlantic.com/business/archive/2017/03/busyness-status-symbol/518178/.

Benjamin, Walter. 1999. *The Arcades Project*. Cambridge, MA: Harvard University Press.

Berlant, Lauren. 2007. "Slow Death (Sovereignty, Obesity, Lateral Agency)." *Critical Inquiry* (33.4): 754–80.

Berlatsky, Eric. 2009. "Lost in the Gutter: Within and Between Frames of Narrative and Narrative Theory." *Narrative* (17.2): 162–87.

Boellstorff, Tom. 2008. *Coming of Age in Second Life: An Anthropologist Explores the Virtually Human*. Princeton: Princeton University Press.

Bolin, Göran. 2012. "The Labour of Media Use." *Information, Communication & Society* (15.6): 796–814.

Bourdieu, Pierre. 1993. *The Field of Cultural Production: Essays on Art and Literature*, edited by Randal Johnson. New York: Columbia University Press.

Boym, Svetlana. 2007. "Nostalgia and Its Discontents." *The Hedgehog Review* (9.2): 7–18.

Bredehoft, Thomas. 2006. "Comics Architecture, Multidimensionality, and Time: Chris Ware's Jimmy Corrigan: The Smartest Kid on Earth." *Modern Fiction Studies* (52.4): 869–90.

Brooks, Peter. 1992. *Reading for the Plot: Design and Intention in Narrative*. Cambridge, MA and London: Harvard University Press.

Brown, Bill. 2001. "Thing Theory." *Critical Inquiry* (28.1): 1–22.

Brown, Bill. 2016. "A Questionnaire on Materialisms." *October* (155): 11–13.

Brownstein, Carrie. 2015. *Hunger Makes Me a Modern Girl: A Memoir*. London: Virago Press.

Busch, Kathrin. 2012. *Passivität*. Hamburg und Lüneburg: Textem Verlag.

"Cardboard Box." 2018. *National Toy Hall of Fame*. Albany. Accessed July 3, 2018. http://www.toyhalloffame.org/toys/cardboard-box.

Carey, James W. 1988. *Communication as Culture*. Boston: Unwin Hyman.

Cates, Isaac. 2010. "Comics and the Grammar of Diagrams." In *The Comics of Chris Ware: Drawing Is a Way of Thinking*, edited by David M. Ball and Martha B. Kuhlman, 90–104. Jackson: University Press of Mississippi.

Chun, Wendy Hui Kyong. 2011. *Programmed Visions: Software and Memory*. Cambridge, MA: MIT Press.

Chun, Wendy Hui Kyong. 2016. *Updating to Remain the Same: Habitual New Media*. Cambridge, MA: The MIT Press.

Chute, Hillary, and Marianne DeKoven. 2006. "Introduction: Graphic Narrative." *MFS – Modern Fiction Studies* (52.4): 767–82.

Chute, Hillary, and Patrick Jagoda, eds. 2014. Special Issue of *Critical Inquiry* (40.3).

Chute, Hillary L. 2010. *Graphic Women: Life Narratives and Contemporary Comics*. New York: Columbia University Press.

Chute, Hillary L. 2014. "Panel: Graphic Novel Forms Today – Charles Burns, Daniel Clowes, Seth, Chris Ware." *Critical Inquiry* (40.3): 151–68.

Claudio, Esther. 2011. "Would You Admit It? (on Chris Ware's Cut-Outs)." *The Comics Grid: Journal of Comics Scholarship*. Accessed April 14, 2014. http://blog.comicsgrid.com/2011/02/would-you-admit-it/.

Collins, Jim. 2010. *Bring on the Books for Everybody*. Durham and London: Duke University Press.

Corbett, Philip. 2016. "It's Official: The 'Internet' Is Over." *Times Insider – The New York Times*, June 1. Accessed January 6, 2018. https://www.nytimes.com/2016/06/02/insider/now-it-is-official-the-internet-is-over.html?_r=0.

Crary, Jonathan. 2014. *24/7: Late Capitalism and the Ends of Sleep*. London and New York: Verso Books.

Crawford, Richard. 1993. *The American Musical Landscape*. Berkeley: University of California Press.

Dechow, Douglas R., and Daniele C. Struppa, eds. 2015. *Intertwingled: The Work and Influence of Ted Nelson*. Cham: Springer International Publishing.

Denson, Shane, and Andreas Jahn-Sudmann. 2013. "Digital Seriality: On the Serial Aesthetics and Practice of Digital Games." *Eludamos: Journal for Computer Game Culture* (7.1): 1–32.

Derrida, Jacques. 1996. *Archive Fever: A Freudian Impression*. Chicago: University of Chicago Press.

Deuze, Mark. 2011. "Media Life." *Media Culture Society* (33.1): 127–48.

Diederichsen, Diedrich. 2010. "Kreative Arbeit und Selbstverwirklichung." In *Kreation und Depression: Freiheit im gegenwärtigen Kapitalismus*, edited by Christoph Menke and Juliane Rebentisch, 118–29. Berlin: Kulturverlag Kadmos.

Dinnen, Zara. 2018. *The Digital Banal: New Media and American Literature and Culture*. New York: Columbia University Press.

Dyer, Richard. 2007. *Pastiche*. London and New York: Routledge.

Ebeling, Knut, and Stephan Günzel, eds. 2009. *Archivologie: Theorien des Archivs in Philosophie, Medien und Künsten*. Berlin: Kulturverlag Kadmos.

Eco, Umberto. 1986. *Semiotics and the Philosophy of Language*. Bloomington, IN: Indiana University Press.

Eco, Umberto. 1989. *The Open Work*. Translated by Anna Cancogni. Cambridge, MA: Harvard University Press.

Eglash, Ron. 2002. "Race, Sex, and Nerds: From Black Geeks to Asian American Hipsters." *Social Text* (71/20.2): 49–64.

Eisner, Will. 2008. *Comics and Sequential Art: Principles and Practices from the Legendary Cartoonist Will Eisner*. New York: W.W. Norton & Company.

Elliott, Jake. 2013a. "Interview: Kentucky Route Zero's Mountain of Meanings." Interview by Nathan Grayson. *Rock, Paper, Shotgun – PC Gaming since 1873*, January 22. Accessed August 11, 2015. http://www.rockpapershotgun.com/2013/01/22/interview-kentucky-route-zeros-mountain-of-meanings/.

Elliott, Jake. 2013b. "Kentucky Route Zero Interview: Choice and Introspection in the Magic Realist Adventure." Interview by Phillipa Warr. *PC Gamer – PC Gamer Reviews, News, & Features*. PC Gamer, January 18. Web. Accessed August 11, 2015. http://www.pcgamer.com/kentucky-route-zero-interview-choice-and-introspection-in-the-magic-realist-adventure/.

Elsner, John, and Roger Cardinal. 1994. "Introduction." In *The Cultures of Collection*, edited by John Elsner and Roger Cardinal, 1–6. London: Reaktion Books.

Engberg, Maria. 2014. "Digital Fiction." In *The Johns Hopkins Guide to Digital Media*, edited by Marie-Laure Ryan, Lori Emerson, and Benjamin J. Robertson, 138–43. Baltimore: Johns Hopkins University Press.

Ensslin, Astrid. 2013. "Playing with Rather Than by the Rules: Metaludicity, Allusive Fallacy, and Illusory Agency in the Path." *In Analyzing Digital Fiction*, edited by Alice Bell, Astrid Ensslin, and Hans Kristian Rustad, 75–93. New York and London: Routledge.

Ernst, Wolfgang. 2013. *Digital Memory and the Archive*, edited by Jussi Parikka. Minneapolis and London: University of Minnesota Press.

Feldman, Brian. 2014. "The Triumphant Rise of the Shitpic." *The Awl*, December 17. Accessed January 6, 2018. https://www.theawl.com/2014/12/the-triumphant-rise-of-the-shitpic/.

Fink Berman, Margaret. 2010. "Imagining an Idiosyncratic Belonging: Representing Disability in Chris Ware's 'Building Stories.'" In *The Comics of Chris Ware: Drawing Is a Way of Thinking*, edited by David M. Ball and Martha B. Kuhlman, 191–205. Jackson: University Press of Mississippi.

Fitzpatrick, Kathleen. 2011. *Planned Obsolescence: Publishing, Technology, and the Future of the Academy*. New York and London: New York University Press.

Fleischer, Rasmus. 2015. "Towards a Postdigital Sensibility: How to Get Moved by Too Much Music." *Culture Unbound* (7): 255–69.

Florida, Richard. 2004. *The Rise of the Creative Class: And How It's Transforming Work, Leisure, Community and Everyday Life*. New York: Basic Books.

Foster, Hal. 2010. "An Archival Impulse." *October* (110): 3–22.

Foucault, Michel. 1972. *The Archaeology of Knowledge and the Discourse on Language*. Translated by A.M. Sheridan Smith. New York: Pantheon Books.
Foucault, Michel. 1980. "'The Confession of the Flesh.' A Conversation with Alain Grosrichard, Gerard Wajeman, Jaques-Alain Miller, Guy Le Gaufey, Dominique Celas, Gerard Miller, Catherine Millot, Jocelyne Livi and Judith Miller." In *Power/Knowledge: Selected Interviews and Other Writings 1972-1977*, edited by Colin Gordon, 194–228. New York: Pantheon Books.
Frahm, Ole. 2010. *Die Sprache des Comics*. Fundus-Bücher 179. Hamburg: Philo Fine Arts.
Freedman, Ariela. 2015. "Chris Ware's Epiphanic Comics." *Partial Answers: Journal of Literature and the History of Ideas* (13.2): 337–58.
Fricke, David. 2013. "Beck's Long Road to 'Morning Phase.'" *Rolling Stone*, November 21. Accessed May 9, 2015. http://www.rollingstone.com/music/news/becks-long-road-to-morning-phase-20131121.
Galloway, Alexander. 2012. *The Interface Effect*. New York: Polity.
Gardner, Jared. 2006. "Archives, Collectors, and the New Media Work of Comics." *MFS: Modern Fiction Studies* (52.4): 787–806.
Gardner, Jared. 2012a. "Comics from the 19th to the 21st Century: An Interview with Jared Gardner (Part Two)." Interview by Henry Jenkins. *Confessions of an Aca-Fan: The Official Weblog of Henry Jenkins*, February 9. Accessed June 7, 2014. http://henryjenkins.org/2012/02/comics_from_the_19th_to_the_21_1.html.
Gardner, Jared. 2012b. *Projections: Comics and the History of Twenty-First Century Storytelling*. Stanford: Stanford University Press.
Gazzard, Alison. 2013. *Mazes in Videogames: Meaning, Metaphor and Design*. Jefferson, NC and London: McFarland & Company.
Gitelman, Lisa. 1999. *Scripts, Grooves, and Writing Machines: Representing Technology in the Edison Era*. Stanford, CA: Stanford University Press.
Gitelman, Lisa. 2008. *Always Already New: Media, History, and the Data of Culture*. Cambridge, MA: The MIT Press.
Goiunova, Olga, and Alexei Shulgin. 2008. "Glitch." In *Software Studies: A Lexicon*, edited by Matthew Fuller, 110–19. Cambridge, MA: The MIT Press.
Gordinier, Jeff. 2008. *X Saves the World: How Generation X Got the Shaft but Can Still Keep Everything from Sucking*. New York: Viking – Published by the Penguin Group.
Graycar, Laura. 2011. "A Visit to Thomas Demand's Studio." *The Iris – Behind the Scenes at the Getty*, October 3. Accessed March 4, 2018. http://blogs.getty.edu/iris/a-visit-to-thomas-demands-studio/.
Groensteen, Thierry. 2007. *The System of Comics*. Jackson: University Press of Mississippi.
Groensteen, Thierry. 2011. *Comics and Narration*. Jackson: University Press of Mississippi.
Halberstam, Jack (Judith). 2007. "Gender." In *Keywords for American Cultural Studies*, edited by Bruce Burgett and Glenn Hendler, 116–20. New York and London: New York University Press.

Hamilton, Caroline. 2010. *One Man Zeitgeist: Dave Eggers, Publishing and Publicity*. New York and London: Continuum.

Hansen, Beck. 1997. "Beck: The Rolling Stone Interview." Interview by Mark Kemp. *Rolling Stone Magazine*, April 17.

Hansen, Beck. 2002. "*The Heartbreak Kid*." Interview by Dorian Lynskey. *Blender Magazine*, October issue.

Hansen, Beck. 2012a. "A Q&A with Beck Hansen, Author of Song Reader." Interview with McSweeney's Books. *McSweeney's – Daily Humor almost Every Day*, December 5. Accessed January 22, 2018. http://www.mcsweeneys.net/articles/a-qa-with-beck-hansen-author-of-song-reader.

Hansen, Beck. 2012b. "Beck Explains 'Song Reader,' an Album Fans Perform Themselves." Interview with Jacki Lyden. *NPR: National Public Radio*, December 29. Accessed May 7, 2015. http://www.npr.org/2012/12/29/168263920/beck-explains-song-reader-an-album-fans-perform-themselves.

Hansen, Beck. 2012c. "A Preface to a Song Reader." In *Song Reader: Twenty New Songs by Beck*. San Francisco: McSweeney's Publishing.

Hansen, Beck. 2012d. "Title of This Song." In *Song Reader: Twenty New Songs by Beck*. San Francisco: McSweeney's Publishing.

Hansen, Beck. 2012e. "Why Did You Make Me Care?" In *Song Reader: Twenty New Songs by Beck*. San Francisco: McSweeney's Publishing.

Hansen, Mark. 2004. *New Philosophy for New Media*. Cambridge, MA: The MIT Press.

Hansen, Miriam. 1991. *Babel and Babylon: Spectatorship in American Silent Film*. Cambridge, MA: Harvard University Press.

Haraway, Donna. 2000. "A Cyborg Manifesto: Science, Technology, and Socialist-Feminism in the Late Twentieth Century." In *The Cybercultures Reader*, edited by David Bell and Barbara M. Kennedy, 291–324. London and New York: Routledge.

Harbach, Chad. 2014. *MFA vs. NYC: The Two Cultures of American Fiction*. New York: n+1/Faber and Faber.

Harvie, Jen. 2013. *Fair Play: Art, Performance and Neoliberalism*. New York: Palgrave Macmillan.

Hayles, N. Katherine. 2002. *Writing Machines*. Cambridge, MA: The MIT Press.

Hayles, N. Katherine. 2008. *Electronic Literature: New Horizons for the Literary*. Notre Dame: University of Notre Dame Press.

Heidegger, Martin. 1983. *Die Grundbegriffe der Metaphysik: Welt – Endlichkeit – Einsamkeit*. Frankfurt am Main: Vittorio Klostermann GmbH.

Herzogenrath, Bernd. 2015. "Media|Matter: An Introduction." In *Media Matter: The Materiality of Media, Matter as Medium*, edited by Bernd Herzogenrath, 1–16. New York, London, New Delhi, and Sydney: Bloomsbury.

Horkheimer, Max, and Theodor W. Adorno. 1989. *Dialectic of Enlightenment*. 1944. Translated by John Cumming. New York: Continuum.

Huhtamo, Erkki, and Jussi Parikka, eds. 2011. *Media Archaeology: Approaches, Applications, and Implications*. Berkeley, Los Angeles, and London: University of California Press.

Hutcheon, Linda. 1989. *The Politics of Postmodernism*. New York: Routledge.

Hutcheon, Linda. 2000. "Irony, Nostalgia, and the Postmodern." *Methods for the Study of Literature as Cultural Memory; Studies in Comparative Literature* (30): 189–207.
Hyde, Emily, and Sarah Wasserman. 2017. "The Contemporary." *Literature Compass* (14.9): 1–19.
Iser, Wolfgang. 1978. *The Act of Reading: A Theory of Aesthetic Response*. Baltimore: Johns Hopkins University Press.
Iser, Wolfgang. 1986. "Fictionalizing Acts." *Amerikastudien Jahresindex* (31.1–4): 5–15.
Jameson, Fredric. 1991. *Postmodernism, Or, The Cultural Logic of Late Capitalism*. Durham: Duke University Press.
Jenkins, Henry. 2006. *Fans, Bloggers and Gamers: Essays on Participatory Culture*. New York and London: New York University Press.
Jenkins, Henry. 2008. Convergence *Culture: Where Old and New Media Collide*. New York: New York University Press.
Jenkins, Henry, and David Thorburn. 2003. "Introduction: Towards an Aesthetics of Transition." In *Rethinking Media Change: The Aesthetics of Transition*, edited by Henry Jenkins and David Thorburn, 1–16. Cambridge, MA: The MIT Press.
Joas, Hans. 1996. *Die Kreativität des Handelns*. Frankfurt am Main: Suhrkamp.
Johnson, Steven. 2005. *Everything Bad Is Good for You: How Popular Culture Is Making Us Smarter*. London: Penguin.
Jordan, Rieke. 2019. "'Her Leg': Chris Ware's Body of Work." In *PathoGraphics: Narrative, Aesthetics, Contention, Community*, edited by Susan Squier and Irmela Marei Krüger-Fürhoff. University Park: Penn State University Press. (Forthcoming).
Joyce, Lindsey. 2016. "Kentucky Route Zero: Or, How Not to Get Lost in the Branching Narrative System." In *The Play versus Story Divide in Game Studies: Critical Essays*, edited by Matthew William Kapell, 17–27. Jefferson: McFarland & Company.
Kelleter, Frank. 2012. "Serien als Stresstest." *Frankfurter Allgemeine Zeitung*, February 4d.
Kelleter, Frank. 2016. "Four Theses on the News." In *Knowledge Landscapes North America*, edited by Christian Kloeckner, Simone Knewitz, and Sabine Sielke, 211–27. Heidelberg: Universitätsverlag Winter.
Kelleter, Frank. 2017. "Five Ways of Looking at Popular Seriality." In *Media of Serial Narrative*, edited by Frank Kelleter, 7–34. Columbus: The Ohio State University Press.
Kelleter, Frank, and Daniel Stein. 2012. "Autorisierungspraktiken seriellen Erzählens – Zur Gattungsentwicklung von Superheldencomics." In *Populäre Serialität: Narration – Evolution – Distinktion: Zum seriellen Erzählen seit dem 19. Jahrhundert*, edited by Frank Kelleter and Daniel Stein, 259–92. Bielefeld: Transcript Verlag.
Kember, Sarah. 2016. *iMedia: The Gendering of Objects, Environments and Smart Material*. London: Palgrave Macmillian.
"Kentucky Route Zero: TV Edition for Nintendo Switch." 2018. *Nintendo.com*, n.p.

K-Hole. 2013. "Issue #3: The K-Hole Brand Anxiety Matrix." *K-Hole*, January 2013. Accessed April 4, 2018. http://k-hole.net/dh/v=3.

Kirschenbaum, Matthew. 2008. *Mechanisms: New Media and the Forensic Imagination*. Cambridge, MA: The MIT Press.

Kittler, Friedrich. 2010. *Optical Media*. Cambridge: Polity Press.

Koepnick, Lutz. 2014. *On Slowness: Toward an Aesthetic of the Contemporary*. New York: Columbia University Press.

Kohlenberger, Judith. 2015. *The New Formula for Cool: Science, Technology, and the Popular in the American Imagination*. Bielefeld: Transcript American Culture Studies.

Kopytoff, Igor. 1986. "The Cultural Biography of Things: Commoditization as Process." In *The Social Life of Things: Commodities in Cultural Perspective*, edited by Arjun Appadurai, 64–91. Cambridge: Cambridge University Press.

Kuhlman, Martha B. 2010. "In the Comics Workshop: Chris Ware and Oubapo." In *The Comics of Chris Ware: Drawing Is a Way of Thinking*, edited by David M. Ball and Martha B. Kuhlman, 78–89. Jackson: University Press of Mississippi.

Lenk, Hans. 2000. *Kreative Aufstiege: Zur Philosophie und Psychologie der Kreativität*. Frankfurt am Main: Suhrkamp.

Lenoir, Tim. 2004. "Foreword." In *New Philosophy for New Media*. Cambridge, MA: The MIT Press.

Levy, Lester. 1971. *Flashes of Merriment: A Century of Humorous Songs in America, 1805–1905*. Norman: Oklahoma Press.

Levy, Lester. 2013. "Overview – The Lester S. Levy Sheet Music Collection." *Sheridan Libraries Special Collections*, Johns Hopkins University, n.d. Accessed March 6, 2018. http://levysheetmusic.mse.jhu.edu/about/overview.

Limits & Demonstrations. 2013. N.p.: Cardboard Computer, LLC.

Lott, Eric. 1993. *Love and Theft: Blackface Minstrelsy and the American Working Class*. New York and Oxford: Oxford University Press.

Luhmann, Niklas. 1982. "Autopoiesis, Handlung und kommunikative Verständigung." *Zeitschrift für Soziologie* (11.4): 366–79.

Lund, Jamie. 2013. "Fixing Music Copyright." *Brooklyn Law Review* (79.1): 51–106.

Manoff, Marlene. 2004. "Theories of the Archives from Across the Disciplines." *portal: Libraries in the Academy* (4.1): 9–25.

Manoff, Marlene. 2006. "The Materiality of Digital Collections: Theoretical and Historical Perspectives." *portal: Libraries in the Academy* (6.3): 311–25.

Manovich, Lev. 2001. *The Language of New Media*. Cambridge, MA: The MIT Press.

Margini, Matt. 2017. "'Hamlet on the Holodeck,' Twenty Years Later." *Second Read – The New Yorker*, August 30. Accessed October 2, 2017. https://www.new yorker.com/books/second-read/hamlet-on-the-holodeck-twenty-years-later.

Mauro, Aaron. 2010. "'Mosaic Thresholds': Manifesting the Collection and Production of Comics in the Works of Chris Ware." *ImageTextT: Interdisciplinary Comics Studies* (5.1): n.p.

Maxwell, Kate. 2016. "Beck's Song Reader: An Unbound Music Book." *Literature Unbound* (8.1): n.p.
McCloud, Scott. 1993. *Understanding Comics: The Invisible Art*. New York: William Morrow, an Imprint of HarperCollins Publishers.
McCloud, Scott. 2000. *Reinventing Comics: How Imagination and Technology are Revolutionizing an Art Form*. New York: Perennial.
McFall, Liz. 2004. "The Culturalization of Work in the 'New' Economy: An Historical View." In *Identity in the Age of the New Economy: Life in Temporary and Scattered Work Practices*, edited by Torben Elgaard Jensen and Ann Westenholz, 9–33. Cheltenham: Edward Elgar Publishing Limited.
McGurl, Mark. 2009. *The Program Era: Postwar Fiction and the Rise of Creative Writing*. Cambridge, MA: Harvard University Press.
McRobbie, Angela. 1994. *Postmodernism and Popular Culture*. London: Routledge.
Merve. 2014. "Re: Kentucky Route Zero's Theatricality Takes Center Stage in Its Third Act." *The AV Club*, May 14. Accessed August 12, 2015. http://www.avclub.com/article/kentucky-route-zeros-theatricality-takes-center-st-204554.
Miodowski, Mark. 2015. *Stuff Matters: Exploring the Marvelous Materials That Shape Our Man-Made World*. New York: Houghton Mifflin Harcourt Publishing Company.
Mitchell, Alex. 2014. "Defamiliarization and Poetic Interaction in Kentucky Route Zero." *Well Played – A Seriously Weird Special Issue* (3.2): 167–86.
Mittell, Jason. 2006. "Narrative Complexity and Contemporary American Television." *Velvet Light Trap* (58): 29–40.
Mittell, Jason. 2012. "Comprehension." *Complex TV: The Poetics of Contemporary Television Storytelling*. Media Commons Press, Open Scholarship in Open Format, August 3.
Monod, David. 2016. *The Soul of Pleasure: Sentiment and Sensation in Nineteenth-American Mass Entertainment*. Ithaca and London: Cornell University Press.
Moynihan, Colin. 2005. "The Cube, Restored, Is Back and Turning at Astor Place." *New Times*, November 19. Accessed October 3, 2017. https://www.nytimes.com/2005/11/19/nyregion/the-cube-restored-is-back-and-turning-at-astor-place.html.
Murray, Janet. 1997. *Hamlet on the Holodeck: The Future of Narrative in Cyberspace*. Cambridge, MA: The MIT Press.
Nealon, Jeffrey N. 2012. *Post-Postmodernism: Or, The Cultural Logic of Just-in-Time Capitalism*. Stanford: Stanford University Press.
Nelson, Ted. 1981. *Literary Machines*. Sausalito: Mindful Press.
Ngai, Sianne. 2012a. "Network Aesthetics: Juliana Spahr's *The Transformation* and Bruno Latour's *Reassembling the Social*." In *American Literature's Aesthetic Dimensions*, edited by Cindy Weinstein and Christopher Looby, 367–92. New York: Columbia University Press.
Ngai, Sianne. 2012b. *Our Aesthetic Categories: Zany, Cute, Interesting*. Cambridge, MA and London: Harvard University Press.

O'Donnell, Kevin. 2006. "Beck's Rock & Roll Puppet Show Hits NYC." *Rolling Stone Magazine*, October 19. Accessed December 17, 2017. http://www.rollingstone.com/music/news/becks-rock-roll-puppet-show-hits-nyc-20061019.

Ong, Walter. 1997. *Orality and Literacy: The Technologizing of the Word*. New York: Routledge.

Parales, Jon. 2002. "David Bowie, 21st-Century Entrepreneur." *The New York Times*, June 9.

Parikka, Jussi. 2011. *Media Archaelogy: Approaches, Applications, and Implications*. Berkeley, LA, London: University of California Press.

Parikka, Jussi. 2012. *What Is Media Archaeology*. Cambridge and Malden, MA: Polity Press.

Parikka, Jussi. 2013. "Archival Media Theory: An Introduction to Wolfgang Ernst's Media Archeology." In *Digital Memory and the Archive*, 1–22. Minneapolis and London: University of Minnesota Press.

Parkins, Wendy, and Geoffrey Craig. 2006. *Slow Living*. Oxford, New York: Berg.

Peters, John Durham. 1999. *Speaking into the Air: A History of the Idea of Communication*. Chicago: University of Chicago Press.

Peters, John Durham. 2015. "Proliferation and Obsolescence of the Historical Record in the Digital Era." In *Cultures of Obsolescence: History, Materiality, and the Digital Age*, edited by Babette B. Tischleder and Sarah Wasserman, 79–96. New York: Palgrave Macmillian.

Popova, Maria. 2015. "In Defense of Boredom: 200 Years of Ideas on the Virtues of Not-Doing from Some of Humanity's Greatest Minds." *Brain Pickings Weekly*, March 16. Accessed August 24, 2015. http://www.brainpickings.org/2015/03/16/boredom/.

Raeburn, Daniel. 2004. *Chris Ware*. New Haven: Monographics – Yale University Press.

Reckwitz, Andreas. 2017a. *Die Gesellschaft der Singularitäten: Zum Strukturwandel der Moderne*. Berlin: Suhrkamp Verlag.

Reckwitz, Andreas. 2017b. *The Invention of Creativity: Modern Society and the Culture of the New*. Translated by Steven Black. Cambridge: Polity Press.

Reed, Arden. 2017. *Slow Art: The Experience of Looking, Sacred Images to James Turrell*. Oakland: University of California Press.

Reynolds, Simon. 2011. *Retromania: Pop Culture's Addiction to Its Own Past*. London: Faber and Faber Ltd.

Ricoeur, Paul. 1991. "Appropriation." In *A Ricoeur Reader: Reflection and Imagination*, edited by Mario J. Valdés, 86–98. New York, London, Toronto, Sydney, Tokyo, and Singapore: Harvester Wheatsheaf.

Ritzer, George, and Nathan Jurgenson. 2010. "Production, Consumption, Prosumption." *Journal of Consumer Culture* (10.1): 13–36.

Robbins, Derek. 2000. *Bourdieu & Culture*. London, Thousand Oaks and Greater Kailash: SAGE Publications Ltd.

Roeder, Katherine. 2012. "Building Stories: Stories about Art and Buildings, and Growing Up." *The Comics Journal*. Accessed May 7, 2014. http://www.tcj.com/building-stories-stories-about-art-and-buildings-and-growing-up/.

Rosa, Hartmut. 2013. *Social Acceleration: A New Theory of Modernity*. Translated by Jonathan Trejo-Mathys. New York: Columbia University Press.

Rosa, Hartmut, and William E. Scheuerman, eds. 2009. *High-Speed Society: Social Acceleration, Power, and Modernity*. University Park: Pennsylvania State University Press.

Rose, Frank. 2011. *The Art of Immersion: How the Digital Generation Is Remaking Hollywood, Madison Avenue, and the Way We Tell Stories*. New York and London: W.W. Norton & Company.

Rosen, Jody. 2012. "Introduction." In *Song Reader: Twenty New Songs by Beck*. San Francisco: McSweeney's Publishing.

Rougeau, Michael. 2013. "Making 'Kentucky Route Zero,' a Magical Realist Adventure in Five Acts." *ANIMAL – Art, New York City, Culture, Politics, and Opinion*, December 12. Accessed August 11, 2015. http://animalnewyork.com/2013/game-plan-making-kentucky-route-zero-magical-realist-adventure-five-acts/.

Salmon, Chris. 2006. "I'm Always in Danger of Being Dismissed as a Clown." *The Guardian*, September 21. Accessed January 31, 2016. http://www.theguardian.com/arts/features/story/0,,1877277,00.html%22%3EBeck.

Sanjek, David. 2001. "They Work Hard for Their Money: The Business of Popular Music." In *American Popular Music: New Approaches to the Twentieth Century*, edited by Rachel Rubin and Jeffrey Melnick, 9–27. Amherst: University of Massachusetts Press.

Sattler, Peter R. 2010. "'Building Stories' and the Art of Memory." In *The Comics of Chris Ware: Drawing Is a Way of Thinking*, edited by David M. Ball and Martha B. Kuhlman, 206–22. Jackson: University Press of Mississippi.

Sattler, Peter R. 2012. "Building Memories: Mine, Hers, and Ours." *The Comics Journal*, November 2. Accessed June 9, 2014. http://www.tcj.com/building-memories-mine-hers-and-ours/.

Scholz, Trebor, ed. 2013. *Digital Labor: The Internet as Playground and Factory*. New York and London: Routledge.

Schoonmaker, Kara. 2007. "Hypermedia." *The Chicago School of Media Theory – Theorizing Media since 2003*, n.d. Accessed May 24, 2014. http://lucian.uchicago.edu/blogs/mediatheory/keywords/hypermedia/.

Schwartz, Joan M., and Terry Cook. 2002. "Archives, Records, and Power: The Making of Modern Memory." *Archival Science* (2): 1–19.

Silva, Joao. 2016. *Entertaining Lisbon: Music, Theater, and Modern Life in the Late 19th Century*. New York: Oxford University Press.

Sloane, Sarah. 2000. *Digital Fictions: Storytelling in a Material World*. Stamford: AblexPublishing Corporation.

Solberg, Dan. 2014. "Road to Two5Six: Tamas Kemenczy." *Kill Screen – Videogame Art & Culture*, May 14. Accessed August 11, 2015. http://killscreendaily.com/articles/road-two5six-tamas-kemenczy/.

Spacks, Patricia Meyer. 1995. *Boredom: The History of a State of Mind*. Chicago and London: The University of Chicago Press.

Squier, Susan M. 2008. "So Long as They Grow Out of It: Comics, the Discourse of Developmental Normalcy, and Disability." *Journal of the Medical Humanities* (29.2): 71–88.

Starre, Alexander. 2015. *Metamedia: American Book Fictions and Literary Print Culture after Digitization*. Iowa City: University of Iowa Press.

Sterne, Jonathan. 2012. *MP3: The Meaning of a Format*. Durham and London: Duke University Press.

Stewart, Susan. 1993. *On Longing: Narratives of the Miniature, the Gigantic, the Souvenir, the Collection*. Durham and London: Duke University Press.

Stewart, Susan. 1994. "Death and Life, in That Order, in the Works of Charles Willson Peale." In *The Cultures of Collecting*, edited by John Elsner and Roger Cardinal, 204–23. London: Reaktion Books.

Taylor, Timothy D. 2012. "General Introduction." In *Music, Sound, and Technology in America: A Documentary History of Early Phonograph, Cinema, and Radio*, edited by Timothy D. Taylor, Mark Katz, and Tony Grajeda, 1–8. Durham and London: Duke University Press.

Terranova, Tiziana. 2008. "Free Labor: Producing Culture for the Digital Economy." *Social Text* (18): 2–63.

Thurtle, Phillip, and Robert Mitchell. 2007. "The Acme Novelty Library: Comic Books, Repetition, and the Return of the New." *Configurations* (15.3): 267–97.

Tinker, Emma. 2008–09. *Identity and Form in Alternative Comics, 1967–2007*. PDF Accessed May 8, 2014. http://emmatinker.oxalto.co.uk/thesis/.

Tomasula, Steve. 2010. "Where We Are Now: A Dozen or So Observations, Historical Notes, and Soundings for a Map of Contemporary American Innovative Literature as Seen from the Interior." *Études Anglaises* (63.2): 215–27.

Tompkins, Jane. 1985. *Sensational Designs: The Cultural Work of American Fiction, 1790–1860*. New York and London: Oxford University Press.

Ulin, David L. 2012. "Chris Ware Ups the Ante with 'Building Stories.'" *Los Angeles Times*, October 28. Accessed January 20, 2016. http://articles.latimes.com/2012/oct/28/entertainment/la-ca-jc-chris-ware-20121028.

Versaci, Rocco. 2007. *This Book Contains Graphic Language: Comics as Literature*. New York: Continuum.

Virilio, Paul. 2006. *Speed and Politics*. Cambridge, MA: The MIT Press.

von Gehlen, Dirk. 2011. *Mashup: Lob der Kopie*. Berlin: Suhrkamp Verlag.

von Gehlen, Dirk. 2013. *Eine neue Version ist verfügbar – Update: Wie die Digitalisierung Kunst und Kultur verändert*. Berlin: Metrolit.

Ware, Chris. 1999. *Acme Novelty Library #13*. Seattle: Fantagraphics Books.

Ware, Chris. 2001. *Jimmy Corrigan: The Smartest Kid on Earth*. New York: Pantheon.

Ware, Chris. 2012a. "A Life in A Box: Invention, Clarity and Meaning in Chris Ware's 'Building Stories.'" Interview by Calvin Reid. *Publisher Weekly*, September 28. Accessed May 4, 2014. https://www.publishersweekly.com/pw

/by-topic/industry-news/comics/article/54154-a-life-in-a-box-invention-clarity-and-meaning-in-chris-ware-s-building-stories.html.

Ware, Chris. 2012b. *Building Stories*. New York: Pantheon.

Ware, Chris. 2012c. "Chris Ware on Building a Better Comic Book." Interview by Christopher Irving and Seth Kushner. *Graphic NYC*, March 6. Accessed May 7, 2014. http://www.nycgraphicnovelists.com/2012/03/chris-ware-on-building-better-comic.html.

Ware, Chris. 2012d. "'I Hoped That the Book Would Just Be Fun': A Brief Interview with Chris Ware." Interview by Chris Mautner. *The Comics Journal*, October 10. Accessed October 12, 2014. http://www.tcj.com/i-hoped-that-the-book-would-just-be-fun-a-brief-interview-with-chris-ware/.

Ware, Chris. 2012e. *Multi-Story Building Model*. Outremont: Drawn and Quarterly.

Ware, Chris. 2012f. "Work Hard and Be Kind." Interview by Tavi Gevinson. *Rookie Magazine*, November 29. Accessed May 6, 2014. http://www.rookiemag.com/2012/11/chris-ware-intervie/.

Ware, Chris. 2014. "The Last Saturday." *The Guardian*. Accessed September 7, 2015. https://www.theguardian.com/books/ng-interactive/2014/sep/13/-sp-chris-ware-the-last-saturday-graphic-novel.

Whitehead, Dan. 2013. "Where the Road Takes You: Investigating Kentucky Route Zero – Jake Elliott of Cardboard Computer Opens Up about His Surreal Indie Adventure." *eurogamer.net*, January 28. Accessed August 1, 2015. http://www.eurogamer.net/articles/2013-01-28-where-the-road-takes-you-investigating-kentucky-route-zero.

Widiss, Benjamin. 2013. "Comics as Non-Sequential Art: Chris Ware's Joseph Cornell." In *Drawing from Life: Memory and Subjectivity in Comic Art*, edited by Jane Tolmie, 86–111. Jackson: University Press of Mississippi.

Wilde, Autumn de. 2011. *Beck*. San Francisco: Chronicle Books.

Wilde, Lukas R.A. 2015. "Distinguishing Mediality: The Problem of Identifying Forms and Features of Digital Comics." *Digital Comics*. Special Issue of *Networking Knowledge* (8.4): n.p.

Willis, Simon. 2013. "Chris Ware: Everyday Genius." *The Economist*, September–October. https://www.1843magazine.com/content/features/simon-willis/chris-ware?page=full.

Wolf, Gary. 1995. "The Curse of Xanadu." *Wired*, June issue, n.p.

Wolf, Mark J.P. 2012. *Building Imaginary Worlds: The Theory and History of Subcreation*. New York and London: Routledge/Taylor & Francis Group.

Wolk, Douglas. 2007. *Reading Comics: How Graphic Novels Work and What They Mean*. Philadelphia: Da Capo Press.

Worden, Daniel. 2010. "On Modernism's Ruins: The Architecture of 'Building Stories' and Lost Buildings." In *The Comics of Chris Ware: Drawing Is a Way of Thinking*, edited by David M. Ball and Martha B. Kuhlman, 107–21. Jackson: University Press of Mississippi.

The Young Englishwoman. 1869. London: Ward, Lock, and Tyler.

Index

Abercrombie & Fitch   17, 18
Adorno, Theodor W.   10–11, 16–17, 18, 30 n.40, 115
aesthetics   xiii n.5, 3, 10, 15, 20, 37, 41, 49 n.7, 49–50, 78, 91–2, 99, 102, 115, 120, 126–7, 129, 136, 137, 139, 141, 145, 150, 158, 159, 166, 168
afternoon, a story   5 n.7
Agamben, Giorgio   xi, x n.3
Amateur Work, Illustrated   170
Anderson, Benedict   105–6, 114, 118
Anderson, Kelli   170 n.5
Apperley, Thomas   149
appropriation   7 n.8, 111
Arendt, Hannah   4–5 n.3
art
    as commodity   16–17
    competence   21–2, 124, 149, 150, 151
    and consumerism   116
    high art   17
    interaction through art   139–44
    performance art   20 n.21
Asterios Polyp   55 n.12
Atlanta (FX)   23 n.24
Atlantic   12
audience   5, 92, 121
    and celebrities   113, 115, 116
    and naturalization   20 n.21
    and planned confusion   12, 24
authenticity   18, 22, 67, 97, 97 n.11, 117
authority   25, 25 n.28, 36, 68 n.17
authorship   2, 18, 68, 82, 84, 112, see also failing author
auto-poetic systems   151, 156

Babbitt, Ben   128
Bachelard, Gaston   55, 55 n.13
Bal, Mieke   45
Ball, David M.   25, 25 n.28, 26 n.32
Banash, David   xiii n.5, 93 n.8
Banita, Georgiana   137
Baudrillard, Jean   45, 46
Bauman, Zygmunt   100–1, 125 n.1
Beatles, Popular Music, and Society, The   82
Beatles, The   17, 18, 82
Beck-Gernsheim, Elisabeth   13 n.15
Beck, Ulrich   13 n.15, 15 n.17, 20 n.20
being
    being busy   12–13, 22
    and collecting   45
Bellezza, Silvia   12
Benjamin, Walter   47, 52, 72, 125
Berlant, Lauren   138
Berlatsky, Eric   61, 61 n.16
Berman, Margaret Fink   136 n.17
Bildungsroman   41, 41 n.3
biography   15 n.17, 21 n.22
Boellstorff, Tom   152 n.27
Bong Load Records   97
boredom   23–4 n.25, 90, 126, 126 n.4
Borges, Jorge Luis   159 n.39
Bourdieu, Pierre   22, 23–4, 25, 91, 124, 149
Bowie, David   82, 87, 100 n.12
Boym, Svetlana   94, 132, 132 n.14
branching narratives   134–5, 143, 158, 162 n.42
Bredehoft, Thomas   65, 68
Brief Wondrous Life of Oscar Wao, The   23 n.24
Bring on the Books for Everybody   9 n.11, 10

Index

Brooks, Peter   7, 7 n.8
Brown, Bill   33–4, 94, 169
Brownstein, Carrie   89, 111
Brunetti, Ivan   25 n.29
Buckley, Jeff   108
Building Stories   x, xiii, xiv, xv, xvi–xvii, xviii, 14, 18, 21, 22, 25, 30, 32, 33, 34, 35, 127, 136
   affective response   91
   analog memories   75–80
   barn cut out   66
   Browsing   51–6
   centerpieces   56–62
   collecting and remembering   46, 78
   collection and practical memory   45–51
   comments on digitization processes   39
   commodification   52–3
   cover design   53–4
   curatorial labor   74–5
   curatorial practices   77–8
   curio cabinets and cut outs   62–9
   cute things in   49–50
   dream   51–4, 55, 59, 65–6, 72
   fake collection   45–6
   format   39–40
   impossible collections   69–75
   inset panels   61–2
   keepsake box   47, 48, 51–6, 65, 68, 70, 71, 76, 82, 118
   modernism in   50 n.8
   narrating house   54–5
   narrative gap   63–4
   panels and gutters   59–60, 67–8
   protagonist is the imagined author of book   58–9
   reader as curator and architect   72–3
   reader's competences   82
   space and time in   59–61, 67
   timeline   41 n.1
   visual discomfort   56
   zoetrope   63–4, 167, 167 n.3

Calder, Alexander   32
Cale, John   108
Campbell, David   86
cardboard   xviii, 163–74
Cardboard (Google)   xviii, 163–4, 166–8, 171 n.6
Cardboard Computer   22, 26, 30, 37, 127, 129, 148, 165, 171
Carey, James   161–2 n.41
Cash, Johnny   108
Cates, Isaac   43, 44
celebrated failures   25, 25 n.28, 26, 27
celebrities   92
Chamberlain, Lula   139–40, 142–3
Choose Your Own Adventure books   6–7, 143
Chun, Wendy Hui Kyong   xviii n.6, 35 n.46, 148–9
Chute, Hillary   79 n.24
Citizen Kane   153
Claudio, Esther   67
Cohen, Leonard   108
Coleridge, Samuel Taylor   153
Collins, Jim   9 n.11, 10
Colors   86
comics, *see Building Stories*; graphic narratives
commodification   23, 50, 52–3, 101, 114
commodity
   art as   15–17
   and object of consumption   114–15
   passive commodity   115–16
competence
   art competence   22, 124, 149, 150, 151
   hip competence   23–5
   reader's competences   82
   slacker competence   121–4
connoisseurship   16–17, 18, 22, 120, 140

contemporariness, the   x–xii, xi n.3, xi n.4, xiii, xix, 1, 2, 4, 7, 9, 12, 17, 22, 30–1, 33, 34, 39, 49, 75, 82, 85, 94, 98, 102, 107, 134, 155, 156, 168, 172–3
copy/cover song   117
creative labor   84, 107, 121
creative writing   15, 15 n.18, 52, 57, 58
creativity   xiv, 2, 10–18, 26, 91–2
  and development   13
  as dispositif (see dispositif)
  economization of   101
  geographical influences of   13
  institutionalization of   15–16
  self-creativity   13, 63, 115
creativity complex   15
Crosby, Bing   106
cultural biography of things   20 n.22
cultural capital   12, 17, 22, 90, 91, 122
cultural memory   156–7
curator/curation   xiii–xiv, xv
  planned confusion   2–9
  reader   10–18, 72–3
curatorial labor   2, 9–10, 14, 17, 19, 74, 82, 100, 142, 150, 170, see also labor
curatorial reading   126, 142, see also curatorial labor; reading
cuteness   43–4, 49–50, 80, 91
cut out   62–70, 74–6, 121–2, 137

Dark Knight, The   5 n.5
data and narrative   150 n.25
Daydream (Google)   166 n.2
deep media   6
DeKoven, Marianne   79 n.24
Demand, Thomas   173, 173 n.8
Denson, Shane   153, 153 n.28
de-skilled laborer   19–20, 24
digital aesthetics   78
digital archive   117–21
digital culture   94, 165, 169, 173
digital fiction   5–6 n.7

digital graphic novella   78
digitality   xix, 32, 33, 75, 164, 172
digital media   33, 135, 153
digital moment   1, 2, 31, 33, 34, 100, 116
digital nostalgia   94, 96
digital technologies   4, 6, 33, 36, 42, 75–6, 78, 82, 84, 92, 93 n.8, 141, 165, 168
digitization   xix, 3, 5 n.4, 31, 34, 33 n.43, 39, 82, 94, 100, 101, 115, 118
Dinnen, Zara   35, 76 n.21, 149, 172
dispositif   xvii, 12, 14, 14 n.16, 15, 16, 26, 91
Dyer, Richard   96 n.10, 97 n.10
Dylan, Bob   82

Eco, Umberto   5, 31–2, 36–7, 40–1, 113, 159 n.36, 161 n.40, 168
Egan, Jennifer   6
Eglash, Ron   23 n.24
Elliott, Jake   128, 131, 131 n.11, 133, 135, 148
Emerson Drug Company   105
Engberg, Maria   6 n.7
Ensslin, Astrid   133–4 n.15
Entertainment Weekly   26
Ernst, Wolfgang   ix, 34, 77, 156
experimental memory, see memory

failing author   25–9
failure   2, 12, 24–6, 26 n.32, 27, 36, 119
fans   106, 122
  investment of   82
  labor of   5
Feldman, Brian   xix
fiction   1, 3–4, 5–6 n.7, 12, 52, 58–9, 72, 95 n.9, 103, 121, 122, 124, 139, 155
Fitzpatrick, Kathleen   30, 31, 31 n.42, 32
flânerie   130–1, 161
Fleischer, Rasmus   102 n.13

Florida, Richard   12–13
Fordism   xiii n.5
Foucault, Michel   14 n.16
Frankenstein, inset panels
   in   61 n.16, 61–2
Freedman, Ariela   41 n.3
free time   5, 10–13, 173
Fricke, David   98–9

Galloway, Alexander   10, 142 n.21,
   142 n.22, 149, 159 n.37
gaps   109 n.23
   narrative gap   63–4
   serial gap   70, 71–2, 74
Gardner, Jared   48, 68–9, 69 n.18,
   71–2, 140
Gazzard, Alison   160 n.39
geeks and nerds   29 n.38
gender   27–30, 50, 50 n.9, 90, 171
gender neutrality, in designing of
   pastimes   29 n.38
Gesamtkunstwerk   14, 18
Gevinson, Tavi   46
Gift Time Is All the Time   95, 96
Gitelman, Lisa   ix, 27, 28, 28 n.34
   Always Already New   ix
Glass, Ira   54 n.11
glitches   7, 144–50
Glover, Donald   23 n.24
Goiunova, Olga   149
Gondry, Michel   124
Gordinier, Jeff   88
graphic narratives   1, 21, 24, 29–30,
   34, 39, 43 n.5, 50, 51, 52,
   53 n.10, 55, 55 n.12, 63–4, 73,
   77, 79 n.24, 82, 136, 137
Graycar, Lauren   173 n.8
Grayson, Nathan   131
Groensteen, Thierry   43, 60
Guardian, The   71, 78

"Hallelujah"   108
Ham (artist)   121–3
Hamilton, Caroline   22, 32, 33, 121
Hansen, Al   86

Hansen, Beck   xix, xv, xvii, xviii, 18,
   19, 24, 26, 27, 28, 33, 34, 37,
   98, 127, 170
   artistic and countercultural
      circles   86–7
   career   85–6
   conscious stance against
      elitism   87
   indie rock field   85–93
   puppet doppelgänger   88
   Song Reader (*see Song Reader*)
Hansen, Bibbe   86
Hansen, Channing   86
Hansen, Mark   xiii n.5, 34 n.43, 35
   n.47, 138 n.20
Hansen, Miriam   28 n.36
haptic experience   3, 30 n.41, 32–3,
   63, 100, 101, 127, 169
Haraway, Donna   50
Harbach, Chad   15 n.18
Harvie, Jen   19 n.20, 19–20,
   20 n.21, 24
Hawkins, Taylor   121
Hayles, N. Katherine   30 n.41, 165
Heidegger, Martin   93
Herzogenrath, Bernd   x n.2
hip competence   22–5
Horkheimer, Max   16–18, 30 n.40,
   115
Hutcheon, Linda   96–7 n.10, 135
Hyde, Emily   xi, xi n.4, xii
hypermediacy and
   immediacy   102 n.14
hypertext   151 n.26

incompleteness   42, 71, 136,
   136 n.18, 157–8
individualization   1, 12, 49, 98, 101,
   106, 113, 128
Information, The   88, 98
interaction/interactivity   xv,
   xvi–xvii, 1–6, 8, 9, 14, 16 n.19,
   30 n.41, 39, 75, 76, 77, 81, 94,
   116, 127–30, 133, 135, 139–44,
   151, 157

internet viii, xi, xix, 36, 51–2, 75, 77, 99, 121, 125–6, 127, 163, 169, 173
Irving, Christopher 63
Iser, Wolfgang 3 n.1, 23 n.25, 109 n.23

Jackson, Shelley 5 n.7
Jahn-Sudmann, Andreas 153, 153 n.28
Jameson, Fredric ix, 96 n.10
Jenkins, Henry 102
Johnson, Steven 4 n.2
Joyce, Michael 5 n.7
Junot, Díaz 23 n.24
Just Kids 82

Kelleter, Frank 8–9 n.10, 21 n.23, 36, 68 n.17, 156 n.34
Kember, Sarah 171 n.6
Kemenczy, Tamas 128, 141
Kentucky Route Zero ix, xiii, xiv, xiv, xvi, xviii, 14, 18, 21, 22, 24, 26, 30, 32, 33, 34, 35, 127
  black screen 144–50
  branching narratives 134–5
  choice 133
  code and narrative 149
  delays and detours 128–9
  "Museum of Dwellings" 144–5
  nostalgic deferral, deferring nostalgia 130–5
  self-referentiality 156
  slowness 125–7, 136–9
  untold stories and parallel possibilities 157–62
  XANADU xv, 151–8, 165
K-Hole 11–12 n.13
Kingelez, Bodys Isek 173
Kirschenbaum, Matthew 158
Kittler, Friedrich 155 n.31, 167
Koepnick, Lutz xi–xii, 126, 158
Kohlenberger, Judith 30 n.39
Kopytoff, Igor 20–1, 20 n.22, 113
Krakauer, Siegfried xiii n.5

Kuhlman, Martha 43
Kushner, Seth 63

Labo (Nintendo) xviii, 163–4, 165, 166, 168–72, 174
labor and work, distinction between 4 n.3
  creative labor 84, 107, 121
  curatorial labor 2, 9–10, 14, 17, 19, 74, 82, 100, 142, 150, 170
  of fans 5
  and play 142 n.22
  productivity of 4 n.3
legitimation/legitimization 20, 21 n. 23, 24–5, 27, 81
leisure/spare time xvii, 13
  definition of 10–11
  and work 4–5, 12, 20, 28, 81, 122, 173
Levy, Lester 105
Limits & Demonstrations 139, 140–4, 145
liquid modernity 100–1
Little Golden Book 42
"Loser" 85
Lost Buildings 54 n.11
Lott, Eric 104 n.15
Luhmann, Niklas 154 n.29, 156, 156 n.33
Lund, Jamie 107 n.18
Lynch, David 135 n.16

McCartney, Sir Paul 121
McCloud, Scott 59, 60, 64, 68, 70
McGurl, Mark 15–16
McRobbie, Angela 133
McSweeney's 21, 26, 32, 33, 71
Madonna 86 n.3
Mailer, Norman 23 n.24
Manovich, Lev 150 n.25, 159 n.37
Margini, Matt 160
Marxism 24 n.26
Marx, Karl 5
Mashup 107–8

mass culture   17–18, 49–50, 92, 107, 113–17
mass entertainment   27 n.33, 28 n.36, 173
mass media   48, 92, 127
mass products   117, 166
material desire   9, 12, 29
material flexibilities   2, 55
materiality   30 n.41
   and mediality   35
material openness   1, 2
Mauro, Aaron   69 n.18
Maxwell, Kate   94, 102 n.14
Mazzucchelli, David   55 n.12
media
   as historical objects   ix–x
   and pastness   x
media archaeology   28 n.35, 34, 93 n.8, 173
media-commons.org   31
media history   34, 103, 114 n.25, 115, 163, 166, 171, 172
Mellow Gold   97–8
memory   xviii, 44–5
   cultural memory   156–157
   experimental memory   xvii, 47, 55–56, 72
   practical memory   47
   thinking around a   67–8
MFA v. NYC   15 n.18
Midnite Vultures   85, 97
Mittell, Jason   7 n.9, 7–8, 16 n.19
modernism   xi, xviii, 1, 17, 29, 32, 50, 50 n.8, 95 n.9
Monod, David   27 n.33, 105 n.16
Morning Phase   86
Moynihan, Colin   143 n.23
multi-activity societies   20 n.20
multiform narratives   159–61
Multi-Story Building Model   xvii, 72–4, 98
Murray, Janet   6, 151 n.26, 159 n.38, 159–61

music
   composition and sound recording, distinguishes between   107 n.18
   dematerialization of   100
   digital culture   94
   formats   94, 99–100
   slacker music   89
Mutations   85, 97

narrative complexity   6 n.7, 7–9
narrative desire   7, 7 n.8, 9
naturalization   20, 20 n.21, 173
"Nausea"   88
Nealon, Jeffrey   17–18, 97, 97 n.11, 112 n.24
Nelson, Ted   151 n.26
neoliberalism   9, 12, 26, 30 n.40, 127
new media   x, xviii n.6, 35 n.47
New Philosophy for New Media   138 n.20
New Yorker, The   26, 70, 71, 126
New York Times, The   26
Ngai, Sianne   49, 74, 126, 157, 166
niche   22, 24, 27, 28, 103, 113, 129 n.8
niche audience   19–20, 171, 172
niche capitalism   18
Nintendo   128 n.6, 132 n.13, 163, *see also* Labo (Nintendo)
nostalgia   xix, 94–7, 130–5
"Nothing Compares 2 U"   108

O'Connor, Sinéad   108
Odelay   85, 97, 104
O'Donnell, Kevin   88
One Foot in the Grave   86, 97
Ong, Walter   152 n.27
open artwork   5, 36
openness   1, 2, 32, 34, 36–7, 43, 62, 127, 168
open-source   31 n.42, 32, 164
open structure   39–40, 41
Open Work, The   31, 32, 159 n.36

Parales, Jon   100 n.12
Parikka, Jussi   156, 169
Paris Review, The   26
participatory culture   xv, 5 n.7, 32, 84, 101, 102, 112, 117, 120
participatory theater   19
pastiche   96–7 n.10
pastimes   1, 4, 9, 13–14, 27, 29, 29 n.38, 74, 80, 94, 105, 129, 169–70, 173
Patchwork Girl   5 n.7
Peters, John Durham   ix, 28 n.35, 140, 155, 157
phonograph   27, 28, 28 n.35, 114, 118
Pinsker, Joe   12
pirating   84, 94, 109, 109 n.22
planned confusion   2–9, 12, 16, 18
Planned Obsolescence   31 n.42
Plato   152 n.27
play
   and labor   142 n.22
   and work   8 n.10
Porompka, Stephan   10
postmodernism   xi, 86 n.3, 95 n.9, 97 n.11, 125 n.1
practical memory   47
pre-internet life   xviii, 132, 133
print capitalism   77 n.22, 106, 114
"product to process"   30–7
proletaroid intelligentsia   24, 24 n.27
prosumption, prosumer   5, 5 n.4, 17
purchasing power   20
purposelessness   16, 17, 18, 30 n.40
Pynchon, Thomas   132 n.12

Raeburn, Daniel   54–5, 66
reader-response theory   2, 3, 13–14
reading   3
   as cultural technique   1
   curatorial reading   126, 142
   as a game   129–30
   open reading   36
   as overlap between free and unfree time   13–14

Reading for the Plot   7
reception aesthetics   2–3
Reckwitz, Andreas   xvii, 10, 13, 15, 20–1, 26, 28–9, 29 nn.37, 38, 90 n.6, 91–2, 114, 115
Reed, Arden   144
Reid, Calvin   52
remembering   39, 44, 46–7, 57, 59, 76–8
restorative and reflective nostalgia   132 n.14
Reynolds, Simon   100, 117–18
Reznor, Trent   108
Ribisi, Marissa   86
Ricoeur, Paul   7 n.8
Robbins, Derek   21–22
Roeder, Katherine   53
Rolling Stone   88
Rosa, Hartmut   126 n.3
Rose, Frank   4 n.2, 5 n.5, 6
Rosen, Jody   95, 119
Rosenthal, Tony   143 n.23
Rougeau, Michael   131 n.11, 148

Sattler, Peter R.   47–8, 56, 58–9, 72
Schoonmaker, Kara   75 n.20
Schwartz, Delmore   159 n.38
Sea Change   86
second modernity   13 n.15
self   11–12, 13, 14, 15 n.17, 36, 45, 113
self-creativity   13, 63, 115
self-culture   13
self-deprecation   2, 25, 26, 27–8, 36, 53, 66, 73, 78, 87–8
self-referential system   22, 112, 123, 156
self-technologies   13–14
September 23rd, 2000   42
serial agents   156 n.34
serial gaps   70, 71–2, 74
serialization   21 n.23
sheet music   27, 29, 34, 94, 127, 140, 165, 169, 172, *see also Song Reader*

Shelley, Mary 61
Shulgin, Alexei 149
singularities 17, 20–1, 26, 29, 29 n.37, 171
  aestheticization of 30 n.40 and banal 172
skilled and unskilled readerships 22
Sloane, Sarah 5–6 n.7
sloths 125–6, 126 n.2
slow art 144
slowness xviii, 125–7, 136–9, *see also Kentucky Route Zero*
Smith, Patti 82
social media xix, 5, 6, 36, 56, 75–6, 79, 94, 129, 155, 167
Solberg, Dan 141
song cover 107–13
Song Reader ix, xiii, xiv, xv, xvi, xvii, xviii, 14, 24, 26, 27, 33, 34, 35, 127
  ads in 95–6
  affective responses 92
  and *Building Stories* 82
  canonization 83, 84
  conceptual slacker 113–17
  cover pages 101
  cover songs 85
  and creativity 91–2
  digital nostalgia and analog nostalgia 96–7
  effort and effortlessness 90–1
  and gender 90
  hipster marionette and ventriloquist 88–93
  inspiration for 83–4
  investment 81
  materiality and immateriality in xviii, 98–100
  "mode retro" pastiche style 96–7
  negotiations of music's materialities and ephemeralities 93–101
  online archive and its digital ruins 117–21

online renditions 119–21
participatory culture 84
reader's competences 82
sheet music 82–3, 101–7
shunning the elitism of rock stardom 90
slacker competence 121–4
"Title of This Song" 107–13
universality and access 103–4
song reader 81, 83, 90, 91–2, 95–6, 99–101, 103, 106, 109–13, 116, 117, 121–2, 124, 165
songreader.net 119–21
"Sound and Vision" 87, 89
Spiegelman, Art 54, 60
"Spinning coin" 143
splendid failures 25–6, 27
Spotify 32, 117
Squier, Susan 53
Starre, Alexander 34, 34 n.45
star system, emergence in twentieth century 92–3
Stein, Daniel 21 n.23, 68 n.17
Sterne, Jonathan 94, 109, 109 n.22
Stewart, Susan 47, 64, 72, 150–1
Stockhausen, Karlheinz 32
"strange-making" media 150–7
stylistic transparency 43, 44
Switch (Nintendo) 164, 168

taste 20, 24, 45, 49, 103
technology, *see also* digital technologies
  and gender 23 n.24, 28
  and nostalgia 94–5
This Book Is a Camera 170 n.5
This Book Is a Planetarium 170 n.5
Thorburn, David 102
time and space, in comics 59
Timothy McSweeney's Quarterly Concern 77 n.22
tinkering 9, 63–4, 163, 168, 170, 172
"Title of This Song" 120

Tomasula, Steve   30
Tompkins, Jane   27
Topshop   18
Touch Sensitive   78 n.23
"Toy-Cons"   168

Ulin, David L.   39, 40–1
unfinished objects/works   xii, xiv, 2, 4, 9, 19
unfree time   11–13
unmodern   33–4, 169
Updating to Remain the Same   xviii n.6

verbal art   133 n.15
versionings   31 n.42, 31–2, 36
vertical embedding   61, 61 n.16
Virilio, Paul   126 n.3
virtuality   152 n.27
von Gehlen, Dirk   31, 107–8, 108 n.20, 108 n.21, 111, 117

Wainwright, Rufus   108
Ware, Chris   x, xv, xvi–xvii, 6, 14, 24, 25, 26, 27, 30, 37, 44, 87, 88, 98, 122, 137, 156, 167, 170
   Building Stories (see *Building Stories*)
   characters' bodily ailments   53 n.10
   characters' inscrutability and shapelessness   43–4
   Jimmy Corrigan—The Smartest Kid on Earth   xvii, 62, 63–4, 137
   Last Saturday, The   6, 78–9
   on memories and architectural construct   54
   style, and discomfort   44
   use of diagrams by   43
Wasserman, Sarah   xi, xi n.4, xii
Welles, Orson   153–4
A Western Harvest Field by Moonlight   97
Whitehead, Dan   128, 148
Willis, Simon   25 n.29
Wolk, Douglas   43
work
   feminization of   50
   and labor   4 n.3
   and leisure   12–13
   and play   8 n.10

YA novels   6
Young Englishwoman, The—A Volume of Pure Literature, New Fashions, and Pretty Needlework Patterns   170
YouTube   15 n.18, 117–18, 119, 120

www.ingramcontent.com/pod-product-compliance
Lightning Source LLC
Chambersburg PA
CBHW052042300426
44117CB00012B/1932